Margin / Alias

Language and Colonization in Canadian and Québécois Fiction

Two critical discourses central to current Canadian literary theory emerged in the late 1960s and early 1970s: postcolonialism as a political paradigm and postmodernism as a literary practice in Canadian and Québécois fiction. Sylvia Söderlind considers the current debate about the relationship between these two discourses, and proposes a methodology that makes it possible to identify and distinguish between features pertaining to the two.

The theoretical question she poses is whether and how it is possible to determine the degree of what writers and critics variously call 'linguistic alienation,' 'alterity,' or 'marginality' in literary texts. Literary studies of marginality generally focus on theme, but Söderlind shows that a text's thematic claim to marginal status is not always corroborated by its textual strategies. Her proposed methodology is used to determine when and to what degree a text's claim to marginality is justified, as opposed to when it is used as an 'alias.'

The author draws on the theory of 'minor literatures' outlined by Gilles Deleuze and Félix Guattari and, in particular, on their concepts of territoriality. Their theories are combined with methodologies more immediately applicable to literary texts, notably the semiotics of Yuri Lotman and Boris Uspenskij and the deconstruction of Jacques Derrida. The textual analyses of novels by Leonard Cohen, Hubert Aquin, David Godfrey, André Langevin, and Robert Kroetsch yield some perhaps unexpected results, which are elucidated through a consideration of a wider corpus.

The study opens up to an inquiry into the possibility of reading from the margin, a strategy solicited by certain kinds of postmodern and postcolonial texts. It concludes with some provocative questions about the postmodern critic's relationship to the literary text and its author.

SYLVIA SÖDERLIND is a member of the Department of English at Queen's University.

THEORY / CULTURE

General editors: Linda Hutcheon and Paul Perron

Sylvia Söderlind

MARGIN/ALIAS

Language and Colonization in Canadian and Québécois Fiction

University of Toronto Press

Toronto Buffalo London

© University of Toronto Press 1991
Toronto Buffalo London
Printed in Canada

ISBN 0-8020-5903-1 (cloth)
ISBN 0-8020-6845-6 (paper)

Printed on acid-free paper

Theory / Culture 6

Canadian Cataloguing in Publication Data
Söderlind, Sylvia, 1948–
    Margin/Alias : language and colonization in
Canadian and Québécois fiction

(Theory/culture)
Includes bibliographical references and index.
ISBN 0-8020-5903-1 (bound) ISBN 0-8020-6845-6 (pbk.)

1. Canadian fiction – 20th century – History and
criticism. I. Title. II. Series.

PS8199.S64 1991   C813'.5409   C91-094687-6
PR9192.5S64 1991
                        76654

This book has been published with the help of a grant from the Canadian
Federation for the Humanities, using funds provided by the Social Sciences
and Humanities Research Council of Canada.

O Tongue of the Nation! Why don't you
speak for yourself?

LEONARD COHEN

Contents

Acknowledgments

No exploration can be undertaken without guides, and my warmest thanks go out to those who have helped me along the way, beginning with Olov Fryckstedt, who inspired me and showed me the road to Canada. Among the many who contributed to the successful completion of the journey are Peter Nesselroth, whose patience and support were greatly tried by my stubbornness, Linda Hutcheon whose perspicacity is only matched by her generosity, and Ben-Z. Shek and Frank Watt who kindly let me into their own territories. The advice of Leslie Monkman and Marilyn Randall on specific parts of the manuscript was invaluable, even when unheeded. Many friends at the Centre for Comparative Literature at the University of Toronto have contributed unwittingly in one way or another; I want to especially thank Barbara Havercroft for her friendship and for all the helpful references slipped under my door. For his generosity with encouragement, ideas, computer hints, and editing expertise, I want to thank Frank Burke, and for their patience with my moods, Wylie and Tyler Burke.

To the Department of External Affairs, whose generous award made it possible for me to come to Canada in the first place, my thanks are joined by my apology for never wanting to leave. A grant from the Advisory Research Committee at Queen's University allowed me to enter the age of technology.

I cannot adequately express the gratitude I feel towards my big and wonderful family in Sweden, without whose help – moral as well as material – this expedition would never have reached its goal. To my niece Agneta Helmius I owe a particular debt for helping make my discovery of Canada such an exciting adventure. The most special thanks I reserve for my daughter Angelika, whose quiet but unfailing sense of perspective is to be credited for – as far as possible – curbing my pomposity. I hope that one day her faith in me will be rewarded with something more fun than a book without a plot.

MARGIN/ALIAS

Writing in the Margin

The discourse of colonization that coloured so much Canadian and Qué-bécois writing and criticism during the sixties and seventies has more re-cently come to be used in a wider critical debate as a new master narrative for any discussion of marginality or otherness. Ethnic, racial, sexual, social minorities of all kinds are currently being talked about – less often talking about themselves – as 'colonized,' and metaphors of territorial subjection and occupation are bandied about as the focus of attention shifts from the centre (the 'metropolis') to the margin (the 'colony'). This is both under-standable and useful, but it is also problematic, as the struggle for the as-sertion of difference itself risks becoming hegemonized in this blanket adoption of one paradigm based on economic or cultural and ethnic grounds which reduces to metaphor the oppression of groups whose subjection is founded on other reasons. The discourse of marginality always involves various degrees of metaphorization; at the extreme the margin becomes a figure for the centre, the 'real' marginal becomes a margin/alias – a marginal in name only. The heuristic effectiveness of the colonization paradigm as a critical tool will, I hope, be demonstrated here, but whether its dangers can be avoided is more uncertain. Canada may indeed offer a good test case for its usefulness for criticism. It may seem presumptuous to speak of the country as if its political situation were equivalent to, for instance, that of former colonies in the third world. Canada's past is, as the ambivalence of its literatures often indicates, a double one: it has been colonized by the French and British but it is also a colonizer of its indigenous peoples. There is no doubt that Canada in most ways is part of what is generally considered as the colonizing part of the world, the industrialized West. Yet, while economically advantaged, Canada is 'colonized' in a specifically cultural and linguistic sense: the Canadian or Québécois writer has no other language than that of the perceived colonizer, whether English or French. No refuge is to be found outside the linguistic territory of the metropolis; no political gesture can be defiantly made by recourse to minority languages, and no common tribal or precolonial past can be conjured up as a challenge in the effort to establish a national/cultural identity.

One reason for the relative absence of explanations of the obvious formal differences between the country's two literatures is the lack of a methodology pertinent to the specific cultural and linguistic situation in places like Canada, in which 'new' literatures must try to find their own expression within the confines of an 'old' language. My objective here is to establish such a methodology and to test it by applying it to texts that are thematically similar but formally unique, so as to explain, as far as possible, the nature and cause of their differences. In a wider sense my discussion is situated within the current post-structuralist debate, for which the postcolonial situation is particularly relevant; the struggle for identity in a situation where self-representation is always tainted with alterity, because imposed by an alien centre, poses problems for a discourse that wants to do away with both subjectivity and representation. In current critical terminology, postcolonial writing is, or at least should be, subversive, and cultural marginality is often seen as a precondition for subversion. (Didacticism and a good degree of moralism are frequent companions of the Western critic of postcolonialism and I do not claim to be an exception.) A methodology attentive to the subversive potential of postcolonial literatures must by necessity subscribe to a view of language which allows for resistance, and my approach implies a pragmatic view of the position of the subject in language as an agent with a degree of control over his or her medium, a control that, while never complete, can be measured. This position is, however, I believe, less a matter of choice than a consequence of a given linguistic or cultural situation.

The obvious point of departure for any study of postcolonialism in the case of Canada is the turbulent period of the late sixties and early seventies when, against a political background of events too well known to mention, the quest for identity intensified and the terms 'Canadian' and 'Québécois' came to be used, with what from a post-Meech Lake perspective seems like prophetic clarity, to define two distinct cultures. The struggle for self-definition was, during this period, brought into a specifically North American context and steeped in an ideological discourse focusing on the problems of colonization in all its aspects. This also coincided with the appearance of postmodernism as a major literary movement, within which the novels I will be considering have indeed often been placed. The parallels between practices labelled postcolonial and those labelled postmodern are striking, as is the infrequently acknowledged debt much post-structuralist theory owes to earlier theories of colonialism. The novels I will be reading were written before postmodernism entered mainstream criticism, however, and to most of them any overt interest in postmodern aesthetics is secondary to their preoccupation with the politics of cultural colonization.

The fact that the texts I have chosen to analyse participate in two major discourses begs the question of their interrelationship. Are they more post-modern than postcolonial, or vice versa? The postmodern decentring of the subject is sometimes seen as inimical to the postcolonial need to assert a cultural identity in terms defined from within the minority situation. I would argue, however, that any statement of identity is an assertion of difference, and that the postmodern interest in the ontology of difference is central to the postcolonial situation. Some critics claim that postmodernism is a Western appropriation of postcolonial practice, and it may be suggested that its itinerary has been analogous to that of many other colonial raw materials – tobacco, for instance; used for purposes of communion or contestation in the colony, it is refined – made fashionable – and commodified by the metropolis before being returned where it came from, stamped and legitimated with the imperial seal of approval. While this view implicitly aligns itself with the controversial critique of postmodernism as an apolitical or, worse, colonizing, aesthetics, it nevertheless allows, albeit somewhat cynically, for the use of the former as a model for the latter. Although some of the theories that have informed my proposed methodology have been – with good reason – accused of Eurocentrism, their adoption for the study of the literatures of a former settler colony remarkably resistant to the influence of indigenous cultures may be justified. I do not, therefore, see any contradiction if, at the outset, I refer to texts as at times postcolonial and at times postmodern; the novels I will be reading are in fact both.

My definition of postmodernism is indebted to Linda Hutcheon's identification of a literary practice that simultaneously and self-consciously uses and abuses the conventions of what is usually called the realist mode of fiction and that counters ruling master narratives with a multitude of non-totalizing and provisional alternatives. Most important, it refers to a literature that questions its own status as art, and its relation to the world, and, acutely aware of its own imprisonment in language, hence ideology, problematizes the crucial notion of representation. Its simultaneous reliance on and contestation of existing patterns explain the frequent accusations levelled at its perceived lack of political engagement. Without agreeing to this view, I will argue that the political force of the texts I will be studying is due more to their participation in the discourse of colonization than to their status as postmodern. Much of this force comes from a concern with recuperating a lost history, a preoccupation which seems to run counter to the questioning of historiography so typical of postmodernism. Although, as a result of the double gesture of use and abuse of existing patterns, irony has been identified as the predominant mode of both movements, it often seems less acute in Canadian and Québécois texts than, for instance, in many of their American counterparts. Irony is an index of the author's position vis-à-vis his/her own utterance. In light of my view of alterity as an effect of a linguistic situation, one way to distinguish between the two possibly contradictory projects may be by identifying the writer's position within the text; that is, by raising the spectre of intention and resurrecting the 'dead' author.

My discussion distinguishes rather broadly between postmodernism as a – primarily American – literary practice and post-structuralism as its – primarily French – theoretical counterpart, both of which have followed a similar movement from margin to centre and back again. The term post-colonialism may seem self-explanatory and neutral; its application is, in fact, here as in most criticism, limited to the literature produced in former colonies that assumes a position of resistance to the metropolis. Its use thus indicates a critical stance that probably overlooks a great deal and may well be based on an imperialist assumption that any writing of importance produced by former subjects must be focused on their contestatory relationship to the absent master; like so much terminology it may reveal more about the critic's desire than about the literature to which it is applied.

Because my main objective is to establish a practically useful methodology, I have opted to concentrate on a limited number of novels rather than presenting a large number of superficial readings. Like any corpus, mine is eclectic and no more immune to charges of arbitrariness than any other. The choice of texts is motivated by their suitability for a concrete and practical reading for alterity. I have chosen texts, written during the crucial period of self-definition, which in some way adopt the discourse of colonization as a – literal or figurative – paradigm within which to pursue the quest for identity. All the novels are concerned, more or less explicitly, with the definition of a Canadian or Québécois identity (and consequently with the question of difference) and with the search for a language in which to express its specificity.

In chapter 1 I will present some of the theoretical problems involved in defining alterity from a literary point of view and will suggest a methodology applicable to individual texts. The remaining chapters contain textual analyses, beginning with a programmatic reading of Leonard Cohen's *Beautiful Losers* (1966), which marked the entry of literary postmodernism into the country and whose straddling of French and English cultures ensures it a unique position in a non-existent, truly inclusive Canadian canon. Because my emphasis is on language, it is necessary to provide a comparative framework that will permit an investigation of linguistic difference. After the first demonstration reading I have for that reason chosen to pair off Québécois and Canadian novels that seem to take similar directions but which, on a closer analysis, reveal themselves as representative of divergent tendencies. In chapters 3 and 4 I discuss two texts that share a certain ideological intertext and that both take recourse to a real postcolonial situation – in Africa – as an analogue to the one at home: Hubert Aquin's *Trou de mémoire* (1968) and Dave Godfrey's *The New Ancestors* (1970). Chapters 5 and 6 juxtapose two texts that discuss the same problem in a specifically North American context: André Langevin's *L'Elan d'Amérique* (1972) and Robert Kroetsch's *Gone Indian* (1973). In chapter 7 I will extend the discussion to a wider corpus and offer some speculations regarding the status of the two literatures, and in the conclusion I return to some of the theoretical implications, as well as more personal questions, raised in the course of my study.

CHAPTER ONE

Mapping the Territory

Each language draws a magic circle round the people to which it belongs, a circle from which there is no escape save by stepping out of it into another.

WILHELM VON HUMBOLDT

In simple terms, the aim of the following is to establish whether and, if possible, how, the linguistic effects of alterity can be measured in literary texts, alterity being understood at this point in a broad sense as an inherent aspect of marginality and a central concept in the discourse of colonization. In order to better define in what it consists, I will begin, as it were, with its opposite, the concept of territoriality, a notion implicit, although defined in different ways, in many theories of culture and language. In this introductory section I shall discuss those theories that are most relevant for a study of literature and that will help establish a methodology pertinent to the postcolonial situation.

A pragmatic, sociolinguistic approach which would make it possible to determine the degree of 'linguistic alienation' in any society is offered by Henri Gobard, an acerbic French linguist, who traces variations in cultural homogeneity or territoriality to the interrelationship between four 'languages' at work in any society. The language most closely linked to the territory is the *vernacular*, the mother tongue, which is primarily spoken, and whose function is to establish a 'communion' rather than a communication between the interlocutors. Used between peers, it is a language of the here and now, pertaining to the *Gemeinschaft*, a term borrowed from Ferdinand Tönnies to emphasize its privileging of the phatic function; that is, the opening and maintaining of contact between speakers. A literature that emanates from a situation of linguistic colonization is often preoccupied with vindicating a forgotten or devalued vernacular, and its association with oral tradition and storytelling will prove central to my textual analyses.

At the opposite end of Gobard's 'tetraglossic' schema we find the *mythic* or, as I prefer to call it because of the confusion surrounding the term 'myth,' the *sacred* language. Although in most societies the sacred seems far removed from the vernacular, my discussion of their relationship will reveal their shared origin. Even when separate, the two retain a functional commonality: like the vernacular, the sacred language demarcates a realm of beliefs shared by all members of the community. It is a paradigmatic, static, and conservative language; the only signification of its words is sacredness.

Between the vernacular and the sacred we find the *referential* language, which is the locus of culture as defined by sociologists and anthropologists in terms of common heritage or collective memory. Here are included history and customs, canons of art, and literature, etc. – that which literary criticism loosely subsumes under the heading 'intertextuality.' Because culture, as 'heritage' or 'memory,' can only be perceived in retrospect, this is the language of the past. It is also the language of the *nation*, while the vernacular belongs to the *region*, and the sacred to the *beyond*. In modern society, the referential would be primarily the domain of media such as print, while in societies where the collective heritage is transmitted orally, it would be closely aligned with the vernacular.

These three languages are all related to the territory, and in non-dislocated or 'territorial' societies, they are shared by everybody. The fourth 'language' analysed by Gobard, however, the *vehicular* or lingua franca, is by nature non-territorial. Considering the common sociological distinction between culture and society – the former is based on communication, the latter on the division of labour – the vehicular would be the exclusive property of the latter. Gobard calls it the language of the *Gesellschaft*, of expediency or necessity and pure information. As an intermediary language that represents a later stage in the process of socialization, it belongs to the city and to bureaucracy; alienated from any territory, it is addressed by anybody to whom it may concern. Gobard offers a spatio-temporal arrangement of the four languages that I prefer to reverse: it seems more logical to place the vernacular closest to the ground:

	Espace	Temps	Langue
Sacré	Au-delà	Toujours	Sacrée
Référentiaire	Là-bas	Jadis	Nationale
Véhiculaire	Partout	Plus tard	Urbaine
Vernaculaire	Ici	Maintenant	Maternelle

The internal relationship between these four languages can be seen as a measure of the stability of any given society, says Gobard. Originally, and this is still true in oral cultures, they all coincide, and the closer they remain, the more territorial the culture. A linguistically 'alienated' or non-territorial culture, on the other hand, would be characterized by heteroglossia: the languages representing the various levels would be different. Perhaps the most common example of this is the phenomenon of diglossia, where one language – the vehicular – is valorized at the expense of the vernacular. Gobard shows, in line with other theorists of bilingualism, that diglossia is not necessarily alienating in itself, but that alienation takes place when the 'high' language encroaches on the 'low' so as to deterritorialize it. Diglossia is most frequent and obvious in colonized societies, which are also breeding grounds for nationalism, a movement which 'claims to reverse the modern affective imbalance between mechanical and organic solidarity, between Gemeinschaft and Gesellschaft, between the sacred and the secular' (Fishman 10). Nationalism is a movement of reterritorialization, an attempt to reintegrate the various functions of language under the sign of the vernacular, a common phenomenon in periods of unrest in colonized societies seen, for instance, in the rise of *joual* in the literature of Quebec in the sixties. It can also, however, be the result of the transposition of material pertaining to the sacred – or the referential in appeals to historical precedence – into the vehicular, the misclassification of myth as information or fact. It is perhaps not coincidental that Nazism figures in two of the novels I will be reading, *Beautiful Losers* and *The New Ancestors*, as the extreme example of such a brutally territorializing translation between incompatible realms.

Although Gobard's discussion may offer a sociolinguistic model for the study of literature, it needs to be complemented if it is to prove useful for close readings. Theories of territoriality, as it applies specifically to literary texts, are generally outlined against the background of the myth of the tower of Babel, where the *hubris* of humanity was punished by the proliferation of tongues and the subsequent alienation from the Word and the Other. George Steiner points out that every known mythology includes a variant of the Babel myth (*Extraterritorial* 123). The fall into language from what Steiner calls the 'Adamic vernacular' constitutes a central topos of what is commonly labelled postmodern aesthetics, and has taken two opposite directions, both of which we will see actualized in my chosen corpus. Any culture, period, or literary genre reflects an attitude, whether negative or positive, towards the possibility of translation, or what could be called a coefficient of translatability, which will be mirrored in its stance vis-à-vis the two myths: it will be oriented towards Babelian frustration or pentecostal faith.

The problematics of translation are explicitly thematized as part of the discourse of colonization in three of the novels I will analyse – *Beautiful Losers, The New Ancestors*, and *L'Elan d'Amérique* – and are clearly central to the discussion of territoriality as a measure of the closeness between a literary text and the culture and language to which it belongs. In very simple terms, the more territorial a text, the less translatable it would be. A text that is deeply rooted in a particular language and culture is not easily accessible to an outsider; like a name, which has no meaning unless we know to whom it refers, a cultural allusion has no significance outside its context. On the other hand, a purely informative and consequently vehicular or non-territorial text (such as a scientific treatise) is translatable because mainly concerned with supracultural information.

In a broad sense, as Steiner points out, translation is an inherent aspect of communication, which always '"interprets" between privacies' (*After Babel* 198), and the recent interest in translation theory may reflect the growing awareness of the complexities of communication. Most theories of translation rest on a belief in the dual nature of the word, on an opposition between the word and its sense, and thus on a transcendental concept of meaning. More recently, the discussion has focused on the heuristic divisibility of the sign into signifier and signified. The focus of attention is the sense, or the signified, which the translator aims to render so that it remains as intact as possible while changing the signifier. Translatability is thus a function of the arbitrariness of the sign, and the closer or more apparently motivated the relationship between signifier and signified, the more difficult translation becomes. Hence the familiar argument against the possibility of translating poetry. A text which is dependent on sound, rhyme, and metre is obviously more difficult to translate than one depending primarily on content, and we shall see in the following that the two novels that in my view present the greatest problems for the translator – *Beautiful Losers* and *L'Elan d'Amérique* – are also the most dependent on poetic strategies.

Gobard's discussion of territoriality shows that translatability is above all the property of the vehicular language, where emphasis is laid on cognitive content rather than expression. His sociolinguistic schema implies a parallel semiotic one, whereby the languages in the tetraglossic table can be defined in terms of their different relationships between the two sides of the sign. That is, while Gobard's theories deal with the relationships between language, its users, and the world, semiotic theories of territoriality deal with relationships pertaining within language. In the vernacular and the sacred, where communication and signification are secondary to communion and expression, the sign is perceived as natural and indivisible. In the referential language the sign would be charged with connotations to a specific cultural context, while the vehicular would be characterized by a high degree of arbitrariness in the relation between signifier and signified. Because of the primacy of the signifier in the vernacular and the sacred, these 'languages of communion' do not easily lend themselves to paraphrase, the necessary condition for translation according to most pragmatic views, at least since Dryden. While the translatability of the vehicular is a consequence of its openness to paraphrase (i.e. the detachability of the signified from the signifier), Gobard caustically illustrates the unparaphrasable nature of the sacred text by claiming that if we were only concerned with meaning, we might as well say 'okay' at the end of the Lord's Prayer. It is the sacredness and the consequent inexchangeability of signifiers that constrain us to 'Amen.' The sacred text is intimately linked to a specific cultural/mythical territory, and the relationship between signifier and signified is seen as highly motivated and absolute, or perhaps more correctly, the signified is subsumed under the 'pure' signifier, a phenomenon I will discuss in connection with *Beautiful Losers* and *The New Ancestors*. The criterion of a sacred text is precisely its untranslatability; any translation of Scripture must proceed on the level of the signifier, according to Saint Jerome's principle of 'verbum e verbo,' a procedure diametrically opposed to the practical translator's task of 'sensum exprimere de sensu' (*After Babel* 262).

The position of literary translation in this discussion is an intricate and currently hotly debated question. Walter Benjamin, following Hölderlin, would contend that the translation of literary texts should proceed on the model of scriptural translation, a view that would seem to sacralize, and consequently territorialize, literature ('The Task of the Translator'). Taking his cue from Benjamin, and in line with the preceding discussion, Jacques Derrida more recently defines the sacred text as one where 'le sens et la littéralité ne se discernent plus pour former le corps d'un événement unique, irremplaçable, intransférable "matériellement la vérité" ... C'est le texte absolu parce qu'en son événement il ne communique rien, il ne dit rien qui fasse sens hors de cet événement même ... Il est traductible et intraduisible.' ('Des Tours de Babel' 247–8). Because the sacred Word does not communicate but *is* the truth, as Benjamin puts it, nothing can be put over it ('übergesetzt'), but because the truth is universal and absolute, the Word can be infinitely carried over ('übergetragen'). (We encounter here a difficult translation problem: English has no good equivalent of the couple 'traductibilité/Übertragung.')[1] Although this debate, with its strong theological overtones, falls outside the scope of this study, it confirms my contention that the sacred text is untranslatable in the pragmatic sense of the word, which is the one at issue here. For our purposes, therefore, translatability will be seen as synonymous with vehicularity. According to this practical view, translatability and territoriality stand in a relation of opposition: the more territorial a text the less translatable it is.

Gobard's contention that the homogeneity or territoriality of a society can be discerned in the configuration of its four languages is reminiscent of the typology of cultures suggested by the Soviet semioticians Yuri Lotman and Boris Uspenskij. In rapidly changing cultures, they claim, there is an increase in semiotic activity, while stable, homogeneous cultures maintain a higher degree of immediacy between the individual and the world, an immediacy reflected in a perceived relationship of identity between words and things ('On the Semiotic Mechanism of Culture'). The one-to-one relationship between word and thing is particularly typical of magic, which forms part of everyday life in 'primitive' cultures. As civilization progresses, experience becomes increasingly mediated by what Lotman terms 'secondary modeling systems,' in a movement towards what Gobard would call tetraglossia. The original unity of the vernacular and the sacred, seen in magic, is reflected in the formulaic discourse which still serves a phatic function in both: the similarity between proverbs and prayers, swear-words and ritual utterances, etc. 'The power that resides in prayer is of magical origin and kind: the will of the godhead is compelled by the magical force of the word,' says Ernst Cassirer (*Mythical Thought* 229). In the following we shall encounter examples of this link between magic and prayer, most radically in *Beautiful Losers* but also in *The New Ancestors*. Prayer tears down the barriers between humanity and God, between the profane and the sacred, which have been erected with the development of intermediary systems, most particularly print which, in the form of books, has become the repository of the collective memory. As we shall see, Leonard Cohen's novel offers a particularly radical attempt at bridging the gap between the oral/vernacular and the written/vehicular through an unexpected redefinition of translation as prayer.

Walter Benjamin emphasizes the collective nature of oral storytelling as well as its phatic function ('The Storyteller'). Storytelling plays an important role in both Canadian and Québécois fiction but, while it draws on oral tradition, its function has changed quite drastically. In a genuine oral culture with a living folktale tradition, there exists what could be called a communal author- or proprietorship of a referential which is closely linked to the vernacular. Rather than using Benjamin's adjective 'anonymous' to characterize such storytelling, I prefer to see it as collective. The 'community of listeners' which characterizes it does not exist for the novel which, in spite of its individual signature, remains anonymous and alien to the communal situation. The automatic authority of the traditional story, conferred on it by the death of the successive tellers, is akin to that of myth. (The relationship between death and storytelling is parodied, for instance, in Robert Kroetsch's novels which frequently play self-consciously with the incongruity between oral telling and novel-writing.) The novel, says Benjamin, cannot come out of an oral tradition. Anonymity is the criterion of the vehicular language, and the novel is thus, by definition, a non-territorial genre. It can try to operate a reterritorialization through various strategies – by calling on a specific vernacular, sacred, or referential territory – or it can assume its non-territorial character by emphasizing its vehicular, anonymous aspects. The five novels in my chosen corpus exhibit widely divergent, and at times contradictory, uses of these conflicting tendencies.

In Lotman's and Uspenskij's terms, cultures reflect different types of consciousness, and they define as 'mythological' a culture which retains the original unity, before the split between the various functions of language. Although a purely mythological culture could hardly be found, I will use the concept as a heuristic approximation as a way of defining genres in terms of territoriality. Because of its direct and unmediated relationship between word and world, a mythological consciousness would, in this view, be asemiotic or pre-symbolic, perceiving the relationship between word and referent – and in a less pure form between signifier and signified – as motivated, natural and absolute. The dichotomy between the pole of mythological consciousness – or zero semiosis – and its opposite would correspond to that between maximum and minimum territoriality. (The distinction I am adopting here is based on a definition of 'semiotic' as concerned solely with diacritical signification and with the systemic aspect of meaning-production; that is, as divorced from both the reference and the instance of discourse.)

The concept of territoriality is also central to the theories of Gilles Deleuze and Félix Guattari, whose writings are currently hotly debated in the realm of postcolonial theory. While the criticism levelled at the Eurocentrism of their writings is justified from the point of view of the study of third world literatures, it does not, I believe, lessen their validity for the study of new literatures written in Western colonial languages. In the anti-Freudian view of these writers, territoriality or cultural homogeneity is equivalent to 'oedipalization,' because it reflects the split between the individual id and ego. In what amounts to a Deleuzean reading of the myth of Babel, their discussion assumes the existence of an original pre-territorial collectivity. In *L'Anti-Oedipe* they posit a primary deterritorialization in terms of the imposition of state authority on the primitive social machine and the ensuing division of the territory. An ideal, non-territorial culture would be anti-oedipal, subversive, and consequently, according to their radical (or, one might argue, idealist) view, essentially political. Its expression would be found in the 'minor literature,' not to be confused with the common meaning of the term as simply 'non-canonical.' Although a minor literature in Deleuze and Guattari's terms always stands in opposition to the canon, all marginal literature does not come under their definition: 'Une littérature mineure n'est pas celle d'une langue mineure, plutôt celle qu'une minorité fait dans une langue majeure. Mais le premier caractère est de toute façon que la langue y est affectée d'un fort coefficient de déterritorialisation' (*Kafka* 29). Following George Steiner's example, they use Kafka to illustrate the phenomenon. Constrained to write in German, the vehicular language of power and of bureaucracy, rather than in Czech (or Yiddish), Kafka was forced into a position of alterity with regard to his cultural territory.

The fundamental criterion of the deterritorialized language typical of the minor literature is its separation from both the communicative situation and the world. In it the word is uprooted from its referent and the signifier cut off from the signified. It is by definition subversive. Deleuze and Guattari's analysis is interesting, insofar as it deals specifically with literature; what might in ordinary language be non-territorial in a completely innocent way becomes revolutionary when used to subvert literary convention. The subversion of language is characteristic of all truly radical literature, and it is in the nature of the minor literature that it belongs to no school or movement: once the revolutionary devices become canonized, they lose their subversive energy.

The preceding discussion has shown the affinity between the two main aspects of territoriality: first as a measure of the homogeneity of a culture and as a measure of the closeness between word and world, and second, in the realm of semiotics, between signifier and signified. An approach based on the theories presented here would seem particularly relevant to the literatures of Canada and Quebec which both, at least superficially, fit the definition of the minor literature: they are written in languages already hegemonized by long established major literatures with which they do not wish to be identified, or against which they write. Dennis Lee's 'Cadence, Country, Silence: Writing in Colonial Space' anticipates, in a specifically Canadian context, the writings of Deleuze and Guattari, and, like the claims of many Québécois writers that they belong to a linguistically alienated society, it illustrates the appropriateness of the approach I am suggesting here. In my readings I will, on the one hand, examine the 'tetraglossic' constellation of the individual texts, focusing on the relationship among the vernacular (and the profane), the sacred, and the referential (which will be subsumed under the rubric of intertextuality), and the possible role played by the vehicular. The various aspects of the problematics of translation will form an integral part of this discussion.

On the other hand, I will focus on the semiotic aspect of territoriality through a close reading of the rhetorical strategies that predominate in the texts. The relationship between levels of signification will be at the centre of attention: between text and intertext, between form and content, and between signifier and signified. The results of the close readings will allow me to place the individual texts tentatively on a heuristic spectrum ranging from maximum territoriality, or minimum semiotic mediation, to minimum territoriality or maximum semiosis. My theoretical discussion will show that the most convenient indices of territoriality – and for more than purely alliterative reasons – will be myth, metaphor, and metamorphosis. Linked to these are the recently resurfacing concepts of anamorphosis and allegory which will conclude my theoretical discussion.

Myth – Name – Alias

Myth, according to Lotman and Uspenskij, is the product of a consciousness which represents an original state of unity between word and thing, between sacred and profane, and between spirit and matter. In Gobard's terms it would be monoglot, reflecting a stage before the division of languages. In a heuristic spectrum of genres myth would therefore occupy the position closest to the pole of maximum territoriality.

Although the term myth is surrounded by some confusion in current critical debate, all theorists interested in the phenomenon agree on the crucial fact that it is always perceived as natural, as what 'goes without saying.'[2] In myth the relationship between word and referent is always perceived as natural and motivated, and it is essential to distinguish it from literature which is, by definition, a secondary modelling system, to use Lotman's term. Frank Kermode's view of myth is particularly helpful in establishing the crucial distinction between myth and fiction: 'Myth operates within the diagrams of ritual, which presupposes total and adequate explanations of things as they are and were; it is a sequence of radically unchangeable gestures. Fictions are for finding things out, and they change as the needs of sense-making change. Myths are the agents of stability, fictions the agents of change. Myths call for absolute, fictions for conditional assent. Myths make sense in terms of a lost order of time, *illud tempus* as Eliade calls it;

fictions, if successful, make sense of the here and now, *hoc tempus*' (39). Gobard, we will recall, places the mythical stratum of language in the temporal (non-)dimension of eternity. Cassirer explains the difference between mythical and historical time as follows: 'What distinguishes mythical time from historical time is that for mythical time there is an absolute past, which neither requires nor is susceptible of any further explanation' (*Mythical Thought* 106). But, while mythical narratives always deal with something that happened *in illo tempore* and are indifferent to relative time, they nevertheless have a beginning, a middle, and an end. An important aspect of time perceived as meaningful – *kairos* – rather than as simple succession is its dependence on beginnings and endings. Kermode illustrates this with the metaphor of the clock: the *tick* of the beginning creates expectations, built on earlier experience, that a concluding *tock* will follow. The tock is what creates meaning out of the interval; it is the end that makes sense of the middle, and the relationship between beginning and end is what distinguishes the 'tick-tock' from the 'tock-tick,' which is pure unorganized *chronos* (44–6). The relationship between mythical and historical time is relevant to all of the novels I will be analysing, and Kermode's metaphor of the clock will prove particularly pertinent to *L'Elan d'Amérique* and *Gone Indian*.

In myth, as in dreams, temporality is intimately linked to causality. If two events follow each other closely in time, the mythological consciousness will see them as causally related. This mythical convention still governs our reading of narrative; if we are told that the king died and then the queen died, we tend to infer a relation of cause and effect. One could perhaps say that in myth there is no distinction between story and plot, the one implies the other. Myth is, in this way, as Lévi-Strauss has illustrated, a way of making sense of what is at hand, a *bricolage* of temporality and causality.

According to Kermode, literature begins where myth leaves off, with the realization that time is endless and that each ending is a fiction to be ceaselessly disconfirmed and substituted. In the post-Einsteinian age of relativity, myth has become fiction, although fictions 'can degenerate into myths whenever they are not consciously held to be fictive' (39). Kermode uses the example of Nazism to illustrate the pernicious consequences of this transposition between incompatible realms, although he fails to emphasize the most chilling step in that particular story, the vehicularization and consequent bureaucratization of the myth. Kermode's insistence on the perceived fictiveness of fiction seems to make postmodern literature, with its almost obsessive self-consciousness, immune to that dreaded degeneration. There is little doubt that most postmodernist writers share their predecessors' interest in myth, but their self-conscious and ironic use of it, whether or not it is tainted with nostalgia, is clearly a result of the split between what Cassirer would call myth on the one hand and language on the other. It could be argued that the novel is more heteroglot today than it ever was, and certainly as ironic as ever, both of which aspects contradict the myth's claim to monoglossia. Self-consciousness, and consequently irony, the prevailing mode in postmodernism, imply a distancing by definition antithetical to myth, as I have defined the term here.

The attitude of postcolonialism towards myth is perhaps more ambiguous, as is its stance toward irony. Postcolonial literature is often preoccupied with a retrieval of lost myths, a concern no less common (albeit more frustrating because of a perceived lack of indigenous material) in Canada than elsewhere. At the same time it is also frequently busy dismantling both the myths and the literary models of the colonizer; postcolonial parodies of metropolitan canonical texts are by now numerous enough to form their own anti-canon. In my corpus the retrieval of mythologies is particularly visible in *Beautiful Losers* and *Gone Indian*, two novels that show some rather surprising similarities, although the latter seems rather more comfortable with its postmodern irony than the former. One might argue that this is symptomatic of the movement from the primarily postcolonial, ambiguous stance to a greater assurance and interest in postmodern aesthetics that has taken place in the seven years that separate the two.

It is the uncertainty of myth in modern society that has given rise to fictions according to Kermode, and 'on the whole there is a correlation between subtlety and variety in our fictions and remoteness and doubtfulness about ends and origins' (67). The teleological uncertainties and the inquiry into origins so typical of much postcolonial literature (succinctly illustrated in Robert Kroetsch's novels) are thus a corollary of the loss of the stability of the myths which earlier served as unquestioned explanatory systems of the origin and fate of their adherents.

Lotman and Uspenskij equate mythological consciousness with 'proper name-consciousness' ('Myth – Name – Culture' 235). In the beginning was the Word, according to innumerable myths of creation, and in mythological thought, as in fiction, naming equals creation. Proper names constitute a very specific, asemiotic stratum of language: they are not diacritical signs but gain their significance exclusively in terms of their always unique referents. Together with the personal pronouns for the first and second person singular, proper names are, according to George Steiner, perhaps the only universals in language (*After Babel* 97). They constitute the foundation, the absolutely indispensable part, of speech. Naming is, of course, clearly linked to identity, and the postcolonial preoccupation with naming the territory and its inhabitants is well documented. Naming, like myth, is linked to orality, and in oral cultures words have more of the properties of names than of signs: 'One characteristic of the world-view of oral cultures is the assumption that words, uttered under appropriate circumstances have the power to bring into being the events or states they stand for, to embody rather than represent reality. This conviction that the word can create its object leads to a sense that language possesses power over truth and reality.' (Ashcroft, Griffiths, and Tiffin 81). Although Canada can hardly be said to possess an oral heritage, orality plays an important role as a metaphor for territoriality in many of the novels I will discuss; a good example is Dave Godfrey's novel which relies heavily on an African tradition. The use of oral patterns or models presents a problem, discernible in all of the novels I will discuss, of translation between two sometimes incongruous types of discourse, as orality must be made to conform to the requirements of print. This operation is the most frequent example of what I call intersystemic translation, which results from the incorporation of extratextual or paraliterary discourses or media, a common phenomenon in postmodernism. Such borrowings frequently necessitate modifications which can either aim at creating congruity between the incorporated source and the text – that is, strive to make the process invisible – or it can foreground their incongruity. The former would be a territorial strategy, while the latter would be de-territorializing or disjunctive.

The equation between mythological consciousness and proper name is based on the immediate and unique relationship between the word and its referent typical of both myth and name, an immediacy which accounts for their position closest to the pole of minimum semiosis or maximum territoriality on my heuristic spectrum. The discussion about the status of proper names, summarized in Saul Kripke's *Naming and Necessity*, centres on the question of whether names have sense, as opposed to simply reference. Briefly, the view of proper names as asemiotic is based on the notion that they do not have a signified and are therefore not signs. Names thus pertain to discourse or *parole* rather than to *langue*. Many people, places, or objects can share the same proper name without having anything in common; only the act of referring will determine the reference of the name. It is in the instance of discourse – when they leave the name dictionary and become 'embodied' in Alan Gardiner's terms – that names gain their meaning. No metalinguistic operations can be performed on words that have such a direct and singular relation to their referents: names are immune to paraphrase, synonymy (as well as antonymy), and translation.

This discussion is particularly interesting for the study of proper names in fiction, where the reference is fixed within the text, and the name consequently must be replaceable by a description rather than by the ostension of ordinary language. In Roland Barthes' words: 'Lorsque des sèmes identiques traversent à plusieurs reprises le même Nom propre et semblent s'y fixer, il naît un personnage' (S/Z 74). Barthes thus sees the name as a unifying signifier which will assemble its signified in the form of indices of characterization retrieved in the act of reading. However, once the signified has been constituted in the reader's mind, or once the name has become 'embodied,' the signified plays the role of referent and the name functions as it would in ordinary language; the rule of unique reference is as central in most fiction – at least in what Barthes would qualify as readerly texts – as in reality. As Ian Watt points out, this realistic use of names is one of the characteristics that distinguish the novel from romance and allegory, an observation that points to the important role of naming as a generic marker and that I will have occasion to come back to often in my readings.

Fictional names cease to be 'proper' when they become inscribed in a system of intertextual reference. Pamela was robbed of her propriety in more ways than one with the publication of *Shamela*, which turned her name into a sign. (*Joseph Andrews*, of course, did the same.) While Pamela did have a proper name until the appearance of the later works, neither Shamela nor Joseph did, by virtue of their pre-inscribed intertextual signification. They were never more than signs, so to speak. This common parodic device is often used, more or less covertly, in modern fiction, and examples of such intertextual, hence 'improper,' naming will be found in all of the novels I will discuss, most intriguingly, perhaps, in *Trou de mémoire*.

Following Watt, Patricia Parker defines the novel as dependent on 'chronology, spacing, the principle of individuation, and the designating function of proper names' (*Identity of the Literary Text* 96). These elements are interconnected: the proper name as a marker of individuation is dependent on coordinates of time and space. The link between the 'proper' and place, between name and territory, is central to the discussion of the 'proper' as a corollary of property and propriety which is succinctly expressed in Parker's summarization of the Lockean principles of individuation: 'each name in its place and a proper place for every name' (102). The proper name identifies and delimits the boundaries of the self, of the individual territory. But, as Parker demonstrates in her analysis of the ubiquity of names in *Wuthering Heights*, this convention is sometimes undermined even within a fiction which overtly claims to adhere to it. It is not surprising that the postmodern decentring of the subject has influenced the naming strategies in its fictions. We will see that the naming of characters in the novels to be discussed more often than not follows conventions more similar to those usually associated with allegory or romance than with realist fiction. This movement away from what is often seen as the staple of realism – characterization or individuation – into strategies pertaining to genres commonly considered inferior does not mean that the novel is dead, as was sometimes claimed in the early days of postmodernism, but rather indicates that its 'proper' form is not the realism of Dickens, Zola, or Balzac but rather what Linda Hutcheon calls the 'narcissistic narrative' represented to most postmodernists by such canonical texts as *Tristram Shandy* and *Don Quixote*.

It could be claimed that the unconventionality of many proper names in contemporary fiction points to a greater degree of territoriality, to a sense of a more natural link between name and referent. A 'character' like Thomas Pynchon's Herbert Stencil in *V.*, for instance, a typically postmodern, decentred subject, has a name which, in a highly allegorical fashion, speaks this very decentring (Herbert *is* a stencil). This contradiction between the deterritorialization of the subject and what looks like the territorial identity between name and referent may account for some of the paradoxical tensions in much of recent fiction, and it will be seen to have a central, ironic function in *Gone Indian*.

Naming plays an important role in mythical narrative. One of the most universal myths, according to George Steiner, involves a variant of Jacob's struggle with the angel, a hand-to-hand battle between two opponents of equal strength, where the outcome is an act of naming (*After Babel* 225). From a simple introduction to elaborate rites of passage, each naming is a form of initiation and it is perhaps not surprising that, thematically, the preoccupation with naming and identity in several of my chosen texts will be found to coexist with a thematics of initiation, most explicitly in *The New Ancestors*. Revealing one's name or giving a name is an acknowledgment of the Other and, consequently, a statement of identity.

The close identity between name and referent has now been established. But what is the link between the proper name and identity, in the sense of 'self?' Animals have a distinctive way of identifying themselves to others which is different from that used by other members of the flock to call them. The chick will identify itself to its mother by uttering a certain sound, while the hen will use a different signal to call her offspring. There is thus in the animal world a distinction between call-names and 'self-signaling' names (Sebeok). Geoffrey Hartman suggests that a similar distinction may operate in humans. Taking his cue from Lacan's definition of the mirror stage as the moment when the child first identifies with her double in the mirror and (mis)recognizes the connection between her image and her proper name, he posits a similar stage after the entry into the symbolic order. At this point, Hartman suggests, the child would name herself, or adopt an identity felt to be truer than the one imposed in the form of a name given by parents. Hartman's discussion is partly inspired by Walter Benjamin, who felt that he had such a 'personal angel,' an alias appearing anagrammatically in some of his writings. According to both Benjamin and Hartman this 'true' identity would stay latent in the adult and to some extent determine the individual's life. Hartman finally presents the provocative hypothesis that 'literature is the elaboration of a specular name' (108), an idea I will play with in my textual analyses. The theory he presents is inspired specifically by Derrida's definition of literary discourse as 'the transformation of the proper name, *rebus*, into things, into the name of things' (qtd in Hartman 95). My discussion of *Gone Indian* will show this version of the rebus to be related to postmodern allegory, and Hartman's intriguing suggestion regarding the specular name will prove to play both a thematic and an auto-referential role in all of my chosen novels.

In the cases of Hegel and Genet, Derrida's subjects in *Glas*, the key to the personal rebus is constituted by the given name and specific acts of naming imposed by parental authority on the child, which are then transformed into certain words and expressions disseminated in the texts, which thus constitute what might be called the author's signature. The equation of nomination and accusation implicit in Derrida's discussion is mythological, insofar as naming creates identity. This phenomenon will be seen as a central theme used, in radically different ways, in the two novels I will discuss in chapters 5 and 6, *L'Elan d'Amérique* and *Gone Indian*. The specular self, on the other hand, is the result of a self-naming, through which the individual assumes an alias or creates her own fate and, in so doing, transgresses the authority of the father as name-giver. In 'Des Tours de Babel,' Derrida quotes Chouraqui's translation of the Bible's story:

Allons, bâtissons-nous une ville et une tour.
Sa tête: aux cieux.
Faisons-nous un nom,
que nous ne soyons dispersés sur la face de toute la terre.   (213)

It is the *hubris* of the Semites' substituting their own name for that of the father, a felt necessity resulting from the exile from the place of origin, that provokes God's wrath. The link between self-naming and exile (or the attempted resettlement in foreign territory), which is foregrounded in this version of the myth, will turn out to play a central role in André Langevin's novel. The ambivalence of the sacred, then, is seen in the perversion of the name of the father, punished by the proliferation of mother tongues which creates the necessity for translation, that impossible task. In a way translation originates as a guarantee of sacredness, and it is both prohibited and necessary. If Derrida and his deconstructionist colleagues had paid more attention to postmodern texts they might have found that the Babelian stance of the modernists is in the works of their successors frequently redeemed in a pentecostal transcendence of the territoriality of language. It is, in fact, striking how often pentecostal imagery appears in postmodern texts; in my chosen corpus it will be represented by *Beautiful Losers* and, even more clearly, *Trou de mémoire*. Whether this postmodern thematic of linguistic transcendence (or transgression, as most critics would prefer) also may redeem the territoriality of much postcolonial writing is an interesting question, and one that will be pertinent to my discussion of Aquin's novel.

It is becoming apparent that names and their function constitute a rich subject of inquiry into the territoriality of literary texts. Print is, in a sense, a non-territorial medium, insofar as it is not immediately linked to the primary instance of discourse, or even to the time of writing. Or, to put it in Derridean terms, it suffers less from the illusion of presence and transcendence than speech. It is consequently by definition impossible to find a pure 'mythological' or 'proper name' consciousness in literature. The relationship between word and world is always mediated by the text, but the less mediation there is, the more territorial the text will remain. While the polarities posited by my spectrum are thus clearly fictional, they retain a valuable heuristic function.

Although its relevance for an inquiry into territoriality may not be immediately obvious, an analysis along the lines suggested by Derrida and Hartman may make it possible to identify any possible authorial 'self-naming.' Is the author's signature disseminated in the rebus-like fashion identified by Derrida, or is the text, as Hartman suggests, a projection of a specular identity or alias? These questions will lead to some interesting speculations in all of my readings which will, I believe, contain some valuable information regarding the individual writer's perception of his own role and position vis-à-vis his creation, hence of his understanding of his own agency.

Metaphor – Metonymy

'Metaphor has by now been defined in so many ways that there is no human expression, whether in language or any other medium, that would not be metaphoric in *someone's* definition,' complained Wayne Booth in 1978. In fact, metaphor seems to have taken over the place formerly occupied, in turn, by language, laughter, and lying as that which distinguishes the human being from the beast. 'Il est tout à fait exclu qu'un animal fasse une métaphore,' claims Lacan (*Séminaire 3* 248). The renewed interest in the phenomenon of metaphor has indeed led to an inflation of the concept until, at the extreme, it has come metonymically to stand in for literature, if not for human behaviour, in general. It is therefore necessary, in order to preserve its usefulness for critical discourse, and specifically in view of an attempt to place it on a spectrum of territoriality, to decide on a functional definition.

Most theories of metaphor take as their point of departure Aristotle's identification of it as a type of naming: metaphor consists in borrowing a *name* from a *thing* to which it is *proper* and transferring it to another thing, thus substituting an *alien* name for the proper one. In this type of substitution theory metaphor is seen as a kind of 'improper' name, a name uprooted from its proper place. As alien or usurper of what is presumed to be a 'proper' place, metaphor and its movements constitute 'the plot of a Gothic novel.'[3] To Patricia Parker this reveals metaphor as a function of the uncanny, which enters our discussion of territoriality by way of Freud's speculation on the coincidence of 'das Unheimliche' and 'das Heimliche.'[4] According to his view, the sensation of the uncanny arises from our experience of things as alien and familiar at the same time and stems from the surfacing of repressed childhood memories. The circularity that seems inherent in many aspects of my discussion is seen particularly clearly in this curious coincidence of the proper and the improper, the canny and the uncanny. Just as metaphor simultaneously indicates identity and difference, the uncanny is both strange and familiar, alien and original, other and same (as in the famous example of the 'Doppelgänger'). Seen from this perspective, metaphor represents a pre-territorial stage of consciousness, where distinctions between proper and improper are not yet operative because property and identity do not exist.

The idea of metaphor as a substitution trope lies behind what is perhaps the single most influential essay (for literary criticism) on the phenomenon, Jakobson's famous demonstration of metaphor as constitutive of one of the two fundamental aspects of language and the companion-piece to metonymy. According to Jakobson, metaphor and metonymy are the two master tropes, because they reflect respectively the operations of selection and combination. Metaphor works on the paradigmatic axis, as associative substitution, while metonymy, claims Jakobson, works on the axis of syntagmatic combination. This amounts to equating metaphor, in a traditional Aristotelian fashion, with naming and metonymy with predication. Such a view is opposed by advocates of the so-called interaction theories who claim that, although metaphor may technically be a paradigmatic substitution of one word for another, it nevertheless has an effect on the whole syntagm in which it is found. As Paul Ricoeur puts it in *La métaphore vive*, metaphor is a cognitive rather than a simply decorative phenomenon. The change of focus from word to sentence involves a movement from naming to predication: in imposing a new meaning on the sentence metaphor has a predicative function. Metaphor would thus seem to be the product of two distinct operations: naming, which is paradigmatic, and predication, which is syntagmatic. It is consequently less territorial than the proper name.

While in the name identity rules, there is in metaphor always a tension between similarity and dissimilarity, identity and difference, in the relation between tenor and vehicle. Cassirer's identification of the trope as 'the intellectual link between language and myth' (*Language and Myth* 57) is close to Lotman and Uspenskij's view of it as myth 'translated in our habitual forms of consciousness' ('Myth – Name – Culture' 240); both explanations imply a distinction in kind from myth. The idea of metaphor as a kind of translation, a carrying over from one language to another, is essential to my discussion, because it stresses the tension inherent in the trope between similarity and dissimilarity, between proper and improper, which sets it apart from the purely identifying function of the name. Like the name, the metaphor is anchored in reference but it is, according to both Jakobson and Paul Ricoeur, a *split* reference. Metaphor is always ambiguous and requires an effort of construal. (I am clearly limiting my discussion to so-called 'live' metaphors: this definition excludes clichés, dead metaphors, and catachreses which involve no tension at all for the simple reason that they are pure [tenorless] vehicles.) While metaphor, then, recognizes the tension between identity and difference, same and other, it can, as we will see in my analyses, lean towards one or the other of the two poles on my imaginary spectrum of territoriality. That is, it can operate a territorializing conjunction of tenor and vehicle, or it can strive towards the disjunction seen, for instance, in surrealist metaphors, where the split between the literal and figurative is so great as to lead to almost insurmountable difficulties of interpretation. Thus, while metaphor in my schema is always less territorial than the proper name, it can move towards either of the two poles in the spectrum, and my readings will illustrate the difference between conjunctive – territorial – and disjunctive – non-territorial – uses of the trope, or of tropes related to it – especially the oxymoron (notably in *Trou de mémoire*) and the syllepsis (in *Gone Indian*).

The other of Jakobson's master tropes, metonymy, is usually characterized neither by ambiguity nor by tension. Jakobson's definition of metonymy as pertaining to the axis of combination is highly contentious because of its conflation of semantic with syntactic contiguity. Although metonymy involves associative substitution – the substitution of 'hands' for 'sailors' in 'all hands on deck,' for instance, is semantically contiguous but syntactically paradigmatic – both tenor and vehicle belong to the same paradigm, as do 'crown' and 'queen' or 'sail' and 'ship,' to mention only the most common examples. Both metonymy and synecdoche are noun-centred tropes of substitution which have far less influence on the cognitive content of the sentence than metaphor and which are as a rule easier to interpret. There is little tension between tenor and vehicle. Metonymy would thus appear to be primary to and more territorial than metaphor (though contentious, an appeal to children's language acquisition as a model would corroborate this, as Piaget has shown).[5] It is worth remembering that the synecdochic 'pars pro toto' is the general principle of myth and magic, and synecdoche is often seen as near-synonymous with metonymy. As Maureen Quilligan points out, in magic the knowledge of the name (of the victim of a spell, for instance) is as powerful a means of control as the possession of his or her toe-nail (206). This view of the metonymical relationship between the name and its owner does in fact, in the light of our discussion of the territoriality of the name, corroborate a view of metonymy as closely linked to the proper name and primary to metaphor.

Northrop Frye's discussion of the tropological development of literature in *The Great Code* posits metaphor as primary to metonymy, a claim that would seem to be contradicted in his own definition of 'the basis for all ordered categorical thinking' (87) as the identification of a thing as belonging to a class (A is identified as belonging to the class of As), which is a metonymic rather than metaphorical process. In Frye's model, we would seem to find ourselves at the beginning of a Vichian *ricorso*, in which the Enlightenment's insistence on the sharp distinction between subject and object, observer and observed, reality and illusion, is giving place to a post-Einsteinian age of relativity where, as in the age of Homer, such distinctions are not operative. I will contend, however, that the 'first phase' or mythological consciousness, where the word calls forth the thing is fundamentally different from its postmodern, ironic reification. The most obviously post-Einsteinian novel in my corpus is *The New Ancestors*, and my analysis of it will provide an opportunity to observe a postmodern version of myth.

The influence of Jakobson's definitions of the two master tropes can be seen particularly clearly in psychoanalysis, where metaphor and metonymy have come to be seen as synonymous with the two main strategies of the unconscious in the dreamwork, according to Freud – condensation and displacement. Jacques Lacan, who insists that his use of the terms is not figurative, applies them in a very wide sense and contends that the symptom is a metaphor, while metonymy reflects the non-coincidence of desire with its object. Metaphor is the irruption of the signifier into the signified, which involves a crossing of the bar separating the two, while metonymic desire moves between signifiers without connecting with the signified.[6] This implies an analogy between signifier and consciousness, and signified and unconscious. Such a transposition of the terms can only be defined as metaphoric, in spite of Lacan's disclaimer. In this view, metaphor would indeed be more territorial; it indicates the emergence of meaning, the making conscious of the unconscious, while metonymy stays on the surface and resists signification. At the extreme, metaphor has come to be used to define any textual strategy characterized by vertical structures of signification, while texts exhibiting mainly horizontal features are identified as metonymic. This distinction between verticality and horizontality, which Jean-Charles Falardeau saw as typical of the difference between the literatures of Quebec and Canada and which has since then so often been seen as reflective of the opposition between the mythic character of Québécois literature and the realism of its English-Canadian counterpart will be given its postmodern guise in my comparison of *L'Elan d'Amérique* and *Gone Indian*.

Jakobson's claim that literature always oscillates between the metonymic and metaphoric poles has been taken up by David Lodge, who contends that postmodernism resists assimilation into either of the two because of its awareness both of the illusion of metaphor and of the dependence of metonymy on plot, which is a realist convention. This problematic view illustrates the difficulty of generically identifying much of recent fiction, but it would also seem to undermine the whole argument. Has the swing of the pendulum suddenly stopped and, if so, are we witnessing the death, not only of the novel but of literature? I think not. Rather, I see the apparent tropological homelessness of postmodernism as yet another indication that the distinction between the two tropes is not as fundamental as is often thought and that metonymy should be considered a simpler form of, or at least akin to, metaphor. In the following, metonymy will be less important than metaphor, with the exception of my reading of *Gone Indian* which, to some extent, is informed by Lacan's discussion.

Translated into generic terms, my analysis situates poetry, with its dependence on metaphor, close to myth. What has been traditionally seen as the 'proper' form of the novel, represented by realism, occupies, according to Frye, the pole opposite romance in the realm of fiction. The genre that claims transparency and the most neutral relationship between word and world is thus further removed from the territorial use of language than poetry. Its non-territoriality can be illustrated in its translatability. Realism's position opposite metaphor is not a result of its dependence on metonymy, however, as Lodge claims, but rather reflects its sharp division, which opposes it to myth, between spirit and matter. Primarily concerned with the latter, the realist novel is vehicular in Gobard's sense of the word: whether dealing with social or psychological realism, it reflects the split between *Gemeinschaft* and *Gesellschaft* or between id and ego. Poetry, on the other hand, creates a kind of intimacy by fusing the public with the private. As Ted Cohen says, 'a figurative use [of language] can be inaccessible to all but those who share information about one another's knowledge, beliefs, intentions, and attitudes' (in Sacks 7). Although less territorial than the proper name, metaphor is a property of the *Gemeinschaft*, and vehicular language is its enemy. Unlike the poet, the realist novelist is not part of what he or she describes but, even when a narrator is allowed to enter the fiction, the Lockean division between subject and object is maintained. Rather than depending on the problematic opposition between the two tropes, my readings will trace their configuration in terms of conjunction – territoriality – or disjunction – non-territoriality – between tenor and vehicle, hence their striving towards the identity of myth on the one hand, or the difference of what I will call metamorphosis on the other.

Metamorphosis

Our post-Einsteinian era is characterized by the breakdown of the distinction between subject and object, between observer and observed, and between illusion and reality, a breakdown often defined as characteristic of postmodernism. The movement toward undecidability of character and plot in much recent fiction and the undermining of the Lockean (realist) assumptions of individuation coincide with a general movement away from metaphor and culminate in the 'unnaming' typical of much postcolonial fiction, exemplified by the novels of Robert Kroetsch. Similar tendencies are reflected in the diegetic disintegration or absurd proliferation of identity, instances of which will be seen – actualized in different ways – in all the novels I will study. Metamorphosis is the opposite of stable identity and it is not coincidental that Canadian and Québécois fiction abound with metamorphic imagery. 'Metamorphosis is ... an image of what in the Bible is called the fall of man, which traditionally has involved his alienation from nature,' explains Frye (*Great Code* 97). If metamorphosis is the image of the fall, and the postmodern variant of this topos is the fall into language, it is not surprising that the resurfacing of this mythical theme in recent fiction is often linked to the discourse of auto-referentiality. As the original fall reflects humanity's estrangement from nature, so the Babelian 'fall' mirrors the alienation from the absolute Word, and heralds the metamorphic potential of the signifier.

For many contemporary writers the myth of Babel has lost its terror and has come to be seen as a positive metaphor for the recognition of the insufficiency of language and the futility of trying to capture experience in writing, an attitude which, paradoxically, has inspired much innovative and vigorous literature. The 'discovery' of the arbitrariness of the linguistic sign and the post-Babelian loss of faith in language have, according to Steiner, given rise to two opposite trends: 'At one pole we find a "pathology of Babel", autistic strategies which attach hermetic meanings to certain sounds or which deliberately invert the lexical, habitual usage of words. At the other extreme, we encounter the currency of banal idiom, the colloquial shorthand of daily chatter from which constant exchange has all but eroded any particular substance' (*After Babel* 171). The two different tendencies are epitomized by Joyce on the one hand and Beckett on the other. The last three decades have witnessed a growing interest among literary critics in the writers Steiner calls 'extraterritorials' or 'esperantists,' artists like Borges, Beckett, and Nabokov, who are homeless in language because polyglot (*Extraterritorial* 5). These can all be defined as marginal, or as writers of minor literatures, insofar as they are dispossessed, or deliberately 'dispossess' themselves, of a vernacular.

The current canonization of marginality and the view of extraterritoriality as a desirable state may account for the popularity in recent critical theory of Bakhtin's writings on the carnivalesque. The carnival becomes a metaphor for the rejection of the tyranny of meaning and the (Lacanian) inversion of the primacy of signified over signifier in much of postmodernist fiction. Carnival is the realm of metamorphosis, where identity is dissolved and differences break down. In a world where a fool can become king the notion of fixed identity and meaning becomes extremely ambiguous; the signified becomes secondary, and the importance of the carnival for linguistic freedom is actualized in the subversion of the sign. The carnival as an institutionalized deterritorialization for the purpose of liberating the ego from the straitjacket of the superego also constitutes a good model for the mainstream of postmodernism, where language points to its own dissolution and inherent polymorphousness. The carnival and the grotesque have come to exemplify the extraterritorial experience, where the self is dissolved and metamorphosed. In the carnival the world is turned on its head, and the I becomes the Other or, seen from the opposite – anti-oedipalist – vantage point, the Other finally coincides with the pre-oedipal, 'collective' I. It has the same function as the sacrificial crisis in primitive societies, which in René Girard's terms, is a temporary 'effacement des différences' (*La Violence et le sacré* 170), a movement leading *through* undifferentiation to a new differentiation.[7] The momentary return to a pre-territorial state of undifferentiated chaos is a prerequisite for the birth of a new order, which, (like identity) is built on difference, and the ritual is a means of restoring a threatened order. While the liberating and terrifying 'fête' is the locus of metamorphosis, its result is a new distribution of identity and difference. The specifically Christian archetype of metamorphic ritual is the mystery of transubstantiation or the sacrament of the Eucharist which, according to Freud, is a repetition of the original totemic feast on which civilization is built, the slaying and subsequent eating of the father.[8] This particular version of metamorphosis will prove to play central roles in Cohen's, Aquin's, and Godfrey's novels, and we shall see how the transformative power of the word inherent in the sacrament, and reminiscent of the 'primitive' word-magic of myth, will be put to rather surprising uses. In Kroetsch's novel, the carnival will perform a similar function.

As a literary topos, metamorphosis pertains above all to the fantastic and is common in myth and fairy-tale, where it usually implies a movement toward a greater degree of disorder or undifferentiation, but which results in a new order: Narcissus, the patron saint of postmodernism, is resurrected as a flower and the fairy-tale frog becomes a prince again. The metamorphic process can thus be said to comprise two stages: the downward movement toward undifferentiation and the subsequent restoration of a new distribution of identity and difference. When the second phase is missing, which is often the case in postmodernism, the metamorphosis can be qualified as entropic, in an application of Clausius' second law of thermodynamics to the universe which, like every closed system, is moving towards increasing disorder and eventual heat-death.[9] We shall encounter an example of entropic transformation in *The New Ancestors*, a novel heavily influenced by various modern scientific theories. This type of change can be seen as an incomplete metamorphosis: creating chaos out of order, it stops at the first phase.

An instance of accomplished metamorphosis, in which a new order is restored from momentary chaos, will be seen in *Gone Indian*, where the metamorphic process is expressed in terms of 'unnaming.' It can be argued that the movement toward undifferentiation represents a return to the pre-proper, or to a stage prior to the division between self and Other embedded in the proper name, in other words, to a primordial chaos. This would indicate that the non-territorial, the realm of undifferentiation, coincides with the pre-territorial, as the anti-oedipalists claim. It is not surprising that this movement is sometimes seen as common to myth, early infancy and certain types of madness. The schizophrenic, as Deleuze points out and as we shall see exemplified in *Beautiful Losers*, often suffers from the delusion that the body is leaking out of its pores: the distinction between self and world disappears. It is not coincidental that schizophrenia has become a buzzword in recent critical theory as well as a staple of much postmodern fiction; it is the necessary condition of deterritorialization or extraterritoriality in modern society, according to the anti-oedipalists, and we shall encounter it as a central ingredient in *The New Ancestors*. From this point of view, madness represents a healthy reaction against the oedipal split between id and ego and a rebellion against an identity imposed from without. It implies a return to what Lacan terms the pre-oedipal 'corps morcelé,' the body in pieces. This would presumably explain the uncanny effect metamorphic images in literature have on the reader.[10] 'Les métamorphoses,' says Todorov, 'forment ... une transgression de la séparation entre matière et esprit, telle que généralement elle est conçue' (119). Thus, we encounter again the apparent circularity, where the two opposite ends of the spectrum – territoriality/myth and non-territoriality/metamorphosis – seem to coincide. However, because myth recognizes no separation between the material and the spiritual, there can be no question of transgression in that realm. The territorial spectrum may resemble a circle, but it is an open, rather than a closed one; a spiral might be a more appropriate image. The knowledge brought to bear on the operations of thought and language, primarily by Saussurean linguistics, and the division of linguistic functions that has taken place in our modern world, imply, as I stated earlier, that any return to myth – a return to monoglossia from heteroglossia – is impossible. It is true that many postmodern writers – and perhaps none more insistently than Leonard Cohen and Hubert Aquin – try to bridge the gap between the sacred and the profane, but what may seem like a *ricorso* in our post-Einsteinian era is either inevitably tainted with self-conscious irony or presented as religious mystery. Contrary to the anti-oedipalist claim, non-territoriality in literature cannot coincide with pre-territoriality. If the thematic preoccupation with metamorphosis in postmodernism could be found reflected in rhetorical strategies – and I will argue in my analyses that it is – these would be positioned opposite the proper name and yet far from metaphor on the territorial spectrum/spiral and would reflect the disintegration of the relationship between identity and difference which is so essential to that trope.

An investigation of the phenomenon of metamorphosis in modern literature brings us back to Kafka and 'The Metamorphosis.' Unlike the traditional fantastic tale, and in a movement functionally related, though technically opposed, to the Brechtian 'Verfremdung,' Kafka's fiction treats the strange as if it were commonplace. Kafka distrusts metaphor, which he sees as a symptom of the unbearable dependence of word on world: 'Metaphors are one among many things which make me despair of writing. Writing's lack of independence of the world, its dependence on the maid who tends the fire, on the cat warming itself by the stove; it is even dependent on the poor old human being warming himself by the stove. All these are independent activities ruled by their own laws; only writing is helpless, is a joke and a despair' (*Diaries* 200-1). Yet, perhaps because of his awareness of the difficulty of such a project, Kafka almost succeeds in uprooting language from its referential burden. Deleuze and Guattari explain how he does it: 'Kafka tue délibérément toute métaphore, tout symbolisme, toute signification, non moins que toute désignation. La métamorphose est le contraire de la métaphore. Il n'y a plus sens propre ni sens figuré, mais distribution d'états dans l'éventail du mot. La chose et les autres choses ne sont plus que des intensités parcourues par les sons ou les mots déterritorialisés suivant leur ligne de fuite' (*Kafka* 40). What the anti-oedipalists, in their hyperbolic manner, call metamorphosis is thus clearly different from metaphor and represents the split between word and world which reflects the deterritorialization typical of the minor literature. Todorov, following Marthe Robert, claims that the strange effect of Kafka's fictions is the result of his literalization of common metaphors or clichés. People are sometimes described as vermin, and Kafka's father regarded his son as a parasite; consequently Gregor Samsa becomes an insect. Such literalization of metaphor may indeed explain many cases of diegetic metamorphosis in fairy-tales, for instance. As Todorov points out, 'Le surnaturel naît souvent de ce qu'on prend le sens figuré à la lettre' (82). But Kafka's literalization can also be seen as a thematic reification of the word. It would seem as if the word in Kafka's texts has come almost full circle from the original unity of proper and figurative: in a first movement, the proper takes over, eventually giving rise to a metaphor, which is finally undone or re-appropriated – the 'improper' becomes the 'proper.' It may be argued that this metamorphic process could go one step further and re-metaphorize the word in a way different from the first figurative moment. Such an itinerary would reflect, on the level of the word, the movement from myth to metaphor, and finally to metamorphosis. While all of the novels in some way literalize metaphors or figures of speech, the completed circle will, in fact, be illustrated concretely in my reading of *Gone Indian*, where the metamorphic process takes its most radical linguistic expression. In *Trou de mémoire* Hubert Aquin plays on the literalization of figurative expressions, especially clichés, so as both to underscore and mysteriously to overcome the frequent contradictions between a literal and a figurative reading of the same expression in a way which points to the oxymoronic mysteries of polysemy.

Deleuze and Guattari reject Marthe Robert's interpretation of Kafka on the grounds that a literalization of metaphor presupposes the existence of the very trope the author disdains. The shocking power of the writer's language, they claim, results instead from his substitution of intensity for signification. The two stand in a relation of opposition, and intensity is the hallmark of metamorphosis which, consequently, is a-significant. To explain their understanding of the concept of intensity, they refer to Vidal Sephiha, who has studied its use in spoken language, where it is the property of 'tout outil linguistique qui permet de tendre vers la limite d'une notion ou de la dépasser' (113). Sephiha goes on to list several examples of such 'tenseurs': pleonasm, anaphora, progression, paronomasia, hyperbole, as well as the generalizing synecdoche and the passe-partout word, all of which illustrate the movement toward the 'dénotionnalisation' typical of spoken discourse, but none of which is particularly evident in Kafka's style. William Labov, in his study of Black Vernacular English in New York City, points out the frequency of similar devices (notably expressive phonology, quantifiers, repetition, and ritual utterances) in natural narrative. In the oral account of personal experience, Labov shows, intensifiers fulfil a function of evaluation: they reflect the narrator's attempt to convince the audience that the story is worth telling – and hearing. They thus perform an important phatic function, in the same way as similar features documented by Stith Thompson in the folktale, and, one might argue, various regional forms of non-signifying slang (whose Canadian variant might be the source of the McKenzie brothers' 'Take off, eh!').

While all these observations indicate that intensity is linked to expression rather than signification, they contradict Deleuze and Guattari's claim that a language aiming at intensity is less territorial than one aiming primarily at signification. The intensifiers identified by Sephiha, Labov, and Thompson are devices used to subvert a major language, but which eventually come to perform a reterritorializing function. The evolution of *joual* as a literary language in the sixties and seventies illustrates how the deterritorialization of signification becomes a reterritorialization of expression, where intensity turns into a phatic marker of a certain *Gemeinschaft*. While it had a subversive effect in the beginning, it soon became a reterritorialized vernacular, a kind of introverted and apolitical 'thérapie collective,' risking to succumb to the folklorization of otherness.[11] This is in sharp contrast to the 'true' minor literature where the individual Oedipus is directly plugged into the political machine in a way that will turn out to play a central thematic role in *The New Ancestors*. Some of the intensifying strategies listed by Sephiha (notably anaphora, progression, and paronomasia) are usually seen as typical of poetic language, as will be illustrated in what is also the most metaphoric of the novels in my corpus, *L'Elan d'Amérique*. The equation of intensity with deterritorialization is thus problematic. There is an important difference between the territorial intensity of natural narrative and the non-territorial effect created by the Kafkaesque (and Beckettian) avoidance of metaphor.

The metamorphic power of the signifier is reflected in many postmodern texts in frequent punning, which we will see exemplified in different ways in my five chosen novels. The pun always involves some kind of splitting of the sign, usually in the form of polysemic play, as we shall see, for instance, in different ways in *Beautiful Losers* and *L'Elan d'Amérique*. From the point of view of territoriality, the pun is a complex phenomenon and cannot be easily positioned at a particular place on our spectrum. On the one hand, it can be a territorializing device which anchors the signifier in a particular language and hence guarantees untranslatability (as evidenced by the kind of play engaged in by *nouveaux romanciers* like Roussel, Queneau, and Ricardou and, closer to home, Réjean Ducharme). As Ricardou points out, the translation of a signifier-generated text must proceed in a manner different from that of a traditional one; rather than rendering the meaning, it must reproduce the strategies of text generation and, consequently, translation becomes production of new meaning (*Nouveau roman: hier, aujourd'hui* 2:151). The translator of such a text must attempt to reterritorialize it in the target language. The presumed splitting of the sign in the pun thus, paradoxically, foregrounds its indivisibility. A text governed by the signifier is usually not far removed from poetry and is consequently territorial. As Jakobson points out, 'the pun, or to use a more erudite, and perhaps more precise term – paronomasia, reigns over poetic art, and whether its rule is absolute or limited, poetry by definition is untranslatable. Only creative transposition is possible ....' ('On Linguistic Aspects of Translation' 238).

On the other hand, the uprooting of the signifier can aim at deterritorializing the text by freely crossing language boundaries and creating a kind of extraterritorial esperanto, as Joyce does in *Finnegans Wake* and Nabokov, to a lesser extent, in *Ada*. Just as much postmodern metafiction anticipates criticism by integrating critical commentary into the text, one might say that such macaronic writing forestalls translation by, so to speak, translating itself. The clear boundary between source and target language, which is a necessary precondition for conventional translation, is blurred and the task of the translator made impossible. Wordplay can only occur by pitting words against each other, and the new vehicle always carries within it traces of another sign (or other signs).

Anamorphosis – Allegory

Yet another phenomenon sometimes linked to metamorphosis is *anamorphosis*, a concept borrowed from the visual arts by literary critics, and which will be central to my analysis of *Trou de mémoire*. Anamorphosis as a visual strategy is defined as 'a monstrous projection; or a representation of some image, either on a plane or curved surface, deformed and distorted; which at a certain distance shall appear regular and in proportion.'[12] The monstrosity alluded to in the definition points to its affinity with metamorphosis and the uncanny. A narrower description of anamorphosis is offered by Jurgis Baltrusaitis, whose study of the phenomenon has inspired most critical discussion: 'au lieu d'une réduction à leurs limites visibles, c'est une projection des formes hors d'elles-mêmes et leur dislocation de manière qu'elles se redressent lorsqu'elles sont vues d'un point déterminé' (5). Anamorphic techniques thus involve a distortion of form which forces the viewer (or, by extension, the reader) to assume the correct position or distance from which the image can be restored.

The first critic to suggest an analogy between anamorphic art and literature was probably Galileo who, in a tirade against the allegorical poetry of Tasso, saw in both the same contrived quality and deplored the substitution of artifice for beauty (Panofsky 13–14). He strongly disliked the constraint of allegory which, like most anamorphic art, works on two levels – the overt and the covert – that stand in a clear hierarchical relationship. Galileo's linking of allegory and anamorphosis has resurfaced in recent criticism, largely as a result of Jacques Lacan's use of Baltrusaitis' book in his 1964 seminar (published as *The Four Fundamental Concepts of Psychoanalysis*). Building on Freud's discussion of the uncanny, and inadvertently confirming Angus Fletcher's linking of allegory with repetition compulsion (which will prove pertinent to my discussion of *L'Elan d'Amérique*), Lacan and critics following him see anamorphic shapes as signifiers of the unconscious.[13]

Fernand Hallyn, for instance, links anamorphosis to the surfacing of the repressed memory of the 'corps morcelé.' The importance of the gaze is stressed in Lacan's discussion of the phenomenon and is taken up by Timothy C. Murray, who links anamorphosis to voyeurism, which he sees as an ideal mode of reading fantastic literature, whose idiosyncratic logic requires that it be viewed 'askance' in order to make sense. The voyeuristic nature of much contemporary fiction has often been pointed out, and it has sometimes been linked to the influence of cinematic techniques. In film an anamorphic lens is needed to restore the cinemascopic image which is distorted by its compression onto an ordinary film strip. It is perhaps not coincidental that Hubert Aquin, whose novel is the most overtly anamorphic, is also very interested in film, and that the central chapter of Dave Godfrey's novel, which uses overtly cinematic techniques, is also a good example of the 'voyeurism' implicit in anamorphic techniques. Both of these strategies are anticipated, albeit less explicitly, in *Beautiful Losers*.

For the most part, however, the Freudian reinterpretation of the phenomenon fails to distinguish adequately between anamorphosis and metamorphosis, preferring to see both as symptoms of the return to a pre-territorial undifferentiation. What such a conflation overlooks are the connotations of restraint and control implicit in the former which oppose it to the freedom and unpredictability of the latter. Polysemic play can be anamorphic, tightly controlled and manipulative or it can be metamorphic, manifesting the free play of signifiers.

It is not coincidental that both anamorphosis and allegory have re-entered critical debate around the same time, and Galileo's linking of the two will be borne out in my readings. The resurfacing of allegory constitutes yet another link between postcolonialism and postmodernism. As Stephen Slemon indicates, the genre has traditionally 'privileged doctrine and metaphysical system at the expense of "otherness" – if allegory literally means "other speaking" it has historically served as a way of representing, of speaking *for* the "other", especially in the enterprise of imperialism.' ('Post-Colonial Allegory and the Transformation of History' 161). This assimilating function is best reflected in the persistence, traced by Abdul Jan-Mohamed, of the 'Manichean allegory' as the model for the relationship between colonizer and colonized, which will be put to the test in *Beautiful Losers* and *Trou de mémoire*. In this sense of the genre, a new situation is interpreted in terms of a pre-existing master narrative – in the case of colonization the view of a world divided between good and evil, same and other, superimposed on the relationship between white and black. Yet, Slemon insists, because of its transformative force, allegory can be turned into the 'counter-discourse' that will allow for the necessary contestation of such representations.

The postcolonial assertion of the contestatory usefulness of allegory would seem to corroborate Deleuze and Guattari's contention that a minor literature is always hooked on to collective experience, but it entails a problem that is central to the current debate surrounding the term. When Fredric Jameson claims, for instance, that private experience in the 'third world' always becomes an 'allegory of the embattled situation of the public ... culture and society' (69), without clearly identifying the textual signs of this Deleuzian linkage of public and private, it may be argued that he is reading from a centre that continues to deny the existence of individuality in the margin, and that allegory remains an appropriating way of reading otherness. The confusion surrounding the redefinitions of the genre seems to hinge on a fundamental uncertainty: on the one hand allegory refers to a way of reading, on the other to a clearly identifiable genre. I will, in my discussion try to reserve the term for the latter.

In current debate, the resurgence of allegory in both postmodernism and postcolonialism has been accompanied by a change in focus from its hermeneutic level to its linguistic and semiotic properties more symptomatic of a shift in critical concerns than in the conventions pertaining to the genre. This shift in critical interest has led to several attempted redefinitions resulting, I would argue, from a general reluctance to accept the return of a genre so long defined as 'low' and to tackle the problem of intentionality. The genre's dependence on the polysemic potential of words makes it possible, as Maureen Quilligan contends, to see it as inherently hermetic, intratextual and lateral, and we will indeed encounter several examples of the power of puns to generate allegory, most explicitly in *L'Elan d'Amérique*. However, the critical desire to detach the genre from its referential anchoring would also seem to deprive it of the obvious political force that is so visible, at least in its postcolonial form – allegory is, after all, an old form of esoteric writing that has always been potentially subversive. In the following I will therefore reserve the term for a strategy that, by Benjamin and others, is linked to the rebus and to hieroglyphics, to concealment and enigma, all of which show 'the desire to guarantee the sacred character of any script' (*The Origin of German Tragic Drama* 175), and all of which are heavily dependent on authorial intention.

Although it often relies on metaphor, allegory offers less resistance to interpretation; it is territorial insofar as its literal site-specificity is always linked to a pre-existing paradigm which binds the concrete and the specific to the abstract and universal; it reflects the congruity, if not the convergence, of the vernacular – the here and now – and something else, whether a political/referential or sacred territory. While it is as open to parody and other kinds of subversion as any other genre, its striving to overcome differences between the material and the spiritual, mirrored – in spite of its interest in words – in the preference for vertical strategies of signification, marks it as fundamentally conjunctive and territorial, as we shall see in *L'Elan d'Amérique*. Although it always links the particular with the universal or the individual with the collective, that gesture is not, per se, subversive; after all, the colonizer's Manichean allegory is as collective as any attempt to contest it will be.

It may seem surprising that concepts like anamorphosis and allegory, with their connotations of constraint and manipulation, have re-entered critical discourse at a time when the latter seems more than ever determined to stress the openness of interpretation and, in particular in the context of postmodernism, the undecidability of meaning. As I have indicated, however, and as my textual analyses will demonstrate, I see this reappearance as a symptom of the re-emergence of what has been suppressed in most criticism, ever since Wimsatt's and Beardsley's codification of the 'intentional fallacy' – the author's intention. To borrow a Lacanian turn of phrase, anamorphosis, like allegory, is the unmistakable signature of the absent 'father' of the work who, by inscribing his signature, imposes his law on the reader.[14] Similarly, according to Benjamin, from his controlling position, the allegorist can make anything mean anything else. The shift in meaning recent criticism has imposed on these terms, which inevitably connote control and constraint, and not infrequently, didacticism, is, I would contend, a result of the desire to make texts conform to an a priori valorization of certain features considered as inherently subversive – notably openness and indeterminacy – and the consequent attempt to make texts considered radical fit this pattern. It is also, I believe, symptomatic of the critical desire to wrench control of the text from the author – an enterprise I will no doubt engage in myself – which leads to a repression of the acknowledgment of the 'name of the father' of the text. All of the novels I will discuss exhibit allegorical features – in *Beautiful Losers* and *Trou de mémoire* coexisting with anamorphic techniques – associated with the signature of the author. These strategies also involve a certain manipulation of the reader, a troubling fact to which I will return in my conclusion.

This discussion has done little to clarify the possible relationship between postcolonialism and postmodernism. Although I will have to suspend that question in the hope that my readings will throw some light on the confusion, a few observations can be made at the outset. On the one hand, since they are involved in a dialectical relationship with a perceived 'centre,' both projects would seem to suffer equally from the paradox of the double gesture described by Linda Hutcheon – the simultaneous use and abuse of ruling discourses. As Hutcheon points out, the frequent charges levelled against postmodernism's complicity with the conventions it claims to contest follow from its political ambivalence which, I would argue, may stem from the uncertainty of the exact identity of its antagonist. It is easier to identify the metropolis against which the empire writes than clearly to define the 'centre' to postmodernism's margin, except in general terms such as 'realist representation,' a notion that may not be as negatively charged for those who have never had any representations of their own. I would agree with Stephen Slemon's claim that the postmodern (and post-structuralist) negation of representation and consequent valorization of non-referentiality risk devaluing the necessary 'recuperative work' of the postcolonial text ('Modernism's Last Post' 12). While the two projects thus share a contestatory stance, they vary in the form and direction taken by their respective contestations. The political agenda implicit in the postcolonial endeavour may require a territorial mapping and naming to replace those imposed from the centre, while the postmodern text may concern itself with undermining aesthetic practices without any sense of political urgency. Could it be, as Fredric Jameson suggests, that postmodernism represents the logic of late capitalism, and that it is simply the new face of imperialism against which postcolonialism writes? In Simon During's term, the postmodern would then be analogous to the 'postcolonising' antagonist of the 'postcolonised,' often representing the power élite of the former colony ('Postmodernism or Postcolonialism?' 369). Or it could be, as During also suggests, that the two are ways of reading, so that the identification of a text as one or the other depends on what values one brings to bear on them. I will return to these questions in my last chapter and my conclusion, when, in the light of the textual analyses, the presuppositions behind the critical debate surrounding the two phenomena will also have been opened to question.

In the remaining sections of the book I will apply the theoretical ideas presented above to the analysis of the individual texts in a general framework of the ideological discourse of colonization, bearing in mind the specific sense of that term in a Canadian context. Rather than adopting the anti-oedipalist criterion of non-territoriality as a sign of literary merit, I prefer to see it as a heuristic concept representing a phase in the process of maturation in any literature growing out of a situation of marginality and particularly useful for studies of situations of linguistic alienation.

Although in varying degrees, all features of territoriality analysed in this theoretical introduction will be relevant to the five novels constituting my corpus. While all of my textual analyses will have as a common objective to position the text on the heuristic spectrum delineated here, each novel will inspire a slightly different reading. This apparent lack of methodological rigour can perhaps be attributed to the complexity both of the texts and of my critical focus which encompasses thematic as well as formal considerations, though I would prefer to see it as a sign of respect for the difference of each text. The individual chapters will begin with a brief plot summary to refresh the reader's memory and will take as their point of departure the most important signifying structures in the novel under discussion. The readings will vary slightly in emphasis as well as in length. The analysis of *Beautiful Losers* will serve as a model and will hence follow the theoretical discussion fairly closely. After that the complexity of the first juxtaposed pair of novels – *Trou de mémoire* and *The New Ancestors* – requires rather lengthy analyses, while the last two – *L'Elan d'Amérique* and *Gone Indian* – demand less space. My reading of *Beautiful Losers* will cover the spectrum from name to metamorphosis but, for reasons that are purely coincidental, the subsequent readings will reverse the order, beginning with detailed analyses of anamorphosis and metamorphosis in chapters 3 and 4 and concentrating on aspects of naming and unnaming in chapters 5 and 6. In chapter 7 I will trace the territorial constellation of the five novels and make some comparisons to a wider corpus and in the conclusion, finally, I shall return to some of the implications of the suggested methodology for the study of other kinds of marginal writing.

CHAPTER TWO

Beautiful Losers
The Novel as Cure

Leonard Cohen's *Beautiful Losers*, published in 1966, is without doubt *the* quintessential Canadian postmodern novel, and it is with reason that I follow Linda Hutcheon (*The Canadian Postmodern*), to whose reading mine is indebted, in beginning my exploration with it. Although dated in many ways, manifesting the site-specificity of much postmodern fiction, it provides an excellent opportunity to investigate a text which is both obviously postmodern in form and postcolonial in impulse written at a time before marginality had been theorized to the point where theory began more or less blatantly to encroach upon fiction.

Situated in the present of the time and place of writing, the turbulent sixties in Montreal, the plot of this novel is deceptively simple. It concerns three characters and their interrelationships: the unnamed narrator of Book One; his friend and lover, F., who is also the 'author' of Book Two, and his wife, Edith. They are all marginal – an English-Canadian Montrealer, a French-Canadian separatist, and an Indian woman – living in a cosmopolitan Montreal which comes to stand in metonymically for Canada. Edith, one of the last of the 'A ____s,' an Indian tribe on which the narrator, who will be called 'I,' is an expert, has committed suicide by crawling under the elevator in their apartment building, and her husband is writing a journal partly to overcome his pain and grief. The search for a cure becomes a pursuit of the truth about Canada, which eventually widens into an ontological quest. The title of Book One, 'The History of Them All,' recounts the history not only of the main actors in a triangle of friendship and love but of the successive colonizations of the country. Written in the first person and often in an intensely personal tone, it interlaces the psychological drama of the characters with a wider historical/political framework in an allegorical manner similar to that discussed in greater detail in my analysis of *L'Elan d'Amérique* in chapter 5.

The journal is divided into fifty-two numbered entries of varying length. Each representing a day – organized chronologically, though not consecutive – they are as irregular as the narrator's bodily functions or, rather, dysfunctions. Exact time references are scarce, but the time of writing seems to span a period from early fall to early spring, and the place moves from 'I's' sub-basement apartment to a tree-house he has inherited from F. The time told, however, spans centuries, focusing on the present and recent past which is juxtaposed with the history of the seventeenth century. In his attempt to come to terms with his grief, 'I' concentrates his efforts at understanding the successive victimizations which characterize the history of Canada on the Iroquois saint Catherine Tekakwitha, the ultimate beautiful loser who comes to symbolize all kinds of colonization – territorial, racial, ideological, and sexual.

Book Two, which recounts many of the same incidents as the first section, consists of 'A Long Letter from F.,' written by the earlier narrator's (as well as his wife's) friend, mentor, and lover in the Occupational Therapy room of the hospital for the criminally insane where he is incarcerated. At the time of writing of Book One, we are told that F. is already dead; the letter is thus written before the earlier section, but is supposed to be read five years after F.'s death; that is, apparently long after the writing of the journal. There is no indication in Book One that 'I' has read it, and Book Three, entitled 'Beautiful Losers,' will complicate the time scheme even further. It seems to take place immediately after the end of Book One which ends a few days after 6 March, probably in 1966, while Book Three opens with the end of F.'s letter, where all pretensions to narrative verisimilitude break down as F. hears the news of his own escape from the asylum on the radio and reports it in writing before it happens. The temporal and narrative perspectives here become preposterous, in the true sense of the word; F. reports as imminent an event that has already taken place in another medium.

Both Book One and Book Two are written in the first person, by 'I' and 'F.' respectively. The intended reader of Book One is ostensibly the dead F., while the addressee of Book Two is 'I.' The relationship between the two communicative situations is thus one of specularity or reciprocity, and the last Book is, as its subtitle indicates, 'An Epilogue in the Third Person,' entitled 'Beautiful Losers' (287). Here we encounter an unnamed 'old man' who shares features with both 'I' and F. as well as with Catherine Tekakwitha's uncle, about whom stories have been told in the earlier chapters. We also meet a female figure who is the modern embodiment of Edith,

Catherine Tekakwitha and the Egyptian goddess Isis. These unholy trinities represent the outcome of the quest for identity and the truth about Canada that, paradoxically, brings about the complete breakdown of identity in any conventional sense. With this final death of the traditional character comes the first explicit intrusion of an authorial 'I' in the novel. As the characters die, the author is resurrected, and the novel ends, not in the third person at all, but in a new first person which is both singular and plural.

The narrative structure of the novel is thus a *mise en abyme* of the situation of communication, in which I and You are reciprocal and interdependent, specularly related positions reflecting the reciprocity necessary for any sense of identity, while the third person occupies a position outside the instance of discourse; he/she is the one talked about (cf. Benveniste, 'La Nature des pronoms' and 'De la subjectivité dans le langage').[1] From a diegetic intra-textual communication with the I and You positions filled by characters on whom the reader eavesdrops, the text opens up into the real situation of reading, as what seems to be the real author addresses the real reader in a typically postmodern appeal for reader participation. The apparent bilat-erality of the communication is, however, illusory. Books One and Two, though written, are essentially monologues (even if they would qualify as dialogic in the Bakhtinian sense) and the end invokes the radio. Throughout his letter, F. has implored 'I' to 'go beyond' (199), but in the end both their voices are lost and the 'third person' leaves place to the authorial 'I.'

Intertexts

One of the most striking aspects of Cohen's text, and one that has probably had the greatest impact on the critical reception of the novel, is his insistent use of pornography, one of many features that indicate his affinity with Hubert Aquin.[2] His interweaving of this discourse with that of colonization provides a good illustration of the problematic analogy discussed in my introduction between economic and sexual exploitation. It is also used in such a way as to link the present political situation and its concomitant intertextual reference with the historical framework, which centres on the Jesuit missionary endeavour in seventeenth-century New France. Focusing on the violence and cruelty involved as much in the practices of the Jesuits as in the Indian tortures of such famous figures as Brébeuf and Lalemant and on the sexual overtones of both, Cohen emphasizes the sado-masochistic relationship, where the submission to the master is an act of will, which traditionally finds its most articulate expression in the discourse of the pornographer. The pornography paradigm also emphasizes Cohen's (quasi-

Foucauldian) preoccupation with the inscription of power relationships on the body. Like all of the writers I will be discussing, he uses the time-worn equation of colonized territory with female body, but he moves further than many of the others from the purely metaphoric use of this paradigm. As we shall see, he literalizes the metaphor in many different ways, and the bodies of all the beautiful losers we meet in his novel are unmistakably physical, as is the pain inflicted on them.

In Cohen's view the body is characterized by its surfaces and its fissures, from which secretions emanate and by way of which connections are made. All bodily fluids have the ambivalence Bakhtin associates with the carnivalesque; they can all transform into each other and, like the irritated secretions of the oyster, a frequent image in the text, they can all potentially turn into pearls. The incoherence of much of 'I's' journal shows writing as anchored in the body, and it is symptomatic that the secret message sent to F. in the end can only be read after being activated by the nurse's, Mary Voolnd's, lubrications (284).

We encounter in Cohen's novel the first of many scenes of sexual violation we will have to confront in the following chapters, as the stereotypical translation of the colonization paradigm into sexual power relationships seems inevitably to entail the – more or less metaphorical – equation of territorial aggression with rape. This episode explicitly introduces the crucial question of otherness. As a thirteen-year-old 'I's' wife is raped by four men whose enterprise is almost ruined when they 'could not bear to learn that Edith was no longer Other, that she was, indeed, Sister' (77). The realization that the intended victim is the same, that she is both a Christian and a human with familiar emotions of fear and terror, as well as bodily functions, causes the rapists to become impotent. But this recognition only reinforces their desire to victimize her and drives them to rape her with 'index fingers, pipe stems, ball-point pens, and twigs' (77). The rape ensures that Edith stays Other, and the weapons used are not arbitrarily chosen. The Indian is all too often – as in the historical research of Edith's husband – reduced to an index card in an archive of forgotten people; the pipe is a symbol of the white appropriation and commercialization of Indian customs (it recurs in a brief anecdote as a transmitter of syphilis); the ball-point pen is a modern version of the many tools used to colonize by writing, and the twigs are the Indian's own ally, nature, turned against her (they also recur as the tools of self-torture used in Catherine's penitence). This anecdote anticipates the paradigmatic rape in *L'Elan d'Amérique* that I will analyse at greater length in chapter five. Described realistically, both episodes acquire allegorical meanings as woman is equated with the forest in an analogy between sexual and cultural – in this case particularly religious – as well as economic exploitation: 'No wonder the forests of Québec are mutilated and sold to America. Magic trees sawed with a crucifix. Murder the saplings. Bittersweet is the cunt sap of a thirteen-year-old' (73). It is not coincidental that, in yet another foreshadowing of Langevin's equation of rape with economic colonization, the incident takes place in a U.S.-owned quarry.

The rape scene encompasses the paradoxical and self-defeating nature of the colonizing project which in the end produces nothing but losers; the desire to turn the Other into the same must fail since its success would ensure that she can no longer be subjected. Conversely, the colonized must struggle to remain other in order not to be assimilated and hence figuratively devoured.

The pornography paradigm subsumes a plethora of intertexts which are presented as modern equivalents of the religion of the 'Company of Jesus' (6) whose epithet already alludes to the commercial interestedness of its project. The contemporary place of worship is the movie palace, and several episodes in the novel take place in the System theatre, which is also the place from which the final revelation originates. The system remains the same, it is only the elements that change. As the metaphoric syntax of the novel develops, the search for a cure for pain becomes equated with the escape from old systems based on analogy and opposition. The goal of the quest is emblematized in F.'s advice to 'I' to 'fuck a saint'; both are equally self-contradictory, only possible through the conjunction of the sacred and the profane promised by the oxymoronic metaphor.

The link between the pornography paradigm and the political present of the story becomes perhaps most explicit in 'I's' description of a rally in Parc Lafontaine where the separatist project is described, in classical postcolonial terms, as the re-appropriation of a stolen history. The crowd is beautiful 'Because they think they are Negroes, and that is the best feeling a man can have in this century' (150). The idea of 'négritude,' promoted by many African theorists of postcolonialism, and played out in Pierre Vallières' *Nègres blancs d'Amérique* (1969), anticipates the more explicit use of the theme in *Trou de mémoire*. In a way equally anticipatory of Aquin's novel, the political rally turns into a collective orgy, as 'I' engages in a sexual encounter with an unknown hand in the crowd in a manifestation of the liberation from oedipal imprisonment heralded by Deleuze and Guattari's notion of the 'machine désirante' – the collective, hence inherently political expression of desire (*L'Anti-Oedipe* chapitre 1). The bonding with the group entails the loss of the individual ego, which is manifested as the crowd tries to identify him: 'He looks English! – He looks Jewish ... – This man is a sex pervert!' (156). 'I's' auto-erotic command, 'Fuck the English!' (151), becomes literalized, as it were, and 'fucking the English' is suggested as the cure to the political ill. The momentary connection with others is a step in 'I's' education, but the more problematic 'fucking a saint' is the only cure to the ontological malaise. And, as in the case we shall encounter in *Gone Indian*, the protagonist is at this crucial moment on the road to enlightenment, and as his identity is in peril, threatened with having 'the shit beat out of him' (156). Like his fellow academic in *Gone Indian*, the narrator is, as Douglas Barbour has pointed out, caught in the trap of history and hence 'full of shit' (Gnarowski 137). 'I's' stubborn constipation impedes his striving for the emptiness requisite for a candidate for sainthood as a receptacle of grace. As long as he retains his shit, he remains isolated in his own body; it is only by 'being fucked' and 'having the shit beaten out of him' that he can become part of the world. Shit, which equals history, is also associated with memory: 'Constipation didn't let me forget' (47). Memory-loss is a pre-condition for self-loss and, unlike *Trou de mémoire* where these themes recur, they are both desirable to Cohen's protagonist. It could be argued that 'I's' quest is for exactly the same 'trou' that Aquin's narrator tries to get out of, as we shall see in the next chapter.

Catherine Tekakwitha, the saint and emblem of Canada's past on whom the narrator projects his desire, is also an implicit presence in the contemporary geographical setting of the story. The psychodrama involving the three characters takes place in a territory traversed in one direction by Boulevard Saint Laurent, or 'the Main,' which divides the city into east and west and hence, symbolically if not in actual fact, into French and English. (It may be significant for our future discussion to remember that 'the Main' has the same name as the river in which the city is located.) Boulevard Saint Laurent is crossed by Rue Ste Catherine, or 'Ste. Catherine Street' as it is hybridized through French-English contagion (149, 279, 280), in a way which also indicates its role in binding the city together. In yet another implicit literalization, then, finding the truth about Canada also equals 'going down' [on] Saint[e] Catherine.

While the novel's topography is real and local and the historical territory predominantly related to the French colonial past, literary intertexts are frequently culled from the British colonizer's canon. Thus Cohen lets F. place the historical situation in New France in a time-frame which hinges on the demise of British literary figures: 'Shakespeare is 64 years dead. Andrew Marvell is 2 years dead. John Milton is 6 years dead. We are now in the heart of the winter of 1680' (258). British literature seems to die with the rise of imperialism, and Cohen may exemplify the empire's 'writing back.' The time lapse between F.'s death and the reading of his letter is 'Five years with the length of five years' (183), reducing the metaphoricity of the opening lines of Wordsworth's 'Tintern Abbey' to a literal and tautological cliché. Equally parodic is a hidden allusion to Keats in the 'orgy of vase Greeks' that is actualized by contemporary 'restaurant Greeks' (267) in a fashion that will prove central to the generation of the text. One of the objectives of the self-reflexive quest of the novel is to let the 'vase Greeks' step out of the frozen artwork into the orgy of life, or to allow the feature to escape from the enclosure of the temple of entertainment and face the pain of reality. Cohen is himself a 'black romantic' (Djwa, in Gnarowski 94), and his own literary affinities have been frequently, and not unexpectedly, identified as being with such figures as Baudelaire, Rimbaud, Céline, Genet, and, closer to home, William Burroughs, those 'literary criminals' who are frequently aligned with the kind of subculture of which pornography (which also flourishes on the Main) is a part.

Greek and Indian mythologies frequently straddle the boundary between the vernacular, the referential, and the sacred in a way that will be made clearer in my discussion of metamorphosis and translation. On the thematic level, the Indians are linked to the Athenians; Catherine Tekakwitha – soon established as a kind of forerunner of Edith – becomes an analogue of Isis, the Egyptian goddess of truth also venerated in Greece, who appears at the end as the driver of the Oldsmobile that gives the old man a lift to the System theatre. The lifting of the veil of Isis, actualized in the act of oral sex performed on her incarnation by the old man in the epilogue's literalization of 'going down on a saint' and earlier imaged as the lifting of Catherine's blanket, becomes another metaphor for finding the truth about being. Cohen here parodies the allegorical commonplace which invites the reader to see through the textual 'veil' to a hidden level of meaning in a way that will indeed give credit to Quilligan's notion of the genre as based on intra- rather than extra-textual patterns of signification.

The Indian legends that appear in the text are perhaps the most respectfully treated of all Cohen's intertexts. They form a counterweight to the Catholic dogma that causes so much of the suffering in the history of colonization and in the story of Catherine Tekakwitha, and that ravages both the mind and the body. Particularly interesting is the story of Oscotarach, who removes the brains of dead Indians in preparation for the Eternal Hunt. Leslie Monkman has shown the parallels between this narrative and the stages in 'I's' initiation; both bring to mind the Orphic descent, whose centrality is already implied in the theme of 'go[ing] down.' The analogy between Oscotarach and F. is made explicit by the latter: the tree-house where 'I' writes part of his journal and which used to belong to F. is likened to Oscotarach's hut; F. is the 'Head-Piercer' (145) and 'I' is his victim. The period in the tree-house is part of the process of brain removal, an initiation which, like all such rites, as I shall discuss at length in connection with *The New Ancestors*, involves transformations of identity.[3] The legend also contains a link to Edith who eats very little – a sign of sainthood – but loves brains. The education of 'I' by F. is aimed at removing the brain in favour of the body as a site of meaning. The opposite of the cerebral historian, F. is the expert of the body; with the help of Charles Axis he has created himself anew, and he is also the Pygmalion to Edith's Galatea. The book can indeed be read as a fictional elaboration of Norman O. Brown's contemporaneous appeal to a return to polymorphous perversity (cf. Ondaatje 47; Lee *Savage Fields* 67). Frequent imagery also, in carnivalesque fashion, associates the head with the ass, so that the piercing of the head metaphorically equates the piercing of the resisting sphincter and the ensuing loss of memory and ego.

Another important Indian legend is the story of the Andacwandet or 'Fuck Cure' (254). Catherine's sick uncle is rejuvenated by inviting all the young people in the village to have sex in the long house (which is later metaphorically linked to the movie theatre). It is, in a sense, such a cure that 'I' is looking for in his quest to 'fuck a saint' and the ritual will turn out to play a central role in the metaphorics of identity and metamorphosis. F.'s reference to the Andacwandet can also be literalized parodically in the same way as 'I's' 'Fuck the English!' In a way F. is teaching 'I' to 'fuck' the cures available in the systems at hand and to dream up his own, as did Catherine's uncle.

Not surprisingly, an important biblical intertext also runs through the novel, manifested most obviously in metamorphic imagery alluding to the Book of Revelation and frequent references to apocalypse, whose significance will become clear in my discussion of language. Some intertextual clues are more subtle; one of the few dates mentioned, for instance, is 6 March, which is the date of 'I's' 48th journal entry, just preceding the final revelation. The temporal reference is presumably 6 March in the year 66, the three-digit number recalling the name of the beast in the Book of Revelation. There are also a number of explicit references to the Old Testament. But the form of the book is equally biblical. The many allusions to 'Old style' and its implicit counterpart, the New style; the highly prophetic nature of many parts of the narrative; the psalms or prayers and the fact that F.'s section is written in the Occupational Therapy room – referred to as O.T. – and before 'The History of Them All' indicate a parodic inversion of the

Bible. 'I's' story is the New Testament, the history of 'Them All' and particularly of the master, written by his disciple. It is not only the prophetic and mystical books of the Bible that are evoked; references are made to the Cabala, alchemy, and various oriental philosophies in a way which indicates a relationship of analogy between sacred texts concerned with mystery, apocalypse, and revelation.

Naming

The search for Catherine Tekakwitha – beginning as an historian's investigation into the past of Canada and widening into an ontological quest – is expressed in the opening paragraph of the novel in terms of a search for a correct name: 'Catherine Tekakwitha, who are you? Are you (1656–1680)? Is that enough? Are you the Iroquois Virgin? Are you the Lily of the Shores of the Mohawk River?' (3). These attempts at definition constitute a kind of intersystemic translation aimed at finding appropriate analogies or aliases in different explanatory systems, all of which pertain to the intertextual territory discussed above. 'You live in a world of names ...' F. accuses his disciple, the historian and would-be scientist (22). 'Science begins in coarse naming, a willingness to disregard the particular shape and destiny of each red life, and call them all Rose. To a more brutal, more active eye, *all* flowers look alike, like Negroes and Chinamen' (51). The opposition between names and shapes will turn out to be crucial, and the classificatory concept of naming that Cohen plays with here is the modern equivalent of the mythological equation of naming with mastery and control. Knowing Catherine's true name would mean mastering both her and the history she represents, but it would also mean repeating the violence done to her. An opposition is thus established between an active, intrusive, or colonizing way of seeing which is synonymous with naming, and a passive, receptive one. The privileging of the latter is reflected throughout the novel in the emphasis put on receptiveness. The lesson F. wants to teach 'I' is the difficult balancing act which consists in seeing particulars when the only tools available are analogous systems. In order to escape the imprisonment in systems, the narrator must first go through them in a kind of initiation process.

Naming is explicitly and thematically linked to colonization and domination, and the history of Canada is summed up in a 'story' the old man in the epilogue tells a little boy, which consists of the subsequent renamings or translations of Indian tribes by the French and English (294). It is significant that 'I,' in a conscientious attempt at escaping the trap of appropriation, avoids naming the object of his research, the 'A ____ s,' even though they are virtually extinct. The A ____ s become un-names or aliases in a way that anticipates Kroetsch's novel; the Indians are equated with the Athenians of antiquity, and throughout the novel several of the beautiful losers we meet are mistaken for A ____ s. The emptiness of the signifier allows it to receive different meanings; thus, for instance, F. seems to use it as an invective when he calls 'I' 'You poor A ____ !' (22). 'I' is here metonymically equated with that particular body-part that imprisons him in the self, curiously anticipating Robert Kroetsch's situating of the origin of truth in that same anatomical location. The Lacanian sliding of the signified under the signifier, 'A ____ s,' illustrates how possibilities of meaning replace unique reference.

The narrator's desire to know Catherine follows an itinerary leading, by way of analogies, through the various intertextual systems, towards the ontological, oxymoronic project of 'going down on a saint.' The notion of sainthood is central to the book, and its link with possibility rather than definition is clear in the narrator's attempt at explanation, which is dependent on metaphor and imagery – as opposed to naming and classification:

> A saint is someone who has achieved a remote human possibility. It is impossible to say what that possibility is. I think it has something to do with the energy of love. Contact with that energy results in the exercise of a kind of balance in the chaos of existence. A saint does not dissolve the chaos; if he did the world would have changed long ago. I do not think that a saint dissolves the chaos even for himself, for there is something arrogant and warlike in the notion of a man setting the universe in order. It is a kind of balance that is his glory. He rides the drifts like an escaped ski. His course is a caress of the hill. His track is a drawing of the snow in a moment of its particular arrangement with wind and rock. Something in him so loves the world that he gives himself to the laws of gravity and chance. Far from flying with the angels, he traces with the fidelity of a seismograph needle the state of the solid bloody landscape. His house is dangerous and finite, but he is at home in the world. He can love the shapes of human beings, the fine and twisted shapes of the heart. (121–2)

The balance achieved by the saint is the opposite of the imposition of order implied in the act of naming. Naming is part of the 'genital imperialism' (40) that F. tries to teach 'I' to abolish in favour of the kind of intimacy Edith offers with her unfocused kissing of 'I's' body 'in search of nothing but balance' (29). The metaphor of the escaped ski riding the drifts and tracing the surface of the landscape will turn out to have a close equivalent in *Gone Indian*, a text that slips and slides on a frozen ground. The balancing on surfaces seems indeed symptomatic of a particularly Canadian view of a crucial meteorological ingredient in any text from above the forty-ninth parallel; in *Beautiful Losers* the Canadian view of snow as surface (veil that cannot be lifted) is countered by a reference to the penetration of it in the colonizing version of the eternal hunt, 'William's De Luxe Polar Hunt' at the Main Shooting and Game Alley where the American explorers plant their flag in a drift (301).

Paradoxically, the language of desire becomes the tracing of surfaces as the search for the essence hidden behind the name/appearance becomes a love of shapes. It is through an appreciation of the shapes of the body, rather than the names of its parts that 'I' at one precious moment reaches the understanding he yearns for:

> I remember once slobbering over Edith's thigh. I sucked, I kissed the
> long brown thing, and it was Thigh, Thigh, Thigh – Thigh softening
> and spreading as it flowed in a perfume of bacon to the mound of
> Cunt – Thigh sharpening and hardening as I followed the direction of
> its tiny hairs and bounced into Kneecap ... all at once my face was wet
> and my mouth slid on skin; it wasn't Thigh or Cunt or any schoolboy
> slogan (nor was I Fucking): it was just a shape of Edith: then it was
> just a humanoid shape: then it was just a shape – and for a blessed sec-
> ond truly I was not alone, I was part of a family.   (122)

The equation between namelessness and intimacy shows the desired be-longing to 'family' as an anti-oedipal one. The 'pan-orgasmic body' (211) that F. strives for, a precursor of Deleuze and Guattari's desiring machine, finds its analogy in the body politic at the separatist rally and 'I's' anonymous encounter, and later becomes inclusive in the epilogue's allusion to 'Mon-tréal's desire apparatus' (299). The flight from naming is the escape from a language of reason, history, and science into one of desire, magic, and the body, by means of which 'we are part of a necklace of incomparable beauty and unmeaning' (21), tending toward the dissolution of identity and the fusion of bodies. The necklace image is one of the most frequent in the novel, often representing the suffocating yokes of rigid systems, as in the 'necklace of teeth' which becomes the 'eternal wreath' (61) associated with marriage, or that of 'fangs' (64), associated with the monstrous *vagina den-tata* which imprisons both its owner and its victim in genital tyranny and which Catherine finally manages to throw away. Opposed to these images of devouring systems is the possibility of becoming part of the 'sweetest bursting daisy chain' formed by the collective at the rally (154). The difference seems to lie in the system's emphasis on what is being connected, while in the desiring machine the stress is on the connections (the stems of the daisy chain) themselves. That is what F. means when he admonishes 'I' to 'Connect nothing' (20).

The text moves from the language of naming towards that of desire and magic, from signification to expression and intensity, most visibly in 'I's' section. F. distinguishes between the 'old style' and the 'middle style' (237, 238). Although he does not prophesy a new style, he admonishes his disciple to 'go beyond [him]' (199) and to 'not be a magician, be magic' (207) like the 'new Jew' who will be an 'Orphan' with 'not the flaw of naming in his eye' (238). The emblematic, anti-oedipal, extraterritoriality of the Jew is thus clearly equated with the unnaming that is tantamount to magic. It is when 'Magic is afoot' (197) that the tyranny of naming, the imprisonment in systems, is finally overcome. The language of history is that of signification, located in the brain, while the language of desire is one of intensity whose place of origin is the body. The relationship between the two is reflected in 'I's' writing which is only coherent when he tries to detach himself and use the discourse of history. As his personal obsessions keep intruding on his research the style reflects the erratic nature of his bodily functions, dominated by bouts of constipation and masturbatory ejaculations.

The deterritorializing trajectory from naming and signification to unnaming and intensity moves through different stages, the most common perhaps the hyperbolic intensification of comparative metaphors, which are usually quite concrete: 'I hate pain. The way I hate pain is most monumentally extraordinary, much more significant than the way you hate pain, but my body is so much more central, I am the Moscow of pain, you are the mere provincial weather station' (80). The use of intensity here is clearly linked to a phatic communication, which stresses not the meaning of the words so much as the connection between addresser – 'I' – and addressee – F. – but also, by implication, the reader. More striking are the mad prayers or litanies which seek to encompass everything in a non-territorial cosmic language spanning from the sublime to the ridiculous, the sacred to the profane, in a metaphysical inquiry couched in concrete terms: 'Is All the World A Prayer To Some Star? ... May I Suck Cunts For My Gift? May I Love The Forms Of Girls Instead Of Licking Labels?' (114). The pun in the last question reflects the movement from names or labels to shapes discussed above which, not coincidentally, involves the tongue. In a final stage of deterritorialization, syntax and signification break down, leaving a ludic language of pure desire, where sound overcomes meaning. Uprooted from the reference, language here becomes grounded in the physical body, and the following passage is a kind of *mise en abyme* of the itinerary from naming to desire, from 'language' to 'tongue': 'Edith Edith Edith knew your wet rivulets Eeeeddddiiiittthhhh yug yug sniffle truffle deep bulb bud button sweet soup pea spit rub hood rubber knob girl come head bup bup one bloom pug pig yum one tip tongue ...' (81–2). Earlier 'I' has presented the language of the Iroquois, the *Hiro-Koue* – in a translation from the chronicle of Edouard Lecompte (Monkman 58) – as the ideal he presumably tries to emulate: 'They ended every speech with the word *hiro*, which means: like I said. Thus each man took full responsibility for intruding into the inarticulate murmur of the spheres ... at the end of every utterance a man stepped back, so to speak, and attempted to interpret his words to the listener, attempted to subvert the beguiling intellect with the noise of true emotion' (9). The language of the people of the Long House is designed to 'pierce the mysterious curtain which hangs between all talking men' (9) in yet another phatic veil image. The 'noise of true emotion' also figures in the progression from the entrapment in systems, through 'I's' realization that 'All The Systems Are Screaming' (115) to the end where the old man finds that he used to scare the animals 'when he screamed *for* something. Now that he merely screamed, the rabbits and weasels did not frighten' (292). It is when he stops signifying and becomes purely expressive that he becomes part of 'the inarticulate murmur of the spheres,' which is frequently referred to as 'ordinary eternal machinery' (e.g. 41).

The imagery of machinery is pervasive and linked to the anti-oedipal ideal of the body as desiring machine. In the beginning 'I,' in the midst of the throes of constipation, feels his body leaking out of its pores and he becomes dependent on the machinery in his apartment. The notion of ego loss here is a negative version of the experience in Parc Lafontaine, more reminiscent of the schizophrenic's frightening loss of boundaries between self and world than the, albeit ultimately unfulfilled, experience of sexual union at the rally. 'I's' frequent failure to reach orgasm is a symptom of his genital imprisonment; the sexual ideal in Cohen's fictional universe is infinite foreplay, the eternal deferral inherent in the idea of the second coming as something that must remain a promise. Against the genital tyranny of systems is put the notion of play. It is the early 'I's' incapacity to play that makes him turn to the various systems available for protection against this frightening loss of self, and again the System theatre guarantees temporary relief: '... a movie will put me back in my skin because I've leaked all over the kitchen from all my holes, movie will stuff pores with white splinters and stop my invasion of the world ...'(81). Against this simultaneous ego loss and entrapment in the machinery of the mundane world stands the 'eternal machinery of the sky' (266) of which Catherine becomes part at the moment of death and which manifests itself in various ways throughout the novel, from the sky-writing of Charles Axis' promise of rebirth to the final revelation. It is this machine, in which everything is harmoniously interconnected, that the Indians are part of until they are forced to unplug their ears to be tortured with the sermons of the Jesuits with their Manichean, colonizing vision of a divided world. Participating in this desiring machine is tantamount to 'fucking a saint.' This image is clearly apocalyptic, according to Northrop Frye's definition: 'By an apocalypse I mean primarily the imaginative conception of the whole of nature as the content of an infinite and eternal living body, which if not human, is closer to being human than to being inanimate.' (quoted by Douglas Barbour in Gnarowski 143–4). The apocalyptic nature of much postmodern literature will become visible in many forms throughout my chosen corpus, and Cohen anticipates Robert Kroetsch in his equation of apocalypse with unnaming. When Catherine Tekakwitha dies she does so with the names of Jesus and Mary on her lips, but F. knows that she in fact 'perdit la parole' and mispronounced the sacred names at this crucial moment (265); a sign that 'she knew the Tetragrammaton' (265); that is, that she has understood that God's name is an alias. This happens soon after Catherine has partaken of the last sacrament; she dies on Holy Wednesday, 'day of consecration to the mysteries of the Eucharist and the Cross' (264) or, in F.'s words, after receiving the body of the Saviour in his 'Wafer Disguise' (262). The imagery of transubstantiation is connected both with the Cabala and with alchemy, another expression of an apocalyptic world-view, according to Frye. Alchemy will turn out to be highly relevant for *Trou de mémoire*, which, like *Beautiful Losers*, abounds with material metamorphoses, both thematic and stylistic.

Metamorphosis

'The Wafer Disguise' is the paradigm of the many transformations that occur in the novel, which can almost be described as a Canadian version of *The Book of Changes*, with which Cohen has expressed a fascination shared by many of his generation (Gnarowski 73), among them Dave Godfrey who wrote his own version, *I Ching Kanada*, in 1976.[4] Chance or coincidence is transformation, and to many postmodernists it constitutes the real unveiling of providence whose final manifestation in this text becomes a kind of *I Ching*, 'a vision of All Chances At Once!' (305). The saint's tracing of 'the snow in a moment of its particular arrangement with wind and rock' echoes the aleatory arrangements of the three coins, which are comically invoked in one of 'I's pleas for release: 'If sphincter must be coin, let it be Chinese coin' (48), referring to the hole in the middle that would enable his escape from self and memory.

The earliest instance of metamorphic imagery takes place when 'I' recounts an episode in which F. painted a plaster replica of the Akropolis with red nail polish in the first of many chromatic transformations. The desired fusion of spirit and body is anticipated in the explicitly oxymoronic name of the colour – 'Tibetan desire' (12) – reflecting the convergence of the sacred, the Greek temple, and the profane, its cheap commercialization. The metamorphosis exemplifies the frequently parodic sacralization of popular culture which here turns into a true union. The sacramental force of the episode is alluded to when the red of the nail polish is described as a 'transfusion of blood' (12), which magically resurrects the dead ruin. Looking at the metamorphosed temple F. shows 'I' that by squinting his eyes he will be able to see it in a new way:

- That's the way it must have looked to them, some early morning when they looked up at it.
- The ancient Athenians, I whispered.
- No, F. said, the old Indians, the Red Men. (13)

This exchange illustrates the equation between Greeks and Indians, which is worked out thematically and symbolically through the connections linking Catherine Tekakwitha, Edith, and Isis. It also indicates that in order to understand otherness, you have to assume the position of the Other, by looking anamorphically as it were. Instead of turning the Other into the same you must first, as in the invitation extended by Edith, 'be other people' (18). In a situation of alterity, becoming other is paradoxically synonymous with transcending otherness, so that losing yourself equals finding yourself.

The 'akropolis rose' (15) is, in turn, figuratively linked to many of the erogenous zones of the body – including both toes (110) and the 'rosy sphinx hole' (83) whose centrality we have seen – and it echoes F.'s caution to see the differences in all roses which are lost in naming. The importance of *seeing* the 'akropolis rose' may account for the preference of the expression 'going down' (notably on Isis) over the earlier 'fucking' of the saint; the former potentially incorporates the fusion of the oral and the visual which will prove crucial to decoding the text. The Akropolis incident immediately precedes F.'s manifesto for living in the present in which he prophesies the final vision where the figure that is no longer 'I' will be 'coming all over the sky' (15). 'Fucking a saint' is tantamount to learning to 'see the akropolis like the Indians who never even had one' (14–15) and is consequently akin to mystical vision, and both require a shift in position, an anamorphic strategy.

Anamorphic techniques, as I explained in chapter 1 and as we shall see more clearly in connection with Aquin's novel, always depend on an encoded, often violent, perspective, which places the reader in a particular position, and it might be argued that some of F.'s advice to 'I' concerning the reading of certain descriptions in his letter is also the author's advice to the reader as to the appropriate stance towards the reading of the novel, as well as towards life and art in general. 'Just read it through the prism of your personal blisters, and of those blisters choose the one you got by mistake' (244) F. says, again emphasizing the importance of chance. In what is clearly an image of purification, the second reference to 'seeing through the prism' (270) alludes to a blister caused by a burn. The figure of the prism illustrates the breaking down of apparent sameness into particulars that allows for seeing both the 'Clear Light' (305) and the differences that constitute it, and it may also be associated with the frequent references to diamonds which are the alchemical transmutation of 'shit.' When F. claims that all he gives 'I' is diamond, the latter retorts, unwittingly locating the origin of F.'s truth in the very orifice whose refusal to yield its treasures has caused his inability to receive: 'Don't give me this all diamond shit, shove it up your occult hole' (10).

The sacramental overtones surrounding the first metamorphosis recur in several instances, the most famous of which is no doubt the stain which spreads to envelop the universe as Catherine spills a drop of wine at the feast in Quebec after her baptism. This image contains a covert allusion to Revelation 6:12 as the moon turns red and hence, by intertextual implication, equates the wine with blood in a eucharistic transformation. This stain that fills the world is foreshadowed in Edith's prodigious urination at the moment of her rape, which miraculously ensures her impregnability by effecting her tormentors' impotence. Edith's flood turns into blood after the rape, as the incident gains allegorical force and its function as a rite of initiation, similar to Catherine's baptism, as well as a sacrifice, is underscored.

Flood imagery recurs in several instances, and the river, whether the St Lawrence on whose shores Catherine lives and dies and which lends its name to the Main, or the mythical one over which Oscotarach rules, is foregrounded in the epigraph, the line 'Somebody said lift that bale' from 'Ol' Man River' sung by Ray Charles. The river is implicitly linked to the theme of metamorphosis, which culminates in the apocalyptic dissolution of the old man in the epilogue but which finds its most blatant expression in the chant accompanying the Andacwandet (167):

I change
I am the same
I change
I am the same   (166)

The idea of being the same and changing at the same time, recurring in F.'s 'ceaseless' listening to the *rock* group Rolling Stones (189), is the Heracleitean notion of flux; the stones, like the river, constantly change their 'particular arrangement with wind and rock.' Cohen's variant of the idea that you never step twice in the same river becomes the philosophy of Catherine's uncle: 'Each fuck was the same and each fuck was different' (165). It could be argued that Heracleitus' notions of flux, balance, and the fundamental unity of opposites underlie the text. The coincidence not only of same and different but of appearance and essence in the condition of namelessness becomes explicit in the Andacwandet: 'It was a dance of masks and every mask was perfect because every mask was a real face and every face was a real mask so there was no mask and there was no face for there was but one true face which was the same and which was a thing without a name which changed and changed itself over and over.' (167).

Many of the often surprising transformations in the text are brought on by wordplay, of which we will see more in my discussion of translation, and it may be wise to follow F.'s advice – again emphasizing seeing: 'Watch the words, watch *how it happens*' (235). Ol' Man River becomes the old man in the movie theatre who becomes first the projector, then the *ray* of its light beam; he not only makes but becomes the connection between the creator – projector – and the creation – image on the screen – which is magic. The vision in the sky is linked to *Charles* Axis, the body builder and 'creator' of F.; the ray finally becomes a movie of Ray Charles, bent over piano keys that are likened to fishes. This particular metamorphosis seems in fact to have been foreshadowed in the Akropolis incident when, by squinting his eyes, 'I' sees the replica like 'a fantastic jewel ... sending out rays in all directions' (13). Ray and Charles are the two axes of the text; when they cross in the end 'I' attains the 'x-ray vision' that he desires (148) in order to see the 'Clear Light.' The itinerary of the ray through the text surfaces in F.'s account of a visit to the System theatre where 'the unstable ray changed and changed in its black confinement' (281). It is as if *ray* has been on its/his way all this time from its/his birth in the metamorphic coming together of the sacred and the profane in the akropolis rose.

Translation

Metamorphosis is both thematically and stylistically linked to translation in a way that will prove crucial to a determination of the territoriality of the text. The novel flaunts its postmodernity through the inclusion of a number of paraliterary discourses, as if to prove Andreas Huyssen's contention that what distinguishes postmodern art is its bridging of 'the great divide' between high art and popular culture. Many of these incorporations, of music and movies, for example, necessitate modifications or intersystemic translations of the kind seen in the discussion of analogies to conform to the requirements of print. The visual – printed – aspect of the book is thus of crucial importance, not only thematically but, as the presence of anamorphic strategies indicates, also on the level of auto-representation.

If the visual is always important to the postmodern work, the oral is usually an essential aspect of its postcolonial counterpart, which is so often concerned with vindicating the vernacular. As my discussion in chapter 1 indicated, orality is usually associated with naming and is hence a territorial phenomenon. The use of orality in Cohen's novel is quite complex, however, and I will show in the following how the text is founded on the interdependence of the visual and the oral. The clearest translation between oral and visual media takes place at the end of F.'s letter when the action is described as a movie with the radio as protagonist:

(DOLLY IN TO CLOSE-UP OF THE RADIO ASSUMING THE FORM OF PRINT) – This is the radio speaking. Good evening. The radio easily interrupts this book to bring you a recorded historical newsflash: TERRORIST LEADER AT LARGE. (285)

The use of capitals for emphasis at the same time underlines the printed nature of the literary medium which already translates from the presumably handwritten communication in which it all occurs. At this point the self-reflexive aspect of the text takes over and the modicum of novelistic verisimilitude in terms of time, space, and character that has hitherto prevailed vanishes.

A common type of thematic translation is involved in what in fact seems less like a translation than like a transfer of characters between systems or discourses in a way that foregrounds their analogy while at the same time blurring the borders between them. This technique also contributes to the crossing of boundaries between 'fiction' and 'reality' or 'history' – feature and newsreel – and between text and intertext. Thus, for instance, the language of comic strips will invade an otherwise unmarked dialogue, translating the speaker into a cartoon character in a language of emotion and intensity:

- Tell me about Edith when you were telephones.
- No.
- Arrwk! Sob! Ahahah! Sob!   (40)

At times this strategy carries over into the graphic dimension and so loses its vernacular immediacy; the inscription identifies it more clearly as a mythological intertext exhibiting the kind of visual features that are more commonly associated with the sacred: 'Puff! *##! Sob!' (92). Sometimes a transfer from one realm to another will take place by way of an implicit interlingual translation, or perhaps more correctly, by way of a missing translation: thus, for instance, Edith is 'translated' into Isis when she speaks Greek.

The most frequent borrowings of foreign texts are the many quotations from Jesuit histories. The direct incorporation of source texts avoids repeating the Jesuits' own appropriation of Indian history by letting their texts speak for themselves. At the same time it provides a bridge between history and fiction; the Jesuit intertext appears most often in the context of 'I's' research on Catherine who constitutes such a connection. In most instances the French is translated only implicitly through repetition and paraphrase, perhaps as a crutch for readers who are clearly not expected to be bilingual. Hence, translation here is not foregrounded but rather made as invisible as possible while unobtrusively conveying the meaning. The use of French also brings to mind 'I's' decision to begin a chapter of his book with a French phrase from St Paul: 'triompher du mal par le bien' (80), which causes him to claim that 'Foreign languages are a good corset' (81), a statement that indicates that at this stage the recourse to foreign languages plays the same role as the movies in preventing the narrator's self from dissolving. As we shall see, that function is later reversed, as movies and foreign languages both become the magic that will allow the positive fusion of the body with the 'ordinary eternal machinery.' The chosen quotation from St Paul is obviously ironic, as the dichotomy between good and evil is confused as the novel progresses.

Translation is also linked in the book to etymology, one of 'I's' scholarly domains. 'It is my impression that the above is apocalyptic,' he announces after telling about Catherine's spilled wine, before launching into an explication of the origin of the word which equates revelation with sexuality and both with the Isis figure in his conclusion that 'apocalyptic describes that which is revealed when a woman's veil is lifted' (126). A more extensive exploration of etymology occurs in F.'s invocations to history. The rejection of history 'in the middle style' (238) is written in junkie jargon, with extensive footnotes explicating the various terms to the uninitiated, in a parody of 'I's' academic pedantry. The second footnote points out that the word 'Cash' for 'conscience, the brain, or any kind of painful consciousness' is used 'mainly' – pun no doubt intended – on Boulevard Saint Laurent and by 'the criminal element of both French and English extraction' (238). A language that transgresses national and ethnic boundaries is by definition, it would seem, a language of criminals and outcasts, or, in the oedipal paradigm, of orphans. This passing remark also emphasizes the oxymoronic function of the Main; the centre of the city is the locus of marginals. Cohen is playing with his etymologies here, particularly in the secondary footnotes engendered by his use in note 5 of the word 'coprophagist,' Greek for 'shit-eater,' that is, junkie (238). The claim, for instance, that 'peanut' is a term of endearment seems engendered by a transference and subsequent inversion – of the kind implied in the equation shit = diamonds – of the French signifier in 'Quelle cacahuète,' where the first part, 'caca,' lends itself to such fanciful etymology (239). It may also foreshadow the later association of the young prostitutes of the 'desire apparatus' with the 'warm peanuts and Assorted machine' (299). This is one of several examples of signifier-generated bilingual – extraterritorial – wordplay, of which we will see more later.

It is not coincidental that I choose to analyse in relative detail such marginal features as footnotes. As we shall see more clearly in the next chapter, a literalization of marginal writing – that is, an emphasis on the visibly marginal aspects of the text – may be one way of redressing the balance between centre and periphery for the ex-centric writer. The three secondary notes pertaining to the Greek origins of the word 'coprophagist' in this case contain a peculiar subtext which seems entirely incidental and unrelated to the subject matter at hand but which, if looked at closely, underscores the metamorphic paradigm. The first admonishes the reader, 'I,' to think of himself as a 'sponge diver' under the 'fathoms' that threaten to 'crush [his] mossy fumbling' (239). The second, after digressing to the Sanskrit cognates of the Greek word for 'to eat' which associate it with sharing, happiness, and wealth – apparently contradicting all the earlier, cannibalistic associations with eating in the text yet paradoxically confirming them through the shared allusions to communion – seems to run counter to the very etymological enterprise it serves: 'The very words you use are shadows on the sunless ocean floor. None of them carries a lesson or a prayer' (239). The reference to shadows echoes the narrator's final decision with regard to Catherine's identity; by condensing different interpretations of her Indian name, he decides that it means: 'She who, advancing, arranges the shadows neatly' (55), an image that implies an opposition between ordering as mastery and the arrangement of shadows – shapes – traced by the saint.

The sea imagery returns in the third note, where F. sees himself as feeding the submarine receiver of his words and teaching him to breathe with 'silver gills' (239). There have appeared frequent images of fish earlier, usually in connection with Catherine and her virginity, and it would indeed appear that the dive into what Freud might call the oceanic self, the preverbal and pre-oedipal, or Brown's polymorphous perversity, is implied as a psychological analogue to the Orphic descent.[5] F.'s familiarity with this condition may be a parodic literalization of the amphibianism inherent in his French-Canadian identity – his expulsion from Parliament has to do with being a 'Frog' (206); the first adjective used to describe his manner is 'hopped-up' (4) and the nationalist desiring machine at the rally is described as 'frog jelly' (154). But this imagery also pertains to the metamorphoses or sea-changes made possible by seeing words as shapes rather than as carriers of meaning, and it harks back to the earlier reference to the Indians' version of the 'Telephone Dance.' When they have been forced by the Jesuits' threats of hell to unplug their ears and can no longer hear the sounds of nature, 'Like children who listen in vain to the sea in plastic sea shells they sat bewildered' (105). The real sea shells presumably contain the 'inarticulate murmur of the spheres' (9) which is that of the 'ordinary eternal machinery' of united humanity. It is consequently not unexpected to see underwater imagery recurring in connection with the language of desire, earlier associated with woman as ocean and the clitoris – the akropolis rose which can only be seen by diving or 'going down' in a fusion of vision and orality – a pearl to be 'unshell[ed]' (82) by the tongue. This metaphoric complex returns in the sound of 'bubbles above a clam' (185) which is that emitted by men and women together – 'shhh, hiss' (189) – the non-signifying sound of the desiring machine.

Orality and translation are linked in a crucial episode concerning a Greek-English phrase-book, given to F. 'for an oral favor ... performed for a restaurateur friend' (71), which F., in turn, passes on to his disciple. At first glance this incident seems to pertain to the theme of translation as perversion which is implicit in the analogy between naming and colonization. I have pointed to the equation between restaurateurs and Greeks in the allusion to Keats. The association of homosexuality and the athletic body with classic Greek culture is manifested vividly in F.'s description of the possibilities offered by his 'Professional Greek Chair' (202), which seems to associate body-building with pornography and torture. The 'perversion' inherent in the handing down of the scripture is reflected stylistically in the translation of the Greek phrases into an unidiomatic, 'execrable' English (71). (The equation of casual homosexual encounters with perversion is 'I's'.) But the phrase-book is also referred to as a 'prayer book' (71) because, as F. explains, 'Prayer is translation. A man translates himself into a child asking for all there is in a language he has barely mastered' (71). This seemingly para-doxical equation of translation with both perversion and prayer points to two distinct operations. On the one hand there is the vehicular translation – the one concerned with meaning or signification – which aims at mastery and whose result is 'execrable', that is, associated with the 'shit' of history and memory. Prayer, on the other hand, is the opposite of mastery; it is the willing transposition into another realm. It is the person praying who has to be 'carried over,' as in the case of Edith becoming Isis, not the words uttered.

The phrase-book ends 'I's' history. His last, fifty-second, entry consists of the, badly translated, English version of several situations that we are given to understand are taken from the book, with Kateri Tekakwitha in 'I's' mind playing the role of the various personages with whom a Greek tourist might come into contact in an anglophone milieu. (Kateri is Catherine Tekakwitha's Indian name, but it could also be her Greek alias.) We meet Kateri in six rather comical conversations which carry the narrator/imagi-nary Greek to places involving cleansing, communication, and reading. And it is Kateri who, in a reversal of their original roles, asks the narrator to produce his passport and his identity, that is, to name himself, a demand that seems to precipitate his final self-loss. In all of these dialogues the Greek speaker wants to send or receive something. The whole turns into a *mise en abyme* of the difficulty of communication which has figured the-matically throughout and which here ends in silence or rather in a kind of revelation. As the narrator falls into silence and prayer, he invokes not Kateri any longer but God: 'O God, I grow silent as I hear myself begin to pray' (180). Prayer becomes yet another version of the Telephone Dance, a kind of listening inward, and praying is a way of participating in ordinary eternal machinery by refusing mastery and escaping the entrapment of words.

As the narrator withdraws at the end of 'The History of Them All,' the words are left to speak for, or rather, show themselves; Book One ends with a reproduction of a page in the phrase-book, describing a visit to 'the drug-shop' (180). The reproduced page is, mimetically, divided into two columns, one for the Greek original and one for the English translation, and the dialogue concerns cures for different ailments. As silence replaces the earlier almost compulsive writing and talking, indicating 'I's' final achievement of the emptiness requisite for the reception of grace, the quest for shapes rather than names seems to be finally fulfilled. The appearance of the unfamiliar alphabet turns the Greek words on the left into pure signifiers or shapes to the anglophone reader. The very last word in the dialogue is Εὐχαριστῶ, correctly but innocuously translated as 'thanks' (180).[6] The sacramental overtones of much of the earlier metamorphic imagery have already pointed to the paradigm of transubstantiation and the centrality of the 'Wafer Disguise' in which the word becomes flesh – to be eaten in the same way that Edith-Isis is 'eaten.' The reproduced page here thus on the one hand allegorizes the perversion of the sacred through translation, but on the other hand holds out the promise of revelation through the profane by way of an attentive reading of shapes. It is translation, in the sense of being carried over, that allows for the anamorphic seeing from the position of the other in which empty phrases become prayers and the 'akropolis rose' can be seen. It is not coincidental that the Greeks in the novel are 'restaurateurs'; only through their language can the metamorphic potential of the word be restored.

The word Εὐχαριστῶ thus assumes the seminal function alluded to in the narrator's account of F.'s reception of the book – an unholy communion – as it engenders the sacramental imagery disseminated throughout the text and fusing the sacred and the profane, the spirit and the body. In a pentecostal parody, the gift of translation is given with the infusion of 'spirit' in the Shakespearean sense, in which it is metonymically linked with body, and the Greek signifier foregrounds the revelatory powers of the word in a way which, again, shows that the sacred, to the attentive eye, inheres in the profane.

It could be argued that the 'Wafer Disguise' is actualized on this page, that the holy spirit has infused the narrator who is no longer seen as 'I' because, having been given the gift of tongues, he speaks Greek. Pentecostal allusions are found in several instances in an imagery resplendent with baptism by fire and speaking with and in tongues. Throughout the text F. has played the role of a ghost, admonishing 'I' – and the reader – from beyond the grave to 'take [his] spirit hand' (237). A reference to the letter as his 'last *written* communication' (183) also leads us to expect his return in some form. As I indicated in my theoretical discussion, the pentecostal model is not uncommon in postmodernism, and we shall see a more extreme example of the descent of the Holy Ghost in the next chapter. The particularity of Cohen's use of the paradigm is his distinction between the perverted translation which colonizes and subjects and the pentecostal gift of tongues which emphasizes the transformative power of the signifier as it 'translates' the receptive subject.

The contents of F.'s will – soap and fireworks – indicate their baptismal and initiatory function on 'I's' road to Damascus. It could be argued that it is when 'I' has been scorched by the tongues of fire bequeathed to him by F. that he receives the gift of translation and that his seeing through the 'prism' of that purifying blister permits him to resurrect the sacred ruin of the temple. It is above all the polysemic properties of the word 'tongue' with its emphasis on orality that operates the fusion of spirit and body. The signs of sainthood in 'I's' investigation include the resistance of the body to decomposition, and it is significant that many of the saints he lists are found to have their tongues intact long after death.

The descent of the tongues of fire on 'I' anticipates the famous episode in F.'s letter where Edith submits to the will of God – deo volente as suggested by Desmond Pacey (Gnarowski 92) – in the form of the Danish Vibrator which translates her into Greek-speaking Isis. The D.V. is clearly linked to F. as the specular image of the V.D. that drives him insane and eventually kills him in preparation for his second coming.[7] Again the translation into Greek, as in the case of 'I' and the phrase-book, operates the convergence of the sacred and the profane, which is the pre-condition for the loss of self which constitutes sainthood and the subsequent entry into the 'eternal machinery of the sky.'

The phrase/prayer book becomes in the end the central *mise en abyme* of the reading of the novel. The reader must 'translate' herself into the Greek position, as if taking her place in F.'s chair, and perform another 'oral favor' by reading the text aloud 'in Greek,' transferring the visual into the oral again. In modern Greek, the letter B is pronounced V; thus, carried over into the language of the scripture, the words 'bale' and 'veil' would be homonymous. The lifting of the bale about which Ray Charles sings in the epigraph becomes, when pronounced orally (or sung) from such a position, the lifting of the veil. The mystery of being, embodied by Isis, is on the level of the political allegory a question of lifting the ideological veil perpetuating the slavery and colonization of the 'nègres blancs d'Amerique,' as well as of Indians and Jews, all of the 'second chancers.' In a similar but inverted way, Isis' name, when visualized or read as a shape (rather than spoken) 'in English' epitomizes the mystery of being and presence in a way that seems to illustrate the Derridean notion of the 'traductibilité' of the sacred word. It might not be completely outrageous to suggest, in the light of this strategy, that Ray in the end may be a transference of the 'rei' of Heracleitus' 'panta rei'; everything becomes ray because everything flows; all becomes movie.

Inscription

My reading has demonstrated the emphasis on orality, both in the sexual imagery and the play on homonymy. Yet it is only through its *inscription* that the Greek word becomes a pure or sacred signifier and thus gains its transformative force. It is the unfamiliar *shape* of Εὐχαριστῶ that potentially reveals the mystery of being (and it may not be coincidental that it is the letter B that is metamorphosed in the language of Is-is). As Derrida has shown in his critique of Saussure in *De la grammatologie*, writing is the originary supplement, the non-existent origin of language. That is, it is through writing, in the sense of 'grammé,' the trace made visible through inscription, that difference is constituted or revealed. It might be argued, then, that Cohen is anticipating Derrida's treatise on the absence of presence in his fusion of voice and inscription in the revelation of being. This notion is transformed in the end into a strikingly Derridean image of pure being or presence as 'the beautiful waist of the hourglass ... this point of most absence' (305). In F.'s vision at the time of the Akropolis episode, of 'I' 'coming all over the sky,' he elaborated on the particulars, which included 'fuck[ing the saint or Isis] on the moon with a steel hourglass up [his] hole ...' (15), yet again locating the truth about being in that particular body-part whose final emptiness is hence filled – with absence, as the loss of self is equated with the finding of pure being. The waist of the hourglass is also referred to as the 'stem between the two flasks' (305) in an image which confirms the escape from systems foreshadowed in the occultation of the first two letters in the name of the System theatre and emphasizing connections rather than the things connected.

That the voice, whether singing or speaking, is always already writing, is clear not only in the fact that both explicitly written narrations are strongly oral or conversational in nature but also in recurring images that anticipate the final transformation of Charles Axis' sky-written advertisement into Ray's sky-singing. Thus, for instance, at the separatist rally 'the echoes of the young man's clear voice hung above us like skywriting' (150). The convergence of orality and inscription in the realm of the sacred is confirmed when Edith responds to F.'s inquiry 'Who are you?' (231) after the D.V.

has 'gone down' on her, with a Greek inscription from a statue significantly representing both Athena and Isis, at a temple at Sais, which in translation (not provided in the text so as to preserve the sacredness of the pure signifier) produces, according to R.E. Witt: 'I am Isis, born of all things, both what is and what shall be, and no mortal has ever lifted my robe' (231). It should be noted that the inscription contains the word ἀπεκάλυψεν, referring back to the veil etymology.[8] Through her translation into the sacred, Edith is conclusively identified with Isis, as well as with Catherine, whose position she assumes as F. sucks her toes in a repetition of Father Jacques de Lamberville's similar treatment of Catherine (thus perhaps metonymically grounding mystery in the body by showing that magic is a foot). These are Edith's last words; she dies as she must in becoming pure presence – Is-is – as her speech becomes inscribed as pure signifier, and her death precipitates the metamorphic crisis in which 'I' has to lose himself before order can be restored.

It is not coincidental that the crucial last dialogue in the phrase-book situates the mystery of the Eucharist, the ultimate sacralization of the body, in 'the drugshop' (coincidentally ending with a foot in need of nursing). Pain has been the driving force behind the narrator's writing, and the entrapment in memory and 'shit,' with all its consequent bodily symptoms, is what prompts the quest for a cure. The desired medicine is twice shown to be a translation of modern Greek's φάρμακο (pharmako), a term that brings to mind Derrida's deconstruction of Plato's Phaedrus (La Pharmacie de Platon), which I will discuss at greater length in the next two chapters. Signifying both cure and poison, the pharmakon is used by Plato to describe the paradoxical – in Derrida's term, sylleptic – nature of writing, which on the one hand serves as a cure for memory, and hence is a servant of history, but which on the other hand threatens to kill memory by absolving us from the responsibility to remember. The two sides of the coin are actualized in 'I's' archival and historiographic endeavour – the language of systems and naming – on the one hand, and in F.'s advocacy of writing as memory-loss – the language of desire and metamorphosis – on the other.

The pharmakon is embodied in the sacrificial victim, the pharmakos or scapegoat, the beautiful loser whose – saintly but deadly – assumption of the failures and sins of others plays a finally redemptive role. The scapegoat, as I indicated in chapter 1, is, according to René Girard, the centre of the sacrificial crisis on which order is based; I will have occasion to elaborate on its significance in my analysis of The New Ancestors. In Beautiful Losers it is, in line with the pornography paradigm, the women who perform this function. Edith's sacrificial death both brings on the crisis and, indirectly, remedies it; like Isis she is the healer who possesses the magic power to resurrect her dead husband. Her role as cure is clear in the way she is passed, for the purpose of solace, between 'I' and F. 'like a package of mud' (274) in a metonymic identification with Catherine whose death bestows magic healing powers on the soil in which she is buried. Similarly, Mary Voolnd, the last nurse, is mangled by police dogs to ensure F.'s salvation. It is this sacrificial aspect of the *pharmakon* – clearly related to the mystery of the Eucharist – that overcomes the disjunction or alterity inherent in writing by operating the mysterious conjunction of the sacred and the profane, the metaphysical and the physical. The sacrificial crisis leads, as Girard has pointed out, through the momentary effacing of differences – the fusion of identities in the final revelation – to the restoration of order, in this instance the resurrection of the author.

I have until now overlooked the first part of the epigraph: '*Somebody said* lift that bale,' apparently introducing the 'third person,' the slave-driver who returns at the end to whip the reader into interpretive action, into lifting the textual veil. The transformation of the anti-oedipal orphan F. into 'FIRST FATHER PRESIDENT' (284) should perhaps not come as a surprise but rather be seen as an anticipation of the final resurrection of the author as father of the text, as the 'third person' gives place, first to 'we' and then to 'I.' It is, after all, F.'s *will* that 'I' has been charged with and that he ultimately carries out; like the reader after him, he is disciple and executor.[9] But the call to action is paradoxical. The character who sees 'somebody ... making it' in the end is the 'New Jew' working on a 'broken Strength Test' (306), either redeemed from lifting (whether bales or veils) or proving the futility of trying to master the machine. The invitation extended to the reader is to join the exodus of second chancers and 'watch how it happens' with the receptive but attentive gaze which is the opposite of the colonizing one of the 'brutal' or 'active eye.' The lifting of the veil is yet again shown to be a paradox; meaning does not reside behind the veil but rather it is found by paying attention to the texture and the shape of the veil. The reader's engagement with the text-machine should be like that of the Zen student presented with a riddle by the master, who has left his thumbprint in the explosion of his text, rather like F. lost his thumb in blowing up the statue of Queen Victoria. Leonard 'koan' (147) has turned the book into a figurative relic-box for his own saintly body,[10] which in the end is magically resurrected to exult in the game played with the reader. The plea to the reader is the same one extended earlier by Edith to 'I,' to 'be other people' – with the resulting self-loss and assumption of alterity – the invitation whose refusal led to all of 'I's' miseries. To become other is to become A _____, to assume an alias.

The theme of games and their rules converges with the crucial notion of balance in the epilogue's condemnation of the introduction of flippers into the game of pin-ball, which has legalized the 'essential criminal idea' (299) of the second chance by granting the player more control. In its pure form the game depended on wrenching the second chance from fate through the mastery of the 'TILT' (299), the momentary control of angles which may be the pin-ball equivalent of the anamorphic perspective in the visual arts. The first encounter with the novel constitutes an assault; the emotional, even physical impact of the text prevents active engagement, and the analysis I have engaged in is only possible given a second chance to wrest some degree of control from the author, turning the tables the way F. does by wrenching his second chance from the sacrificial body of the last *pharmakos*, Mary Voolnd, who 'buzz[es] ... like an eternal pinball machine' (242). It would seem as if, in the first instance, the author is the sacrificial victim and the text the repository of his mutilated body, but in the end, as the outcome of the metamorphic crisis becomes clear, he reveals himself as the master of ceremonies who, it may be argued, in turn redirects the violence against the reader who becomes the victim of the textual aggression.

As I indicated in the beginning of this chapter, Cohen's novel epitomizes the position of the metropolitan colony as a participant in two, possibly contradictory, discourses. Its part in the postcolonial project is seen in its ambivalent attitude towards history, culminating in the epilogue's offer to rent the book to the Jesuits as a testimonial to Catherine, in a gesture which, however parodically, validates the historiographic endeavour. Its simultaneous participation in a postmodern aesthetics is, I would argue, reflected in the final assumption of control by the author whose claim to speak for a collective is soon obscured by the return to the first person singular and whose presence is revealed in the anamorphic strategies that oblige the reader to assume the receptive position. The seemingly communal welcome to the reader in the last paragraph is offset both by the authorial I's central and superior positioning ('I will plead from electrical tower ... from turret of plane ...' [307]) and the admission that he is alone.

The tension between the two projects – the postcolonial assumption of alterity and the postmodern assertion of mastery – may explain some of the complexities and paradoxes that characterize this text. On the political level, it actualizes both the territorial striving towards a grounding in indigenous reference and the simultaneous deterritorialization of the signifier necessitated by linguistic homelessness. The movement away from naming and metaphor, represented by the many instances of linguistic metamorphosis I have documented, begins with the literalization of the Orphic descent into the 'going down' which grounds the ontological quest in the body. Like all the other transpositions of signifiers between languages, this translation/ perversion from myth to pornography is only possible through the splitting of the sign. Rather than emphasizing the disjunctive properties of language, however, the coincidences of signifiers and shapes across language boundaries demonstrate the sacred and transformative power of the word. In the final analysis, the itinerary of Cohen's novel leads through the political to the ontological, which is its main concern – a fact which, if we are to believe Brian McHale, marks it as indisputably postmodern.[11]

In its marginal position on the Main, the novel straddles yet another border, incorporating features typical of both the Québécois and the Canadian novels I will be discussing in the following chapters. The colonial historical reference, with its French religion and British literature, and the predominantly American nature of their contemporary equivalents all add to its inclusive Canadianness, and will be seen to be shared by writers from both cultures. I will argue, however, that the fact that the conjunction of the sacred and the profane, which all of the novels seem in some way to desire, can only be achieved through a linguistic deterritorialization marks it as more Canadian than Québécois. That it should be read 'in Greek' actually underscores its Canadianness, a paradoxical point that I hope the following analyses will elucidate. The emphasis on the vernacular and the almost obsessive use of pornography and blasphemy are features most visibly shared with the next novel I will be discussing, *Trou de mémoire*, but the recourse to a specific sacred language only incidentally linked to the referential and vernacular territories of the rest of the text is a peculiarity it shares, in varying degrees, with the other Canadian texts.

CHAPTER THREE

Trou de mémoire
Writing as Sacrament

My choice of two such dissimilar novels as Hubert Aquin's *Trou de mémoire* (1968) and Dave Godfrey's *The New Ancestors* (1970) for a comparison of the formal expressions of the colonization paradigm is motivated by their shared participation in a discourse of revolution and, more important, perhaps, by their choice of African former colonies as analogues to the situation in their home countries. While the continent is hardly unknown territory in Canadian fiction, the use of Africa as a model on which to test the problematics of cultural colonization is a good illustration of the typical identification with the real struggle for independence – political as well as cultural – in the 'third world,' in an identification with the 'colony' side of the dual identity of the metropolitan colony. One example will illustrate the common critical view of this interest in Africa as an expression of the perceived similarity of problems:

> a very plausible explanation for Canadian fascination with African na-
> tionalism can be found in the fact that many of the conflicts present in
> a newly independent African country have their clearly identifiable
> counterparts in recent Canadian experience. The threat to a firm con-
> ception of national identity posed by conflicting tribal, racial, or re-
> gional loyalties; the continual onslaught on national self-confidence that
> emanates from forces that have capitulated to the assumptions of co-
> lonial inferiority; the need for perpetual resistance against economic,
> ideological and political domination by larger powers – all of these
> consequences of being caught between two worlds are familiar compo-
> nents of Canadian national life. (Downey 15)

The disregard of difference and the metaphorization of the phenomenon of colonization reflected in this critical stance also neglect the metropolitan side of the country as well as its role as colonizer vis-à-vis its own indigenous peoples. The Canadian interest in Africa may very well be a symptom of the lack of paradigms for the curious situation of the metropolitan colony and must be seen as a result of a search for analogies rather than read as a direct equivalence.

Québécois writers, on the other hand, generally prefer to set their discussions of colonization at home, in spite of their preoccupation with African colonialism and the writings of Albert Memmi, Frantz Fanon, and Jacques Berque. Hubert Aquin's interest in these writers is well-known, and it is shared by Dave Godfrey, about whom William New says: 'In substance, as Godfrey realizes, Fanon describes Canada's tense identity as well as Africa's – both permeated by a foreign (American) culture to the point of selfconscious uncertainty' (*Articulating West* 233).

While *Trou de mémoire* is set mainly in Montreal and is firmly anchored in a Canadian political and historical frame of reference, Godfrey's novel is set almost entirely in a fictionalized version of the former British colony of Ghana. In Aquin's text, the former French colony and neighbour of Ghana, the Ivory Coast, appears as a mirror image of Quebec. Both writers visited the countries they write about and show a thorough knowledge of their history, politics, and culture, and the two novels offer an opportunity for an analysis of colonialism from a British and a French standpoint, although the identification in Aquin's novel of Quebec with a former French colony is more explicit than any kinship between Canada and Ghana in Godfrey's. The African setting lends itself to the treatment of certain phenomena which occur, either thematically or metaphorically, in the two novels: tribalism, neocolonialism, exploration of dark continents, etc. On a superficial level, they also share several minor themes and images. Quite violent in tone, they revolve around murders with strong political motivations and with allegorical overtones. Yet again we encounter rape as a central metaphor, connected with a loss of memory, symbolic of the colonizer's appropriation of the colony's history. The theme of orphanhood, present in *Beautiful Losers*, is implicit in *Trou de mémoire* and, as the title indicates, quite explicit in Godfrey's novel. The thematic analogy already discussed in the context of Cohen's text between the private/emotional and the public/political spheres also recurs in both, in a way equally reminiscent of the Deleuzean notion of the collectivized Oedipus.

Trou de mémoire reflects many thematic and formal preoccupations which recur in the author's other novels, thus forming a link with the whole of Aquin's oeuvre. *The New Ancestors*, on the other hand, stands out as Godfrey's only novel. Thematically it carries on the interest in cultural colonization reflected in the author's short stories, but formally it constitutes a clear break with the earlier fictions, such as those in *Death Goes Better with Coca Cola* (1967). While both Aquin's and Godfrey's novels look like examples of postmodern metafiction, they differ in the degree and explicitness of their self-consciousness. Writing, reading, and editing are all overtly thematized in *Trou de mémoire*, while *The New Ancestors* relies on stylistic strategies in an implicit discussion of writing, which is only one aspect of a broader discussion of language. The two texts are structured around formal and metaphoric paradigms involving distortion and change, but the models chosen originate in vastly different areas. Aquin adopts his basic formal pattern, anamorphosis, from the visual arts, while Godfrey's notion of metamorphosis comes from the realm of biology and physics.

The formal problems in the novels stem above all from a confusion as to the chronology and 'truth' of the events narrated as well as from the highly fragmented narration. There is an inversion of the relationship between fact and fiction, which is dissolved in the end. In *Trou de mémoire* the Ivory Coast is a 'real' place; there are allusions to existing places and historical events, all contributing to the reality effect. Yet the African part of the novel functions as a mythical reflection of a real situation, which is that of Quebec. In *The New Ancestors* the relationship is reversed: the fictional country 'Lost Coast' has a real referent – Ghana – and the fiction disguises a real historical and political context. On the other hand, one part of the novel, the voyage up the river Niger in the section called 'In the Fifth City,' is set in an undisguised location with very precise referents, a place which plays the same mythical role as Africa, or the Ivory Coast, in *Trou de mémoire*.

Although the intricacies of the narration make a summary of the novel rather difficult, *Trou de mémoire* can be divided into four narrative sections, each pertaining to a different narrator who is also implied in the story. The main narrative belongs to Pierre X. Magnant, a pharmacist and politically active 'indépendantiste' living in Montreal, who murders his English-Canadian lover, Joan Ruskin, by injecting her with sodium pentothal. The murder takes place in the Redfern laboratories of McGill University, where Joan works as a microbiologist. During the night immediately following the crime, Magnant writes what becomes the bulk of the novel in the form of an autobiography. His intention, we are told, is to cover, rather than reveal, his crime, but his attempt only succeeds in disclosing his guilt, and the autobiography becomes a confession. There is some confusion as to chronology, but the murder takes place in 1966. Information about Joan Ruskin is scant and sometimes contradictory, and the motivation for the murder remains ambiguous. Magnant's account reveals less about his personal background than about his thoughts and feelings, particularly on the subject of Québécois history and politics, colonialism, revolution, and crime. The narrator's claim that he is heavily drugged makes his discourse even more opaque.

Magnant's journal contains several addresses to the reader and seems intended for publication. It is supplemented by two brief fragments from a more intimate diary, the 'cahier noir,' which does not appear intended for publication and whose contents to some extent contradict the main narration. In an editorial note we are told that Magnant has committed suicide, and we are consequently in the presence of a posthumous confession.

The novel opens with a prefatory letter from Olympe Ghezzo-Quénum, a pharmacist from the Ivory Coast, who has decided to write to Magnant after reading a newspaper report about a speech he had given in Montreal and being struck by the many similarities between the two men. Although there is no indication that Magnant ever reads it, the letter establishes a pattern of doublings and mirrorings and introduces the main characters. Olympe does not appear in Magnant's account, but as a pendant to it we are presented with that of the African, who recounts how he has met Joan Ruskin's sister Rachel in Lagos, where she works in a hospital. Through her he had heard about Magnant. After Joan's murder, Rachel, or RR as she is called, feels herself pursued by her sister's assassin, whom she knows to be Magnant, and leaves Lagos with Olympe. In Lausanne RR disappears, and Olympe, believing her to be in danger from Magnant, seeks the help of the uncomprehending Swiss police. Returning to his hotel after a night in jail, he finds that RR has reappeared. She tells him about having been raped by Magnant but does not remember the details of the experience. Leaving Lausanne for Paris, Olympe subjects her to a 'narco-analyse' to make her remember what happened, and she relives the trauma of the rape in a series of attempted, incomplete repetitions of the original crime.

In the end they return to Montreal where Olympe, on RR's advice, looks up Magnant's editor, a certain Charles-Edouard Mullahy. Their conversation, reported by the latter, eventually reveals that Magnant staged his own death in order to work clandestinely for the revolution in the identity of the editor. We are also led to believe that RR is pregnant as a result of the rape. Magnant/Mullahy and Olympe both die, presumably by suicide, while RR remains as sole survivor and final editor. In reading and ordering the documents constituting the novel, RR has been transformed: she decides to change identity and becomes Anne-Lise Jamieson, Québécoise, eagerly awaiting the birth of the child she claims is Magnant's.

Both Magnant's and Olympe's writings have been extensively and obtusely annotated, first by the editor, that is, presumably Mullahy, and then by RR. As Magnant's narration proceeds, it becomes increasingly evident that the editor has played a part in the described events. He intervenes with his own 'reconstructed' version of certain happenings, particularly in 'L'Incident du Neptune,' where he, by interviewing witnesses to the bizarre incident barely discussed by Magnant, produces a 'true' version. On another occasion, shortly after the crucial, central fragment which does not belong to either of the two narrators, the editor intervenes again, revealing more of himself and his role in the story.

The central fragment is written by RR, who presents a version of events which blatantly contradicts Magnant's story. According to her, Joan was her lover and an expert in the theatrical use of techniques of *trompe-l'oeil*. RR herself does not respond to the name of Rachel Ruskin and is furthermore the real author of the confession of Magnant, who is nothing but a figment of her imagination. At the end of the text RR reveals that she smuggled this apocryphal fragment into the office of the editor in order to confuse him. Like Olympe's prefatory letter, RR's apocryphal passage, which forms the link between Magnant's and Olympe's narrations, functions as a *mise en abyme* of the novel.

The basic structure of the text is thus reminiscent of that of *Beautiful Losers*, consisting of two main narratives that are closely related through devices like reflection, repetition, and doubling. The similarity or near-repetition of the central events – the murder and the rape – is paralleled in other, less explicit, repetitions of incidents, metaphors, etc. that show the narrations to be specular versions of each other in the same way as the characters. The two sections are framed by the prefatory letter and the editorial discourse and *mises en abyme* in the central apocryphal passage which overtly misleads the reader, but which covertly functions as a guide to the interpretation of the novel as a whole.

Anamorphosis

The proliferation of doublings and mirror images in *Trou de mémoire* has provoked a considerable amount of criticism aimed at disentangling the identities of the characters and particularly of the narrators. The mirroring, or doubling technique, is found not only in narrative and formal structures,

Hans Holbein, *The Ambassadors*. Reproduced by courtesy of the Trustees, The National Gallery, London, England

however, but is a modality of the fundamental principle of anamorphosis, mentioned in chapter 1, which underlies the novel as a whole. Though no direct reference is made to Baltrusaitis' book in the novel, Aquin's familiarity with it has been shown by Patricia Smart, who in her important study points out certain passages lifted more or less verbatim from that work.

The anamorphic techniques are both explicit and implicit and pervade all levels of the text. The most important anamorphic work described is the younger Hans Holbein's painting *The Ambassadors*. Its central role is emphasized by its position in the text: it forms the focus of the discussion of anamorphosis as an art form, contained in RR's apocryphal fragment. It is here that passages from Baltrusaitis appear, including some of his comments on Holbein and on *The Ambassadors* in particular.

The two French ambassadors to England pose on either side of a table displaying a number of instruments pertaining to the arts and sciences of the time: the trivium and the quadrivium. The serenity and stiffness of the image are disturbed by the anamorphic shape floating above the floor in the centre of the picture. Seen from a particular angle, this obscure shape is restored as a cranium, a fact which has led most critics to interpret the painting allegorically. Against the opulence and worldly knowledge of the ambassadors stands the mystery of death. A barely visible silver crucifix, situated in the continuation of the line of vision invited by the restored anamorphosis, suggests the theme of resurrection.

One of the most important aspects of Holbein's picture, pointed out by Baltrusaitis, is its dramatic and hermeneutic properties. He describes the viewer's perception of it and the reversal that occurs as the 'figure cachée' is discovered, and 'reality' is revealed as an illusion. According to Baltrusaitis, the 'Mystère des deux ambassadeurs' is a drama in two acts (105). First, the spectator looks straight at the picture, focusing on the obvious and interpreting it as a realistic representation of two ambassadors of knowledge. The feeling of uncertainty, evoked by the presence of the anamorphosis, only increases as she tries to identify it by getting closer. Dissatisfied, the viewer retreats but, upon leaving the room, casts a last glance at the painting. From this oblique angle, the figure of death, which had remained hidden, suddenly stands out. The work is consequently reinterpreted in allegorical terms as an example of the *memento mori* or *vanitas vanitatum*.

The painting works on several levels of the text as a thematic and structural *mise en abyme*, and various interpretations of it are offered; its auto-referential role becomes increasingly explicit as the novel proceeds. RR's piece on *The Ambassadors*, which emphasizes its dramatic properties, clearly puzzles the editor, who professes to distrust painters who resort to the techniques of *trompe-l'oeil*. His bewilderment leads him to assume that RR's analysis of it contains coded clues that might help him understand Magnant's text which, he is led to believe, may in fact have been inspired by the painting. Thus, for instance, the ambassadors could be Joan and Magnant, held together by nothing but the 'tissu' of words that constitutes Magnant's account and by the anamorphosis in the centre: 'Cette forme est le centre secret de cette grande composition, un peu comme le meurtre de Joan est le socle sombre du roman. La forme pâle indiscernable qui flotte au-dessus du sol s'apparente au corp [*sic*] blanc de Joan qui repose sur les dalles froides de la morgue.' (143).

The painting returns indirectly in Olympe's journal, where he pays a visit to the Musée des arts décoratifs on *R*ue de *R*ivoli in Paris and sees some of the objects represented in Holbein's picture. The doubling of Joan and RR becomes clear when Olympe perceives RR's 'tête absente' floating 'entre l'astrolabe et la sphère armillaire' (188), a position closely resembling that of the cranium in the painting.

It is also possible to distinguish a closer relationship between the painting as representation and the form of the novel. The two ambassadors, whose position on the canvas is heraldic, represent the two narratives, Magnant's and Olympe's. Looking straight ahead rather than at each other, they are held together by the weave of the text like the ambassadors by the tablecloth. The central anamorphosis, which is so crucial to the interpretation of the whole, is RR's apocryphal fragment linking the two pendants. Following the rules of heraldic art, the *mise en abyme* is situated in the centre and reflects the surrounding elements. In summing up the most important functions of this particular anamorphosis in the novel, it could be said that as composition, the painting reflects the anamorphic nature of poetic creation; as representation, it reflects the diegesis, both narrative and allegorical; as form, it reflects the structure of the novel; and as object of perception – as 'le Mystère des deux ambassadeurs' – it reflects the act of reading.

The second anamorphic work in *Trou de mémoire* appears on the cover of the book and is, like *The Ambassadors*, taken from Baltrusaitis. This is another image of a cranium, made for a cylindrical mirror. The elongated picture is painted on a horizontal surface and is restored in a mirror placed in the centre. If the mirror is removed, the anamorphosis cannot be restored, and the picture is not perceived. This particular work is a prefatory frame reflecting the construction of the text: the central absence or 'trou' must be filled by the mirror or *mise en abyme* which allows the reader to interpret it. The position of the anamorphosis on the cover of the book also places it within the auto-referential discourse. As the narrator/author commits suicide, the writer, by placing his name within the image of death kills the conventional authorial presence from the outset and thus, it would seem, exiles himself from his work.

The specular structure of the novel resembles the picture on the cover. RR's section constitutes the central mirror in which the surrounding narratives, as well as the editorial commentary, are reflected. Not only does RR's text form a *mise en abyme*, but it is through her that the diegetic unity is achieved. It is the rape of RR that implicates Magnant in Olympe's story, and the rape is nothing but a repetition of Joan's murder. A close study of the two specular narratives shows practically every narrative and metaphorical element to be reflected in both and having their counterparts in the mirror of RR's 'semi-finale.'

Mirroring inevitably implies inversion, and its function is best summed up in Olympe's comment, 'J'écris sur une table surmontée d'un miroir qui me renvoie mes mots à l'envers' (175). While in the cylindrical anamorphosis the restoration is situated in the mirror, Olympe describes the opposite

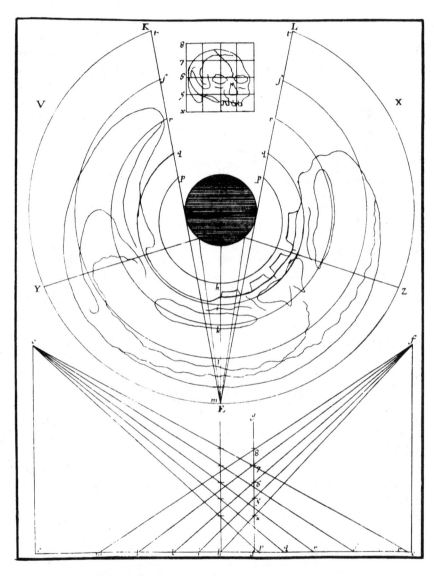

Anamorphosis for cylindrical mirror (by Père du Breuil), used on the cover of
Trou de mémoire

situation, where the mirror operates the distortion/reversal of reality in a way that brings to mind the Lacanian view of the mirror as the source of the misrecognition of self. The exact status of mirror reflection and its corollary, the relationship between reality and illusion, is thus ambiguous. This is further emphasized by the affinity between reflection and masks. Encountering his colonial past in London, Magnant says, 'Ce royal parc à crimes ne faisait que me renvoyer, tel un miroir noir, le masque dogon de mon vrai visage' (82). What the mirror gives back is indeed an inversion, in this case the black mask, or the Olympe version, of Magnant's double identity. Writing is not only reversal but masking, as Magnant writes to mask his crime, 'recouvrir le corps de Joan d'une grande pièce de toile damassée d'hyperboles et de syncopes' (55). This function of writing is generalized by the editor who, in a reference to *The Ambassadors*, equates it with the cloth on the table in the painting (145). This recalls images of murder as unveiling or unmasking, as the lifting up of Joan's dress and discovering her nudity, which then has to be re-covered by writing. There are many echoes here of Cohen's use of the same image and Aquin's revelation imagery is similarly connected to the topos of sex and death.

The most basic pattern combining the doubling with specular inversion is the ambiguous duality between black and white, which becomes a kind of parody of the Manichean allegory. The equivocal use of this chromatic opposition is most explicit in the relationship between the two narrators, the white Québécois and the black African. The distant, though intimate, connections between them are first alluded to by Olympe, who feels that they are 'incroyablement frères' (8). Their relationship thus parallels that of the Ruskin sisters.

The already familiar cliché of the 'nègres blancs' is used ironically throughout the novel as an appropriate emblem of the metropolitan colony, and is crucial to the ambiguous relationship between white and black, as hinted at initially through some of the passing comments in Olympe's letter. Thus, for instance, the whiteness implicit in his geographical origin, the Ivory Coast, is echoed in his 'tendances narcissiques' (9). These markers of whiteness are inversely analogous to Magnant's 'masque dogon' aspect. While Magnant is usually connected with the colour white, Olympe finds it hard to define the exact position of the Québécois in the schema of colonization: not being one of the European colonizers with whom Olympe is familiar, Magnant is not an ordinary 'sale blanc' (9), and he may even be on the 'liste noire' of known revolutionaries (16). Magnant's ambiguous position is a result of his past as both colonized and colonizer, reflected in his strong affinity with London, 'la seule ville qui hante [son] double passé'

(82). His double past is paralleled by that of Olympe, who is a Fon and descendant of the liberator Ghezzo, and whose ancestors are guilty of colonizing the hated Yorubas – hence his black-and-white-ness.

Joan's role in the black/white paradigm is seen in the transformation she undergoes, reminiscent of F.'s chromatic transformation from white to black after death, which reflects her changing position in the political allegory. Alive, Joan is identified by the 'chienne blanche' that she wears at work (26), but after her death she is naked and 'gorgée de noir' (26). In a symoblic extension of her role as defeated Quebec, Joan becomes the very idea of 'pays,' which equates her with Africa and blackness.

The political dimension returns in a metaphor of defeat and defiance which reverses the equation of black/colonized versus white/colonizer. Before being killed, Joan is wearing a 'carré de soie de chez Dior en guise de drapeau blanc' (41). Earlier, Magnant talks about 'le sang noir qui coule dans nos veines et sur nos drapeaux' (35). This reference is interpreted by the editor as alluding to the emblems of Reggie Chartrand's 'Chevaliers de l'indépendance,' the opposite of Joan's white flag of surrender. The political overtones of the black colour are implicit when seen in the context of the 'cri de la race' (22), the xenophobic version of separatism which is the only one Joan pretends to understand. The 'sang noir,' red and black, returns in a series of metaphors. The deliberate and cold-blooded murder is a revolutionary 'projet sanguinaire' (35), a black parody of the 'cri de la race' coming from the laboratory monkeys witnessing the crime.[1]

The image of the 'sang noir' recurs in auto-referential commentary. Magnant claims that he is filling the pages with 'une somme incalculable de petites taches de sang' (52), a comment which immediately leads the literal-minded editor to observe that, in fact, the text is written in the customary manner, 'noir sur blanc' (52). This inversion of the literal and figurative is yet another actualization of the ambiguous relationship between the illusory and the real. The editor underlines the equation between blackness and writing in his own narration, when he finds himself imprisoned in 'l'épaisse nuit d'encre' (139), elaborating the earlier implicit equation between writing and nocturnal time – Magnant spends several 'nuit[s] blanche[s]' (25 e.g.) writing not only his autobiography but his 'cahier noir.'

Closely related to the black and white pattern is the metaphor of the *camera obscura*, whose significance is foregrounded in an editorial footnote concerning the possible affinity between Magnant's text and Nabokov's novel *Kamera Obskura* (48).[2] There are three 'chambres obscures' in Aquin's novel. The first is the hotel room where the initial sexual encounter between Joan and Magnant takes place. Described analeptically, the meeting foreshadows the murder, and the fact that the hotel is called 'Windsor' fore-grounds the political dimension. The Windsor is the territory of the colonizer and Joan's seduction of Magnant is a kind of conquest, which is eventually avenged in the murder/rape. As might be expected, the specular counterpart of the hotel room in Olympe's narrative is the location he imagines for RR's rape, and the 'chambre obscure' in RR's apocryphal passage refers to the room where *The Ambassadors* hangs. In the light of my discussion of the central function of the painting, this particular *camera obscura* is the one into which the reader must look to 'see' the reflection of the external events. A *camera obscura* is in itself an anamorphic *mise en abyme*, an apparatus which reproduces in an enclosed space the image of events taking place outside it. An inverted platonic cave, it reveals the 'truth' to the gaze turned inward. The essential element of the *camera obscura* is the hole through which light is let in; it is through the 'trou' that reality can be seen. Allowing the light to bring out the image in the *camera obscura*, perceiving the truth of defeat and death, brings on a sudden insight resulting in a 'lucidité in-tolérable' (130). It is symptomatic that the black African is 'ivoirien,' an obvious, vernacularizing, pun on 'il [ne] voit rien.' The loss of vision is described as the result of defeat.

RR's equation of lucidity with the allegorical unveiling or lifting of a mask is reflected, in a manner again reminiscent of Cohen's revelation par-adigm, in a series of images which put the blindness/insight pattern close to the masking/unmasking. Magnant's project to cover the nudity of Joan's corpse is a fight against the fatal lucidity, and writing becomes an evasion, even a drug. Magnant's 'nuit nyctalope' (31) provides neither the rest offered by sleep nor the lucidity of daylight. The gaining of lucidity is described progressively in a series of metaphors. When Magnant states in the begin-ning, 'je vois clair' (36), his is the false (white) lucidity of drugs. 'Tout ce qui est lucide doit mourir,' says RR (130), and when Magnant's true identity has been revealed to Olympe, he states: 'Je vois tout en noir' (200) before dying. Lucidity is not 'claire' but 'noire'. The blinding shock recurs when RR, after her rape/defeat, looks at Olympe 'comme si elle était myope ou même complètement aveugle' (168). The near-sightedness echoes the idea of distantiation as necessary for the perception of truth, which, as I will show later, returns in several intertextual references.

Distance is achieved through reading, something which is implied already in Olympe's initial letter, where he talks about 'lucidité rétroactive' (11). All the narrators become readers: the editor reads Magnant's text and RR's apocryphal insertion; RR reads both Magnant's text and the editor's com-mentary, as well as Olympe's journal. This successive overlaying of discourses, through which the editorial commentary distances Magnant's narration, which is further made strange by its reflection in the dark mirror of Olympe's journal and RR's *mise en abyme*, culminates in the reader's final manoeuvring into the only angle from which she can perceive the anamorphosis constituted by the text.

The anamorphic principle extends to the political dimension of the novel, which reflects ideas expressed in Aquin's other writings. To Pierre X. Magnant, revolution and separatism are synonymous. *Trou de mémoire* is often seen as the actualization of the 'prochain épisode' to which Aquin's first novel, with its paralysed vacillation between writing and action, formed the prelude. The second book is indeed far more revolutionary in its form and seems to constitute the convergence of the two earlier opposite poles. A close analysis of the particular metaphors pertaining to the theme of revolution, however, shows this resolution as rather problematic.

In his essay, 'Calcul différentiel de la contre-révolution' (in *Blocs erratiques*), inspired by what was seen as a movement of reaction in Quebec in the spring of 1965, Aquin ironically concludes that the true relationship between revolution and reaction has been reversed in dialectic discourse. With the help of the logic of differential calculus, he affirms that revolution is a permanent phenomenon representing continuity, of which the counterrevolution constitutes a rupture. In a turn of phrase that will prove relevant to my discussion, Aquin defines the counter-revolution as a 'carence du continu' (125). Much later, he returns to the dialectic inversion in terms which reveal his attraction to the existentialism of Sartre. In 'Le Texte ou le silence marginal?' from 1976 (in *Blocs erratiques*), he says: 'En fin de compte et somme toute, c'est le néant qui différencie l'être et non pas l'être le néant' (270). This is the existential assumption underlying the many dialectic inversions in *Trou de mémoire*. In this essay the author emphasizes the analogy with the written page; it is the blank spaces, or the margin, that 'invert' the text. The auto-referential aspect of the black/white duality consequently becomes explicit as a fundamental *mise en abyme* of the existential endeavour of writing, and we shall see later how this reversal is literalized in the text.

The inversion of revolution and reaction is exemplified by Magnant, and its inherent contradictions are reflected in a wide network of metaphors, as well as in a series of idiomatic expressions that appear completely innocuous until seen in the light of the formal structures. The first mention of the permanent revolution is made by Magnant, who declares: 'Je m'installe d'emblée dans la révolution permanente qui a tué ce pauvre Trotsky et qui peut se comparer à la rotation terrestre qui a fait tourner la tête à Galilée'

(58). The ambiguous equation between the revolution and the rotation of the earth is repeated in the figurative expression, 'tourner la tête.' The implicit paradox of the idea of the permanent revolution is further echoed in the frequently recurring expression, 'je tourne en rond' (19 e.g.), a figurative idiom immediately conflated with its literalization, 'je ne fais absolument rien.' The oxymoronic juxtaposition of the figurative and the literal foregrounds the ambiguity of the meaning of 'revolution,' an ambiguity further emphasized by the narrator's actual immobility.

The metaphor of terrestrial rotation and the Galilean intertext generate a network of images centring on the sun, with which, through an initial metaphoric of fire and burning, Magnant identifies: 'Le soleil n'est qu'un imposteur; il me plagie chaque jour ... Le soleil c'est moi! ... Le rumeur veut que le soleil aille se coucher; or, c'est faux, archifaux – et je suis bien placé pour le savoir! Le soleil paqueté mais dextrogyre ne se couche pas. Il mène une double vie – j'en sais quelque chose ... Et puis ce n'est pas si facile qu'on pourrait le croire, au premier abord, d'être soleil: briller, se lever à l'aube, se coucher à l'heure des poules, tourner en rond, c'est une vie de chien!' (24–5). The flagrant contradiction in this passage sums up that of the 'révolution permanente.' The sun is the *trompe-l'oeil* par excellence: since Copernicus we know it is immobile, yet we see it and talk about it as perpetually revolving. The double life of the sun is analogous to the two images in Holbein's painting – the obvious versus the hidden, illusion versus truth.

The sun metaphor is closely linked to the black and white duality. Magnant's narrative is nocturnal: while he is writing his confession in Montreal, the sun is, anamorphically speaking, in Africa. His period of activity consequently coincides with that of his black but diurnal double in the Ivory Coast. But Magnant's sun becomes even more anamorphic, as he eventually drifts from the permanent revolution. His defeatist pole of the solar paradigm is the opposite of the 'soleil victorien' (39) of the British empire, which never set. The Victorian/victorious sun is juxtaposed with the defeat of the sun eclipsed or thrown out of orbit.

This metaphor also partakes of the auto-referential discourse. Having identified with the sun, Magnant says: 'il y a de quoi noircir le disque inflammatoire!' (25). What creates the eclipse is ostensibly 'ce clavier nullement électrocuté, ces frappes plombées qui s'emmêlent en diphtongues strictement allogènes, ces efforts du bout des doigts' (25). Writing is again the eclipse or the mask, which is at the same time the 'miroir noir' through which he sees the other in himself. But the black sun is also the alchemical symbol of the conjunction of opposites, the perfect fusion of black and white, darkness and light, matter and spirit, profane and sacred, which, to Magnant, is writing. The ambiguous status of writing and the novel is evident through Magnant's primary identification with the sun, the light that will penetrate and make sense of the *camera obscura*, and with his own writing. His claim, 'Le roman d'ailleurs c'est moi' (19), is synonymous with 'Le soleil c'est moi!' (24). The anamorphic nature of the novel is thus implicitly confirmed.

Another metaphoric analogy to the permanent revolution is expressed in the 'zombie' code which recurs in obvious patterns and repetitions, as well as in less conspicuous metaphors and idioms. Most clearly it is found in metaphors concerning 'revenants.' In a paradoxical juxtaposition which is a reversed parallel to the 'je tourne en rond' versus 'je ne fais rien,' Magnant exclaims: 'je n'en reviens pas' (19), after which he goes on to extol the virtues of 'revenir': 'Ils reviennent toujours: c'est la preuve même qu'il faut revenir et non pas venir. Ce qui est bon pour les zombies est bon pour moi et il y a belle lurette que j'en reviens du coït parlementaire du pouvoir avec l'opposition, de ce qui peut avec ce qui n'en peut plus. Il faut zombifier à mort la chambre bassement basse du Bas-Canada et tout faire sauter.' (23–4). Yet another pun analogous to the pair 'je tourne en rond' / 'je ne fais rien' and 'il faut revenir' / 'je n'en reviens pas' is seen in the opposition between 'ce qui peut' and 'ce qui n'en peut plus.' The political allegory, here expressed in a sexual code that brings it close to the rape metaphor, seems to posit 'zombification' as a prelude to the revolution. Magnant's outburst is immediately followed by the exclamation 'Maudite machine!,' presumably directed to the typewriter, but also anticipating the later identification of zombies and machines in terms echoing again the 'tourner en rond': 'Je ne cesserai jamais de m'étonner qu'il y ait des gens qui vivent normalement, qui rentrent tous les soirs au foyer pour y prendre le repas eucharistique et qui, perpétuels en cela qu'ils se meuvent, tournent en rond avec un bruit régulier de machine à coudre.' (69). Magnant's aloofness from the man-machines here contrasts sharply with his earlier identification with the zombies and illustrates his entry into revolutionary activity through crime. This development is put in Nietzschean terms, with echoes of Apollinaire: 'le crime de la veille m'avait hissé au-delà de ce qui est humain trop humain, au-delà du bien et du mal aimer' (71). While Magnant gains the status of 'super-zombie' (80), Joan becomes the ever-present ghost and, like the trauma of the conquest, she comes back incessantly to the murderer, who equates death and colonization: 'Je l'ai réduit [*sic*] à l'état mortuaire de colonisé' (37).

Magnant's identification with zombies is echoed in RR's description of how she used to watch her lover Joan's stage sets from a box which 'servait jadis pour les revenants ou les personnages mythologiques' (126). And, she reveals: 'Je jouais sans relâche la "revenante" ... pour "Joan"' (127). Her initials give rise to a zombie-related pun, when Olympe imagines how she 'erre, erre' (154) on the streets of Lausanne where, according to the logic established by the murder (of which it is a repetition), her rape turns her into a zombie. Belonging neither to life nor death, the zombies are the (dis)embodiment of alterity and the ultimate extraterritorials, and the defeat – the Conquest/murder/rape – is the loss of the 'pays,' the territory.

Olympe's identification with zombies or ghosts is brought about indirectly through his use of expressions like 'Je revins sur mes pas' (157). Returning from the zombifying rape, RR looks at him 'comme une enfant qui vient de voir un revenant' (171), a comment which establishes a link between Olympe and Magnant; RR has just been raped by the latter but is looking at the former, who has just described himself 'comme un fantôme' (177).

Whether metaphorically or diegetically, the narrators all die but are resurrected, and the theme of death and resurrection constitutes the most symbolic actualization of the zombie code. Magnant supposedly commits suicide but returns with a new identity, and the editor 'dies,' having implicated himself in Magnant's text to the point where he adopts his style and becomes transformed into a writer: 'je m'étrangle sans un cri ... Je meurs en écrivain' (121). He is 'resurrected' through the reading of RR's text, after which he resumes his editorial identity.

'[L]a révolution est un crime, rien d'autre,' exclaims Magnant (83), and his entry into the revolution is symbolized by the murder of Joan and its repetition, the rape of RR, both of which are foreshadowed on a number of occasions in the text. At the source of his revolutionary activity lies his failure to love Joan. 'A mon réveil, je suis devenu révolutionnaire, faute d'avoir possédé ce soleil aux yeux cernés' (116). Again using the clichéd sexual code to express the dialectics of colonization, Magnant explains how the impotence of defeat leads to revolution: 'Mon comportement sexuel est à l'image d'un comportement national frappé d'impuissance: plus ça va, plus je sens bien que je veux violer' (112). Crime would seem incompatible with the idea of permanence, but Magnant makes the analogy with the permanent revolution: 'Il existe telle chose que le crime permanent, analogiquement du moins: dans les deux cas il doit y avoir préméditation' (84). It is indeed premeditation, rather than the crime itself, that sets the revolutionary apart: 'Pourtant, depuis des semaines et des semaines, combien de fois, super-

zombie, n'étais-je revenu sur les lieux du crime prochain?' (80). The seemingly preposterous notion of 'revenir' in the future is the logical corollary
of an ironic use of Nietzsche's idea of the eternal return.

Crime generates both history and literature which, like this novel and
Cohen's, begin with a dead body.[3] 'On a tort d'enseigner l'histoire de la
littérature selon une chronologie douteuse: elle commence au crime parfait,
de la même façon que l'investigation délirante de Sherlock Holmes débute
immanquablement à partir d'un cadavre.' (82). Literary texts are repetitions
of the archetypal perfect crime but inevitably tainted with imperfection. The
detective novel thus becomes a metonymy for literature and 'Tous les romans
sont policiers' (82). As the inventor of the 'perfect crime,' Sherlock Holmes
has also shown its impossibility. The dialectic relationship between crime
and legality is another of the être/néant analogies, and since crime is only
perceived in its relation to its opposite, the perfect, undetectable crime is
a contradiction in terms.[4] Illuminating the role of the zombies, detective
novels reflect 'une croyance obscure en la vitalité des morts' (82) and corpses
are 'catalyseurs embaumés' (82), agents of change. Sherlock Holmes is more
than Magnant's literary hero and a marker of cultural reference: belonging
to Victorian England, he is a part of the double past. Magnant's identification
with Holmes illustrates his attitude to his writing through the polysemy of
the word 'auteur': 'Sherlock Holmes aurait pu être l'auteur des crimes qu'il
démontait' (81). The affinity between Holmes and his lethal opponent is a
kind of specular inversion: Professor Moriarty could be the 'masque dogon'
of the brilliant detective. The view of the novel itself as a crime is expressed
in Magnant's confession: 'je cours après mon récit comme Sherlock Holmes
après un assassin' (65). Magnant is both murderer and detective, both author
and reader.

Much like Edith's in *Beautiful Losers*, Joan's corpse is source and generator
of Magnant's writing in the same way as the conquest is the source of
revolution. The corpse and the conquest thus occupy parallel positions in
the diegesis and the political allegory. *The Ambassadors* as a *mise en abyme*
of the text holds a similar generating position on the level of form. The
formal isomorphism linking Joan and the perfect crime with the anamorphosis in the painting is clearly expressed by the editor: 'En vérité, son
corps [de Joan] repose en travers du livre, projetant une ombre anomalique
sur tout le récit – un peu à la manière de l'ombre projetée par le crâne dans
le tableau de Holbein. L'ombre contredit les lois fondamentales de la lumiére,
répétant par sa projection invisible un crime parfait!' (143). The inventor
of the perfect crime, Sherlock Holmes, occupies the same place in the
discourse of auto-referentiality, as Magnant reveals: 'Quand j'ouvre un livre,

je ne puis m'empêcher d'y chercher la silhouette cocaïnomane du génie de Baker Street et l'ombre criminelle qu'il projette sur toutes les pages blêmes de la fiction' (82). The emphasis laid on the detective's drug habits underscores his affinity with the narrator. There is thus, in the final analysis, a complete formal congruity linking the corpse, the conquest, the anamorphosis in the painting, and Sherlock Holmes on the various levels of the text, a congruity operated through the formal and rhetorical use of anamorphic techniques.

Magnum Opus

The numerous transformations taking place in the novel, and particularly those involving the characters, are reflected in a metaphoric code pertaining to alchemy, a 'science' for which Aquin has professed a deep interest. Alchemy is often linked to mannerist art with its allegorical bent and, by extension, to anamorphosis. In his essay, 'La Mort de l'écrivain maudit' (in *Blocs erratiques*) Aquin talks about the famous alchemist Paracelsus as his 'doppelgänger' (151), and in *Trou de mémoire* Magnant refers to himself as 'fils et petit-fils d'alchimiste' (65), indirectly establishing a link between the author and his pharmacist narrator. All the 'characters' are involved in pharmacology, medicine, or microbiology, areas related to alchemy and, by extension, to revolution, as Magnant implies: 'Mon activité politique ... me prouve que j'incarne une image archétypale de pharmacien, car je rêve de provoquer des réactions dans un pays malade' (65). Magnant's earlier identification with the pentothal that kills Joan indicates that he is not only the performer of the alchemical rite but also the agent of transformation, the *pierre philosophale* which permits the identification of opposites and makes transmutation possible. Hence his 'discours lapidé' (46) and his confession: 'Par moments, je suis pétrifié' (21). Like the drug or *pharmakon*, the pharmacist/alchemist is an 'agent double' (32) who can produce opposite effects: writing is an alchemical process which can either seduce/cure, like cheap detective novels, 'du crime-parfaitement-écrit' (50), or rape/poison, like true revolutionary texts. In a colonized society the alchemist/writer can either perform the accepted transmutation of the rumblings of discontent into the gold of silence or turn the silence into its opposite, the cry of revolution. In the context constructed by the novel, the corpse is the prima materia, the original chaos which, through transmutation, becomes the magnum opus. In traditional alchemy, the process takes place in a skull; the anamorphic cranium is thus the locus of transformation. Pierre X. Magnant is at the same time the *pierre* philosophale, the unknown ingredient x of the transmutation, and the *magnum* opus; he is agent, material, and product – writer, print, and book.

Both reading and writing operate metamorphoses. Each reading trans-forms not only what has been read but the reader, as RR explicitly states: 'En lisant ce livre, je me suis transformée' (203). Magnant's final identifi-cation with his writing changes him into the black of print: 'je m'étire sur la page' (99). The transformatory power of writing is questioned by the editor, who, nevertheless, finds himself caught and transformed into his own *récit*. The editing process, in which reading and writing converge, ends by placing him 'sous l'empire d'une inspiration malarique qui [le] transforme en écrivain' (121).

As a creator of anamorphoses, and in view of Aquin's use of anagrams, Pierre X. Magnant may well be one himself. According to Baltrusaitis, the creator of the first mural anamorphosis in black and white, to be viewed through a hole in the wall, was a certain Père Maignan. Like Galileo and Huygens, whose isochronic inventions figure metaphorically in the novel, Maignan was interested in the measuring of time and wrote a treatise on *sun*dials. More significantly, however, 'Maignan rapproche le mécanisme de la perspective qui "abuse la vue" de la façon dont nos sens sont "abusés" dans le mystère de la Transsubstantiation' (Baltrusaitis 69-70). Father Maig-nan's views on the subject of anamorphosis reflect Magnant's use of it and illuminate the analogy between the form of the novel and its symbolic sig-nificance.[5]

The alchemical characteristics of transubstantiation have been pointed out by C.G. Jung, who traces the isomorphism between the philosopher's stone and Christ.[6] The 'repas eucharistique' (69) which has already been seen as a symbol of zombification, is reversed in a series of metaphors. Magnant says: 'le crime parfait ... n'est qu'une des nombreuses modalités du grand mystère de la transubstantiation' (49), and this equation is echoed in Olympe's reference to the 'transubstantiation sacrilège' (189) through which he be-comes the alter ego of Magnant by repeating the rape of RR. In this light, Magnant's eucharistic identification with the 'pain total' (pentothal) (29) that transforms Joan and his reference to death as the 'vin magistral' (94) gain added significance. The metaphors involving the metamorphosis of blood into printer's ink partake of the same code and manifest a sacramental view of writing which brings to mind some of Cohen's imagery.

The fact that Magnant writes his manuscript on the 'vert parchemin' (73) of his pharmaceutical company implies a reference to the famous *Tabula Smaragdina* attributed to Hermes Trismegistus, the patron of alchemy. But Magnant's text can also be seen as an apocryphal testament of the same type as the *Aurora Consurgens*, signed Thomas Aquinas and probably written in the thirteenth century. Considered at the time highly blasphemous, the text may be the first to trace the analogy between the alchemical opus and the Christian sacrament: the author calls the alchemical transmutation 'donum et sacramentum Dei atque res divina.'[7] He furthermore sees the philosopher's stone as a drug: 'et est medicina: quae fugat inopiam, et post Deum homo non habet meliorem' (40).

To Magnant the drug is 'un frère' (29). He refers in particular to the *pento*thal which kills Joan and which forms part of a metaphoric network surrounding the number five, and alluding to an analogy between the drug and the *quinta essentia*, the spirit hidden in the *prima materia* which is sublimated into the stone in the *magnum opus*. The number five appears on the occasion of Magnant's first encounter with Joan in room 405 ('quatre cent cinq,' or 'quatre sans cinq') of the Hotel Windsor and in the number of pills that Magnant has taken when he sets out to write: 'Cinq c'est sûrement un de ces fameux chiffres sacrés: sacré, je le suis' (21). This remark indicates not only Magnant's sacred status, but his equation with the number five which will become clear eventually.

The opposition between writing and action, which was so paralysing to the narrator of *Prochain épisode*, appears to be resolved through a – Eucharistic – view of the word as action, in the Christian equivalent of the mythological word magic discussed in chapter 1, and here exemplified in Olympe's superstition: 'En nommant les choses, souvent on les appelle' (10). In Magnant's words, 'Par l'action matricielle de la parole, l'action passe à l'action, râflant d'un geste hâtif tout l'or du silence et le dépouillant, par surcroît, de sa plénitude significative' (57). The 'parole matricielle' will replace the 'langue maternelle,' killed or 'saintciboirisée' by zombifying institutionalized religion. The primacy of the word is expressed even more clearly in Magnant's account of his speech to the crowd, which takes the form of an inverted sacrament: 'les mots que j'ai lancés au public m'ont enfanté. Je suis né à la révolution en prononçant les paroles sacramentelles qui, de fait, ont engendré plus de réalité que jamais mes entreprises ne l'avaient fait. Ma naissance seconde a suivi ce baptême improvisé, de la même façon qu'une confirmation brûlante a succédé, ce jour-là, à notre premier sacrilège' (46). The 'naissance seconde' is part of the ironic use not only of conversion, but of death and resurrection, which runs through the novel and which, through *The Ambassadors*, is linked to the formal strategy of anamorphosis and the symbolism of transubstantiation.

In what is probably the least obvious of the blasphemous uses of Christian symbolism, a clue to the narrator's identity is offered. Initiating his narration in a metaphoric of fire, Magnant identifies himself: 'Je suis, à moi seul, une vivante et interminable pentecôte' (26). The image of *Pent*ecost recurs surreptitiously in several instances. The date of Magnant's speech, 27 May 1966, is the Friday before Pentecost, and the allusion becomes evident in Magnant's reference to 'nos bouches à langues maternelles de feu' (95). Magnant is St *Pierre*, who was the preacher of the first Pentecost, and his rape of the crowd is a blasphemous inversion of the descent of the Holy Ghost – not unlike that of the D.V. going down on Edith in *Beautiful Losers* – as a symbol of Christian love. Magnant's project is to restore to the people 'la langue désaintciboirisée de [ses] ancêtres' (95), to return language to its pre-Babelian purity, before its zombification by the Church.

'[J]'écris au niveau du pur blasphème,' claims Magnant (57). As in *Beautiful Losers*, blasphemy pervades all levels of the text, ranging from common formulaic curses to a highly inventive use of blasphemous inversions which testify to the vitality of the territory from which they are culled. Blasphemy is not possible outside of its dialectic position as the antithesis of the sacred, and the original affinity of the sacred and the profane is particularly obvious in Quebec in the use of 'sacres' which reflect the power and territorial homogeneity of the cultural tradition carried by the Catholic church. As Bakhtin has demonstrated, blasphemy is the hallmark of the carnival, where the territoriality of the sacred is shown in its reversal and its appropriation into the vernacular. The ambivalence of the sacred and the fundamental unity of the two orders of belief, the religious and its inversion, have been discussed by several writers, among others Aquin's mentor, Jean-Paul Sartre who, speaking about another 'saint,' Genet, says: 'Cette volonté exaspérée du Mal se démontre en révélant la profonde signification du sacré, qui jamais n'est plus grande que dans son renversement.'[8] The commonality of desire behind the two extremes is expressed by Magnant: 'Je bascule dans le sur-blasphème avec la ferveur des premiers apôtres' (94), and, later: 'je rêve à la plénitude du viol – comme les mystiques doivent aspirer à l'extase divine ou à l'apparition' (112).

The most obvious and stereotypical actualization of blasphemy is the cliché of religion as opiate of the people, which converges with the pharmacological code. According to Magnant, the Church keeps the people in a perpetual state of zombification 'moyennant 10 à 20 grammes par jour d'eau bénite par voie intraveineuse' (38), a statement that brings to mind Cohen's literalization of the same Marxist dictum in an episode where F. and Edith inject themselves with holy water from Lourdes. Magnant's project of writing a 'hostie de roman' (42) is reflected less explicitly in a number of blasphemous indices, some of which translate the political allegory into a geographical locale, in a manner reminiscent of Cohen's symbolic Montreal topography. The first thing that meets the reader's eyes on opening the novel *Trou de mémoire* is Magnant's name and address heading Olympe's letter. The address, '123, rue Saint-Sacrement,' is foregrounded through frequent repetition, and its significance becomes clear in retrospect. In the final section it is revealed that Magnant has moved to this address from 'rue Papineau.' The move coincides with his 'suicide' and subsequent return alias Charles-Edouard Mullahy. To Magnant, Papineau personifies the defeat of Quebec, and the move symbolizes the narrator's step from the realm of defeat into that of blasphemy/revolution, the escalating triad (trinity?) of the number in the new address culminating in the blasphemous exclamation 'Saint-Sacrement,' by implication at the same time indicating the text's residence in the holy sacrament.

The alchemical enterprise is blasphemous, insofar as the alchemist plays God in giving birth to the philosopher's stone, to Christ. Magnant and, it would seem, Aquin repeat this sacrilege by claiming to give the Word to the people in the disguise of the Holy Ghost. Indeed, seen anamorphically, Magnant's signature under his autobiography could be read as ✱. As the Holy Ghost, Magnant would also, in an implicit bilingual pun, be a 'sacré revenant.'

The ambiguity underlying the central metaphors in *Trou de mémoire* can perhaps be best understood in the light of the idea of *carence*, a term frequently used by such writers as Albert Memmi and Frantz Fanon to describe the experience of colonization. In Memmi's words, 'la colonisation carence le colonisé et ... toutes les carences s'entretiennent et s'alimentent l'une l'autre' (108). *Carence* is thus a global notion implying a number of ways in which the colonized individual is kept in a state of non-being or alterity. The anamorphic character of the concept in the text is evident in a number of patterns pertaining to its different aspects.

'Tel est le drame de l'homme-produit et victime de la colonisation: il n'arrive presque jamais à coïncider avec lui-même' (Memmi 125). While the 'décalage d'avec soi,' as a phenomenon specific to the colonized mentality, is most obviously illustrated in the frequent doublings, metamorphoses, and uncertainties as to the true identity of the narrators, it pervades the text both explicitly and implicitly in several ways. The most insistent actualization of the alterity or condition of extraterritoriality in its broad sense, is the frequency of the preposition 'entre.' (For instance, on page 85 it occurs five times.) The essential in-betweenness underlying the ambiguous positions of the characters has been seen in the double past, the black/white confusion, and the zombies as occupying a place between life and death.

Both Magnant's and Olympe's narrations reflect a progressive sense of otherness, illustrated in the discrepancy between Olympe's initial assertion, 'Je n'en finis plus d'être moi-même' (13), and his 'Mais je suis un autre' (156), reflecting his sense of self before and after the rape/defeat. The insoluble dilemma of the otherness of the conquered is summed up in Magnant's appeal to the crowd: 'révolution ou suicide' (36). The choice is illusory: in a society where the individual suffers from acute alterity murder, or its synonym (according to the metaphorical syntax established in the novel), revolution, is equated with suicide. When 'je est un autre,' murdering the Other is tantamount to killing yourself.[9] The permanent revolution looks like a vicious circle, 'aller et retour ... entre une tentative de révolution et une tentative de suicide' (38), an impasse contrasted with Joan's confident assertion: 'une anglaise ne se suicide jamais' (91).

The final *carence* is that of the narrator, whose identity always turns out to be apocryphal, until we are left with the absence of any narrative voice. Magnant's identification with his novel is undermined by the editor's definition of the text as 'hors roman' (74). If, as the editor maintains, 'Le roman de Pierre X. Magnant se présente à nous comme absence de roman' (74), then the author of that novel is obviously absent, and my analysis of the anamorphosis on the cover of *Trou de mémoire* as an auto-referential *mise en abyme* of the death of the author is validated.

Paraphrasing Lord Durham's famous words, Magnant deplores the lack of an indigenous cultural tradition in Quebec: 'ce pays n'a rien dit, ni rien écrit' (55). This ironically well-documented lack of history and literature, which Quebec shares with most colonized societies, is a result of the 'amnésie culturelle' which, according to Memmi, is symptomatic of the experience of colonization (99) and which Aquin deplores in 'La Fatigue culturelle du Canada français' (in *Blocs erratiques*). In killing memory, the conquest has also killed language, and the revolutionary's difficult task is to restore the two to the people. The title of Aquin's novel can indeed be seen as a correction of the perceived hypocrisy of the Québécois slogan, 'je me souviens.' The linguistic modality of the *carence* is not only the 'aphonie' or the 'baragouinage bilingue' (28) which is the result of assimilation, and which is sometimes expressed in bilingual puns, as in Magnant's situation of Quebec after the conquest as 'entre chien et loup, ... entre ce chien de Montcalm et Wolfe!' (85). It is also the problem of the educated Québécois summed up by Magnant: 'Je parle trop bien pour m'en sortir par un dialecte, trop mal pour m'écouter' (95). Notwithstanding his scepticism towards the use of *joual* and his fear of the folklorization of popular speech, Aquin in this novel uses a vernacular full of anglicisms and colloquialisms to emphasize the homelessness or non-territoriality of the French language in Quebec. This illustrates perfectly the ambiguous status of the vernacular in Quebec at the time (before Bill 101). Deterritorialized insofar as it is bastardized through the encroachment of the vehicular English, it reflects the reality in which it is used. As such it performs a phatic, territorial function.

Olympe, who apologizes for his 'verbalance fonale' (15), would seem, as a Fon, to represent the opposite of Magnant's '*aphonie*.' At the moment of his victimization by association with RR's rape, however, his articulation becomes increasingly 'défectueuse' (164). The silence of the 'aphones' is the opposite of revolution, which is a scream but one that differs significantly from the animal 'cri de la race': 'La révolution ... n'est qu'un immense et inaudible cri, cri funèbre et inédit proféré par une nation ... et non pas le bégaiement informel que je sténotypie avec tristesse sur ces pages pour oublier l'inoubliable nudité de Joan' (57). One of the two oxymorons in this passage, the silent scream, which is another ambiguous analogy to the permanent revolution, engenders a pun. The colonized aspect of Magnant's double past is emphasized, or doubled, by the fact that he is part Cree ('cri') Indian. This is an example of a territorial pun; the homonymy plays on both signifier and signified. Significantly, the Cree were victims of French, rather than English, colonization. The suicidal fate of the double past is illustrated in Magnant's statement, 'Le Cri est mort en moi, scalpé par l'autre clan de ma solution génétique' (37). Murder is again suicide, and Magnant is both perpetrator and victim.

In an inversion connected with the alchemical code, Magnant plays with the proverb identifying silence and gold. Quebec is populated by 'un peuple, aurifié, avec gueule d'or sur fond blême [qui] se tait à force de ne pas vouloir s'exprimer tout haut' (57). The horrified state implied in the pun is a result of the conquest and the ensuing amnesia/aphasia. The state of victimization is illustrated in images and linguistic actualizations of stuttering, hesitation, and aphasia in a clear equation of extraterritoriality and lack of language. The metaphoric code of silence and scream shows revolutionary activity as an inverted alchemical endeavour, an attempt to transmute the gold of silence into its opposite, the cry of revolution.

The affinity between victimization/amnesia and aphasia is illustrated by Olympe's forgetting the name of his hotel at the time of RR's rape and their exile from 'La Résidence,' via 'Les Arromanches' – another name connoting British victory (the Great Armada) – to 'La Bourdonnais,' where RR 'marmonne confusément à haute voix' (177), until they end up in the symbol of Olympe's double past, 'Paris-Home' (187). Paris plays the same role in Olympe's past as London in Magnant's. The itinerary of RR's and Olympe's travels coincides with their assumption of the past and the defeat and is reflected in Olympe's restoration of his anamorphic writing from 'j'écris sur une table surmontée d'un miroir' (175) to 'J'écris sur une table banale' (187). It is the return of memory and the painful recuperation of the past that restores the anamorphosis: the victims step out of an illusion into reality, out of the 'trou' into history.

The reterritorialization of history is analogous to the recuperation of language which becomes equated with the 'pays.' Death or defeat turns Joan into a symbol of the country: 'Notre pays est un cadavre encombrant' (48). The affinity between language and country is expressed in the central metaphor of Lagos which, like Lac Léman in *Prochain épisode*, becomes the *point de fuite* where the formal and diegetic lines converge. Unlike the classic perspectival focus, however, the vanishing point of the anamorphic 'perspective curieuse' is considerably more difficult to discern. The crucial role played by the 'pays' is illustrated in RR's section, where it is described in terms echoing the description of the 'cabinet de vérité' in Holbein's painting.

The access to the island of Lagos is made difficult by the surrounding 'lagunes' and the 'sables mouvants.' The metathetic or graphically anamorphic relationship linking 'langue,' 'lagune,' and 'lacune' is thematized in the insistence on the difficulty of navigating through the obstacle course of the lagoons surrounding the city: 'Je n'ai pas d'autre pays que ces limans noirs qui m'ensorcellent dans leur succession de rédents et d'isthmes décrochés. Oui, mon pays n'est rien d'autre que ces sables mouvants qui encastrent Lagos dans un écrin accore. Né du sable, je tente interminablement de m'y enraciner, mais je m'ensable et je m'emprisonne dans le tracé du littoral et dans les calligrammes deltaïques du rivage' (98). The 'lagunes' are the 'trous,' or 'lacunes,' which must be filled with meaning. The defeated narrator must fight against the 'ensablement' resulting from the 'trou de mémoire,' the absence of language, and the impossibility of making sense of history. It is only by filling the lacunae that he can turn the anamorphic 'lagune' into 'langue' and reach Lagos, the locus of truth.

The vocabulary pertaining to the description of Lagos reflects the opposition between speaking and writing alluded to from the beginning, when Magnant states that 'Ecrire [l']empêche de tout dire' (55). Magnant yearns to reach Lagos, to come to terms with his past and the defeat, yet by writing he covers Joan's corpse, creating the 'littoral,' which is to 'littéral' as 'lagune' to 'langue,' and which prevents the 'enracinement.' The auto-referential aspect of the lagoon metaphor is evident in the editor's insistence on the lacunae in the text. He remarks on the frequent *carences* in Magnant's manuscript and, in his interpretation of *The Ambassadors*, he emphasizes that it is not the substance of the tablecloth that holds the two figures together but rather the 'entrelacs des motifs de tissage' (142).

A footnote foregrounds the fact that Lagos is the capital of Nigeria, the heart of darkness, or the 'nigredo' of alchemy, a place named after the river Niger, whose mouth becomes a symbol for Joan's as the entrance into the 'pays.' Lagos is the home of RR, the unknowable. In yet another typical inversion, Montreal eventually comes to play the same role to Olympe as Lagos to Magnant.

The temporal dimension of the *carence* is perceived both structurally and metaphorically in the novel. There are several inconsistencies concerning the position of events in time, and the chronology is problematic. Olympe's letter, which seems to be written before the events described in the rest of the text, is dated September 1966. Magnant's autobiography is written in the same year, after Joan's death, which – according to Olympe's journal – takes place about three or four months before 14 May, the opening date of the journal, thus around February 1966. The journal's internal chronology is distorted: there are too many 'lendemains' between 30 and 31 May. The events of the 'Note finale,' which presumably occur just after Olympe's and RR's departure from Paris in June of 1966, are firmly anchored in the actual events happening in Montreal in July of 1967. In the end there seems to be a convergence of fictional time with the actual time of writing of *Trou de mémoire*. Basically, there are two orders of time present in the text: the anamorphic one of *carence* and the chronology of objective reality or history. When the two finally converge, and the temporal anamorphosis is restored, fiction and reality coincide.

The central metaphor illustrating the temporal *carence* is directly related to the theme of death and resurrection: 'Conquête est aube noire et longue, deuil blême, face de carême pour ne pas dire sainte face – ce qui revient à double face!!! Le conquis vit entre chien et loup, et pour lui, chien fidèle, il n'y a qu'un jour au calendrier: un samedi saint sans lendemain ... Oui, le conquis s'est taillé une toute petite place entre la mort et la résurrection, il est mort et attend dans une espérance régressive et démodée un jour de Pâques qui ne viendra jamais' (38). The temporal dimension is thus inscribed in the pascal symbolism and is diegetically reflected in the chronology of the events, stretching from February, the beginning of 'carême' in the Christian calendar, until May and the Pentecost, which is always temporally relative to Easter. The symbolism also surfaces in numerous images of waiting and of spectacles without beginning or end.

RR defines herself as 'une anamorphose que nul regard amoureux ne rendra à une forme raccourcie, je veux dire: au temps retrouvé' (130). The restoration of the anamorphosis is analogous to the step out of the time-lessness of defeat into the temporal dimension of history. This is operated through RR's reading and arranging of the fragments constituting the novel: 'me voici en train de le regarder d'un point de vue final qui me fait découvrir la vérité raccourcie de cette perspective que chaque document rallongeait de façon indue' (201). The alchemical transmutation performed by reading also implies power over time, as the alchemist speeds up natural processes in a temporal anamorphosis.

RR's role as editor/catalyst is anticipated when she describes how, by entering the stage, she puts an end to a play put on by Joan: 'Le spectacle était consommé à l'instant même où j'entrais en scène avec fracas' (128). This coincides with an image equating the play with the country and the entry into historical time with exile: 'en quittant mon "théâtre supérieur," je m'étais exilée à jamais de mon pays natal' (128). This image foreshadows Lagos and the metaphor of the 'pays' as 'île exil' [sic] (152) and reflects the paradoxical analogy between distantiation and 'enracinement,' 'pays' and exile.

Intertexts

The high degree of literary self-consciousness in *Trou de mémoire* is reflected in the proliferation of intertextual allusions. The most fundamental ideological intertext of the novel, illustrated in the thematics of colonialism and revolution, reveals the influences of Sartrean existentialism and Marxist theories of colonization. The frequent references to Descartes and Nietzsche anchor the text in the philosophical tradition of Western Europe and the colonialist aspect of the double past. The symbolic territory is, as we have seen, specifically that of Catholicism and the sacraments of the Church. My discussion of blasphemy and its close relation to the vernacular has shown this aspect to be territorial, insofar as it is based on the original unity of the sacred and the profane and reflects the homogeneity of the culture resulting from the influence and position of the Church in Quebec.

The ideological discourse of colonization is exemplified in a historical/ allegorical structure that is clearly territorial, focusing on the figure of Papineau who, to Magnant, personifies defeat and treason and is ultimately responsible for the defeatism of the people of Quebec.[10] The insistence on Papineau, the rebellion, and the conquest is reflected in a number of references which lack significance for readers unfamiliar with Quebec history, and some of which are ignored by the editor. One such example is the mention of Bougainville, ostensibly referring to his role as explorer (93).

Magnant's identification with Bougainville gains an added dimension in the context of the latter's prophecy when, as Montcalm's aide, he predicted the defeat of the French Canadians as a result of their own prejudices.[11]

The complexities of the colonial relationship, discussed in connection with the double past, are foregrounded in numerous references to internal oppression. This is seen especially in the theme of the collaboration of the Church with the colonizer, which is further put in a relation of synonymy with the justice system, as illustrated in the image of the 'procureur de la couronne d'épines' (83). A direct equation between colonial oppression and internal political corruption is operated in an analogy between the Stamp Act and the Quebec Act on the one hand and Duplessis' infamous padlock law on the other (60–1). This 'roi nègre' syndrome, which is a variant of the ambivalence of black and white, is anticipated in Olympe's oxymoronic reference to the police of the Ivory Coast 'noircissant l'horizon de leurs uniformes blancs' (10). It is also reflected in the Cree metaphor: as the Indians were first colonized by the French, who were subsequently colonized by the British, the Fon were once the colonizers of the Yoruba before being colonized by the French.

The simultaneity of Papineau's defeat and its opposite, Victoria's ascension, reflects the anchoring of Magnant's literary heritage in the British tradition of which Sherlock Holmes is the most prominent representative. There is also a clear Shakespearean intertext with implicit references to *Hamlet* (anticipating Aquin's use of this particular play in his last novel, *Neige noire*) and, as seen in a reference to 'tout est silence, même le reste' (56) to *Macbeth*. Both plays are concerned with murder, revenge, and ghosts, prominent ingredients in *Trou de mémoire*. The most puzzling occurrence of the Shakespearean intertext, however, is the insistence on the knocking on the door after Joan's murder. The knocking, which disturbs Magnant in his writing, has no obvious diegetic function, and it is never revealed who, or what, causes it. The insistence on this incident points to a convergence of the Shakespearean intertext with that of one of Magnant's favourite writers, Thomas De Quincey, whose name occurs twice in significant positions (first in Olympe's letter and then in RR's 'Semi-finale'). De Quincey, like Sherlock Holmes, belongs to the British literary part of Magnant's heritage. Of all De Quincey's essays, only one deals with Shakespeare, 'On the Knocking at the Gate in *Macbeth*.' Here De Quincey analyses the knocking in terms reminiscent of my discussion of temporal anamorphosis and *carence*: 'The human has made its reflux upon the fiendish; the pulses of life are beginning to beat again; and the re-establishment of the goings-on of the world in which we live first makes us profoundly sensible of the awful parenthesis that had suspended them' (393). The final collision of the two orders of time is foreshadowed in the Neptune incident, but the discrepancy between them persists until the final convergence.

De Quincey's essay on *Macbeth* anticipates his satirical 'On Murder Considered as One of the Fine Arts' in its considerations of the aesthetics of crime. In Olympe's words, the British writer is a 'perfectionniste du mal' (13). He is, of course, better known for his *Confessions of an English Opium Eater*, in which he traces his fall into addiction in a manner not unlike Magnant's account of his own drug habit.

Another crucial intertextual presence is John Ruskin. The connection alluded to in the name of the two sisters is made explicit when the Swiss gendarme mistakes Joan's name for 'John' (162). Magnant professes his aim to 'faire baroque' (63), and the Ruskin intertext is part of a dichotomy contrasting the 'perspective curieuse' which, to Magnant, pertains to the baroque, reflecting the otherness of the colonized, with its opposite – the gothic that Ruskin prefers. While no explicit reference is made to the opposition between the two styles, it is implicit in the editor's contempt for the techniques of the baroque and its penchant for the *trompe-l'oeil*.[12] In what could be an allusion to Ruskin's *The Stones of Venice*, he points out that the motifs in the cloth joining the two ambassadors in Holbein's painting resemble gothic windows and traces its origin to Venice. The only other reference to the gothic is found in Olympe's journal, where the capsules of amytal, which plunge RR into a near coma, are described as 'ogives' (185). Drugs and the induction of amnesia are thus linked to the gothic, which represents the aesthetics of the colonizer. Joan Ruskin's death and its specular counterpart, RR's rape, eventually lead to Rachel's rejection of her name. In assuming her role as victim, she takes on a new identity and casts off her past as colonizer.

Venice becomes the locus of another intertextual convergence between Ruskin and Marcel Proust, whose presence is more obvious in the thematics of lost time and memory, and becomes explicit in RR's reference to the 'temps retrouvé' as the impossible restoration of anamorphosis. It was Proust's admiration for Ruskin that inspired his writing as Jean Autret has shown.

The main proponent of the baroque in the visual and dramatic arts is Bernini, who not only figures in the novel as a master of sculptural *trompe-l'oeil*, but whose role in the discourse of apocryphy is foregrounded through editorial commentary. Footnotes 2 and 3 on page 49 constitute a *mise en abyme* of this theme: the editor interprets a certain reference made by Magnant as an allusion to a specific work by Bernini, and RR, in turn, contends that the work in question is not by the great sculptor but was executed by his disciples. This mirrors the process of narrative authorization, whereby a fact presented by one authority (Magnant) is interpreted by a second (the editor), only to be refuted by the third and final reader/writer, RR, who replaces it with her own – presumably final – truth, stating that the work of art in question is apocryphal.[13]

Besides its important function on the levels of auto-referentiality and allegory, the baroque also forms part of a wider historical reference centred in the Renaissance and the Reformation. The focus of this particular referential network is Descartes, who is introduced already in Olympe's letter. Baltrusaitis shows Descartes' interest in the techniques of anamorphosis flourishing at the time. One of the French thinker's correspondents on the subject was Galileo, who, as I indicated in chapter 1, disliked the technique, and whose role in the metaphoric of the permanent revolution has been pointed out. The astronomer may constitute a bridge between two intertexts in the same way that Thomas De Quincey links the discourses of drug addiction with both Shakespeare and the idea of temporal *carence*. The essential concept of distantiation in drama, discussed by RR, finds its modern counterpart in Brecht's 'Verfremdungseffekt.' Instead of depicting the heroism and martyrdom of its protagonist, Brecht's *Life of Galileo* concentrates on the 'human, all too human' aspects. Thus, Galileo, for economic reasons, partakes of the discourse of apocryphy by pretending to have invented the binoculars and, at the crucial moment of truth, disappoints his admirers by recanting his convictions rather than risking the judgment of the Inquisition. Descartes, for the same too human reasons, one would assume, withdrew publication of his defence of Galileo upon hearing of his prosecution. It is significant, considering the paradoxical equation of 'enracinement' and exile analysed in the Lagos metaphor, that so many of the intertextual proponents of distantiation, from Descartes to Brecht, at some point lived the experience of exile or extraterritoriality, whether by force or choice.

Magnant's other favourite writer, besides Thomas De Quincey, is said to be Bakunin, whose particular brand of revolutionary anarchism may shed light on Magnant's idea of the permanent revolution. Like his fellow 'perfectionniste du mal,' Bakunin wrote a confession in which he repented his early career in crime. Whether written in earnest or as a ruse to gain clemency from the czar, it resulted in his being exiled rather than executed.

A curious piece of trivia contained in Bakunin's confession makes it possible to see him as yet another bridge between two seemingly disparate intertexts. If Bakunin epitomizes the ideological version of Magnant's revolution, his literary counterpart is Vladimir Nabokov, to whose formal innovations Aquin is heavily indebted. Both exiles, Bakunin and Nabokov represent opposites that converge. The latter's aristocratic forebears were a considerable presence in pre-revolutionary Russia, and one of his ancestors was governor of the Peter and Paul fortress at the time Bakunin wrote his confession there.[14] The Nabokovian influence is perhaps most obvious in the structure of the novel, with its multilayered commentary, which is reminiscent of *Pale Fire*.[15] There are, however, also several parallels with *Kamera Obskura* or *Laughter in the Dark*, the novel mentioned in the text, in which Albinus has the idea of animating the works of old masters in film, as Magnant can be said to animate *The Ambassadors*.

Names

The 'quatuor' formed by the characters in *Trou de mémoire* should be considered as 'la fragmentation d'un sujet en quatre parties, respectivement matérialisées par une diversité de noms propres' (Maccabée-Iqbal 123). The most striking aspect of the names in the novel is their doubleness. The individual Ruskin sisters may seem to be excepted from this rule, but, in fact, Joan has a middle initial which is in itself double, W. (51), and Rachel is always referred to by her double initials, RR. Olympe has a double last name, and Pierre X. Magnant has an unknown middle name, presumably standing for Xavier, but also indicating an unknown property. As I have already shown, Magnant's name is a possible anagram of Père Maignan, and he is also Saint *Pierre* and the *pierre* philosophale, as well as the *magnum* opus. His signature can be read as the pharmacists' ℞ or as ✠ . Magnant's editorial alias, Charles-Edouard Mullahy, with its royal and Irish connotations, must be seen in another context, however. Charles I and Edward VI pertain to the historical context of the Reformation and both figure prominently among the anamorphoses reproduced by Baltrusaitis: the first is made for cylindrical mirror, according to the same principles as the anamorphosis on the cover of Aquin's book which in Baltrusaitis appears opposite a clandestine portrait of the decapitated king. The mirror conceals the picture of a cranium in such a way that when it is removed, the portrait cannot be restored, and the only thing seen is the image of death. The portrait of Edward VI, on the other hand, whose origin is unknown and which must be viewed through a hole, furthermore shows 'les mêmes dilatations [que] le crâne allégorique dans le tableau des Ambassadeurs' (Baltrusaitis 22).

The discrepancy between the British royal names and the Irish last name sums up the colonial pattern in an Irish intertext which – besides its obvious relevance for the discourse on nationalism and colonization – reveals Aquin's great admiration for James Joyce. The episode in which Joan and Magnant go to London is described in terms of the colonial background of the British empire (significantly 'Old Bond Street' is mentioned [61]). Among the places visited are St James Street, St James Place, St James Hotel, and it is in St James Park that Magnant finds his double past. James Joyce returns implicitly in Anne-Lise Jamieson, whose father was Irish. Considering that this is RR's adopted identity and her role in the discussion of apocryphy and authorship, her name recalls Anna-Livia (ALP) as the possible author of *Finnegans Wake*. The green, or Ireland, occurs in Joan's home address, 'avenue Green' (51) and in the colour of Magnant's notepaper, which, as pointed out, also alludes to the *Emerald Tablet* (*Tabula Smaragdina*). Joyce's view of writing as a kind of alchemy may indeed have provided inspiration for Aquin.

The metaphoric itinerary of the text can be said to go from the Ivory Coast to Ireland, from white to green. In light of the many references to flags, it is significant that those of the two countries are mirror images of each other. Charles-Edouard Mullahy may also have a fictive referent in the Sherlock Holmes canon: one of the worst criminals in Holmes' London is a certain Charles Augustus Milverton (of the story of that title), who is in possession of incriminating letters which he uses to blackmail members of the aristocracy. Milverton is shot, in Holmes' presence, by one of his victims, a mysterious woman whose identity is known to the detective but revealed neither to the reader nor to Dr Watson. According to Donald Redmond, the character of Milverton is based on Charles Augustus Howell, a universally disliked person who worked as John Ruskin's secretary (Redmond 145).[16]

Rachel Ruskin is in many ways the unknown quantity in the novel. Her last name is derived from John Ruskin, and her first initial may result from the imperative that she be double. Rachel as a red herring also implies an allusion to the first Sherlock Holmes story, 'A Study in Scarlet,' where the non-existent Rachel leads the detective on a wild goose chase, until her 'identity' is revealed as the German word for revenge, 'Rache,' significantly written with blood on a wall where a murder has taken place. Her double initials also coincide with the 'réseau de résistance,' a Quebec separatist group founded in 1962.[17]

As a martyr of French-English conflict, Joan Ruskin is also an inverted St Joan. This is implied in the description of her corpse as that of an 'enfant morte,' the use of words like 'croisillon' and 'l'arc' to depict the position of her body (28), and the likening of her clothing to 'cuirasses' (46). There may be an indication of this link in her connection with Lagos, in French homophonous with 'La-gosse' (89).[18] The opposition between 'John' and

'Joan' is worked out also in this paradigm. As a heretic and blasphemer, St Joan is the opposite of the patron saint of the 'cri de la race,' St John the Baptist (George Bernard Shaw makes his St Joan the first protestant, as well as the first true nationalist). While Magnant vehemently rejects the celebration of the feast of St John, that of St Joan is celebrated on 30 May, the anniversary of her death, which in 1966 coincided with Pentecost. Reaching Lagos, 'la gosse,' according to this metaphoric code, equals returning to the pre-Babelian virginal 'langue désaintciboirisée,' filling the void and turning 'lagune' into 'langue.'

Olympe Ghezzo-Quénum's name is foregrounded through a footnote referring to his descendance from the liberator of the Fon, Ghezzo, which leaves the other two elements of his name unaccounted for.[19] Considering Aquin's interest in African writing, it is probable that Olympe is a persona of the Beninian writer Olympe Bhêly-Quénum, who is also a Fon.[20] The author of numerous novels and articles on the problems of colonialism and neocolonialism in French West Africa, Bhêly-Quénum lived for several years in France before returning to his newly independent country, Benin, as Minister of Culture. He has also been editor of *La Vie africaine*, to which many of the writers alluded to in Aquin's writings are frequent contributors. Bhêly-Quénum's 1960 novel, whose title, *Un Piège sans fin*, echoes the *carence* discussed above describes the collision of cultures in a colonized society, focusing on the conflict between widely different systems of religion and justice. The protagonist kills a woman, who becomes the innocent victim (*pharmakos*) of his displaced rage. Although Bhêly-Quénum's style is quite distinct from Aquin's, it is significant – considering my discussion of pascal symbolism – that one of the crucial moments in the novel occurs at an Easter celebration, where the murderer intuitively identifies with Christ's passion. The complexity of the culture clash is illustrated, as in *Trou de mémoire*, by the willingness with which the colonized mind embraces the most barbaric aspects of the colonizer's culture.

The name Thomas, which occurs in a seemingly redundant anecdote in the novel, and whose apocryphal nature is emphasized by the editor (59), recalls both Thomas De Quincey and the false author of the *Aurora Consurgens*, Thomas Aquinas. Hubert Aquin's nominal affinity with 'St Thomas d'Aquin,' as well as his relatedness to Bhêly-Quénum and De Quincey, is revealed when Olympe complains that the 'q' on his typewriter 'crée un embouteillage de caractères' (13–14). It is significant that Aquinas' presence in the Catholic mass is represented above all by eucharistic hymns; as indicated already in the context of the apocryphal *Aurora Consurgens*, he is the poet of transubstantiation. It is also possible to see in Aquinas yet another link with James Joyce, whose interest in thomism is well documented.

It is thus possible to detect the dissemination of the proper name of the author in the text, in names of characters and intertextual and symbolic references, as well as in the predominant metaphoric of water and fluidity. The notion of specular identity is discernible both diegetically and formally in the novel, where Joan and RR, as well as Magnant and Olympe, are specular inversions of each other. Magnant's own specular counterpart which, considering the striking affinities between the narrator and his creator, may well be Aquin's own, is, as we have discovered, 'Saint Pierre,' the preacher of the first Pentecost, to whom Olympe constitutes the counterpart, 'l'amuse-gueule de Paul-hors-les-murs' (94). And, in the final instance, the author's own alias is none other than the Holy Ghost. Aquin's image of the ideal relationship between author and reader – a more directly auto-referential counterpart of the rape of the crowd – may be Bernini's famous sculpture of religious ecstasy, which RR in a note renames 'La transverbération de Sainte Thérèse' (49). Like Cohen's novel, *Trou de mémoire* links sainthood with sexual rapture, and Aquin's apocryphal name for what is often seen as the best visual representation of the workings of the Holy Ghost emphasizes the piercing power of the Word, in the religious mystic's revelation of the logos as phallus.

'A la limite, je me demande si la grande innovation littéraire ne serait pas de revenir à l'anonymat ... A lecteurs anonymes, auteurs anonymes,' says Aquin (*Blocs erratiques* 267). The desired disappearance of the author, announced on the book's cover, is expressed in *Trou de mémoire* in the discourse of apocryphy – the transposition of alterity onto the level of auto-referentiality – whereby each narration casts doubt on the preceding, undermining all claims to narrative authority. The metaphoric unity and formal interdependence of the various sections of the text, however, point to a unifying presence superseding the individual narrations. The dialectic of absence and presence is quite explicit in the auto-referential discourse, and its ambiguities resemble those pertaining to the other metaphoric patterns discussed. Thus, for instance, Magnant at one point proclaims: 'je suis parti,' only to translate immediately the figurative expression into its literal, even if pleonastic, counterpart, alluding to the drug-induced sharpening of the senses: 'je suis présent d'une présence réelle' (20), in a convergence of absence and presence that is as Derridean as Cohen's hourglass image. The oxymoronic nature of this pair is of the same type as 'je tourne en rond/je ne fais rien' and 'Je n'en reviens pas/il faut revenir.' The absence/presence dialectic also partakes of the postmodern view of the specular relationship of writing and reading: it is the reader who attributes a presence to the author by establishing a situation of communication in the act of reading.

We have seen how, in spite of the apparent fragmentation, the novel is unified through metaphor and symbol. Generically *Trou de mémoire* can be seen as the convergence of two opposite types of discourse, the autobiographical and the editorial. Autobiography is the story of an 'I,' and in a fictional autobiography the 'I' is constituted within the text. Focusing on the question of the identity of the narrator, such a text is mainly centripetal, incorporating the extratextual only to the extent that it can throw light on the 'I.' Conversely, editorial commentary is fundamentally referential. Marginal footnotes are generally subject to certain conventional assumptions: they are supposed to 'have a notational function,' to be 'connected to and dependent on the text that engenders them,' and to be 'subordinate to' the text (Benstock 209). Interposed between the text and the reader, they serve two basic functions: they comment on the authority of the text by referring to extratextual sources, and they open up a dialogue with the reader on the subject of the text. Thus exclusively geared to the extratextual (the reference and the reader), their movement is essentially centrifugal. As Shari Benstock points out, these assumptions have been subject to parody ever since *Tristram Shandy*, and the ancestors of *Trou de mémoire* in this respect are no doubt *Finnegans Wake* and *Pale Fire*.

Much more blatantly than Cohen in his footnotes, Aquin literally does his writing in the margin. The notes form a grid which, by foregrounding certain elements in the *récit*, serves as a guide to the reading. The supposedly centrifugal discourse, with its wealth of encyclopedic information, turns a mirror to the text, reflecting inward instead of outward, as in a *camera obscura*. Like a palimpsest, the *récit* must be read through the prism of the margin; in *Trou de mémoire* it is indeed the margin that makes sense of the text, and the ironic reversal of the hierarchical relationship between centre and margin is foregrounded in the title of the last 'chapter' of the novel, 'Note finale.' The proper names, on the other hand, which in fiction are expected to create their reference within the text, have been seen to project outward: Magnant, Quénum, Ruskin, Mullahy, and Jamieson all carry a considerable amount of intertextual reference. This specular inversion between the two types of discourse – between the centripetal and the centrifugal, the referential and the non-referential – might be called a generic anamorphosis symptomatic of the alterity of the colonized subject for whom the autobiographical 'I' can never coincide with its representation.

Oxymoron

The presumed 'aphonie' of the text, with its references to hesitation, stuttering, and lying, is counterbalanced by the extreme intensity of the narration, created mainly through hyperbole, progression, and pleonasm, as well as by the profound symbolism that clings to even the simplest idiom. Metaphor is, as I have shown, very much present in the text and often plays a generating role. Françoise Maccabée-Iqbal has, in her inventory of figures and tropes, found numerous examples of repetition, anaphora, accumulation, hyperbole, syncope, ellipsis, metonymy, and neologism. She has also commented on the proliferation of the signifier, whereby one signified explodes into a network of near-synonymous signifiers. These stylistic devices, all aiming at intensity of expression are reminiscent of those listed by Vidal Sephiha as phatic, hence territorial, markers in oral narrative. Maccabée-Iqbal posits a combination of repetition and antithesis as the fundamental generating principle of the language of the novel. Antithesis is, as we have seen in the basic metaphoric patterns (white/black, alive/dead, colonizer/colonized), a problematic phenomenon in *Trou de mémoire*; rather than an opposition, it reflects an ambivalence that paradoxically results in the conjunction of opposites.

The trope that best translates this conjunction is the oxymoron, of which numerous examples are to be found in the text: from clichés like 'nuit blanche' to the central 'inaudible cri' and expressions triggered by polysemy like 'chienne immaculée' (90), to more unusual images, such as 'patinoire brûlante' (43). We have also seen the oxymoronic principle at work in the frequent juxtaposition of the figurative with its contradictory literal equivalent in expressions of the type 'je suis parti / je suis présent' in such a way as to operate their conjunction. It culminates on the symbolic level, where it is expressed in the alchemical opus, symbolized by the black sun, and in the philosopher's stone as the conjunction of the *prima materia* with the *quinta essentia*. Reminiscent of Cohen's 'akropolis rose,' this central symbol mirrors the convergence of the material and the spiritual, the profane and the sacred, whose linguistic expression is blasphemy, the 'sacre.' When Magnant identifies himself as 'sacré,' he indicates his simultaneous status as sacred and damned which characterizes the original unity of the two in the once shared realm of the sacred and the profane/vernacular. The equation of *prima* and *quinta* also confirms the narrator's earlier self-identification with the sacred number: the agent of transformation, the author, can become five others (Magnant, Olympe, Joan, RR, and Mullahy).

Léon Cellier has noted that the oxymoron indeed represents the *coincidentia oppositorum* and, as such, it reflects the ambivalence of the sacred. Derrida, on the other hand, argues that the conjunction of opposites is to be found in the *syllepsis*. According to Dumarsais, whom Derrida purports to follow, syllepsis means the coexistence in the same word of two meanings, one proper and one figurative. Derrida, however, considerably narrows the definition of the trope to mean the coexistence of *opposite* meanings, as in the *pharmakon* ('Pharmacie de Platon' 249). I shall try to clarify the confusion surrounding the definitions of the two tropes in my analysis of *Gone Indian*, which exhibits mainly what I would call sylleptic structures. My definition of the oxymoron follows Cellier's view of it as fundamentally conjunctive and entails a view of syllepsis, of which more in chapter 6, as its opposite, the figure of disjunction.

The mystery of the *coincidentia oppositorum*, the *mysterium coniunctionis*, is in *Trou de mémoire*, as in *Beautiful Losers*, epitomized in transubstantiation, which is expressed aesthetically in the technique of anamorphosis. The liquidity of Aquin's imagery which, as mentioned, is part of the authorial rebus/signature in the text, and which thus counteracts the inscription of the death of the author on the book's cover, also actualizes the conjunction of opposites: 'Dans le liquide, les opposés passent plus facilement l'un dans l'autre. Le liquide est l'élément du *pharmakon*' ('Pharmacie de Platon' 175). If Aquin is liquidity, he is consequently also the element which operates the conjunction; he is, yet again, shown to be the philosopher's stone.

Although Cellier does not use the term *pharmakon* in his discussion of the oxymoron, he points out that the frequent warnings against the excessive use of the trope is peculiarly reminiscent of warnings concerning the use of drugs: 'Ainsi parle un pharmacien en vendant un produit toxique' (14). The oxymoron may thus be a *pharmakon*, but its use is a question of just measure and, unlike in Derrida's definition of syllepsis, there is no undecidability attached to it. The oxymoronic ambivalence of the sacred is not the same thing as duality: the two sides of the coin are interdependent and coexistent. The Christian variant of metamorphosis is expressed in *Trou de mémoire*, more explicitly than in *Beautiful Losers*, through the formal strategy of anamorphosis, and the congruity of form and content is achieved, in the final instance, through the fundamentally religious equation of the *pharmakon* of writing with the sacrament of the Eucharist, which constitutes the *point de fuite* of all the signifying lines in the novel. Through what seems like pentecostal inspiration the potentially manipulative and deterritorializing strategy of anamorphosis is territorialized in a return to the original unity of the sacred and the profane in an act of [un]holy communion, a *sacrée communion* not unlike the one achieved by way of the Greek in *Beautiful Losers.*

The thematic – political – concern with the position of the colonized, the beautiful loser or 'nègre blanc,' and the ensuing discourse of alterity, expressed in non-territorial, disjunctive strategies are in both novels permeated by fundamentally religious concerns that transcend the immediate political situation. A thematic study will invariably stress the revolutionary aspects of Aquin's novel, but I would argue that the reading I have proposed in terms of all the different aspects of territoriality has shown its most radical aspect to be the religious impulse; although it exhibits features that are both non-territorial and territorial, the latter are more fundamental to the author. Aquin's revolution is, in the final analysis, religious and aesthetic before it is political. In both of the novels I have discussed so far, the alterity of the metropolitan colonial subject is redeemed – transformed into art – through the mystery of transubstantiation, but while in Cohen's text the metamorphosis can only be performed through recourse to a scriptural, sacred language alien to the linguistic territory, it is in Aquin's text hidden within the vernacular itself and, it may be argued, within the very lowest part of it.

I have suggested that *Trou de mémoire*, with its insistence on the state of amnesia in Quebec, can be seen as an attempt to counter the official motto, 'je me souviens.' It was, we will remember, the 'q' that created the problematic 'embouteillage' and ensuing confusion of identities in Olympe's letter, and it may not be too fanciful to suggest that we may be witnessing another generative signifier at work. In what seems like a statement of his own intent, Aquin has Magnant explain that 'La seule compensation du conquis absolu serait de comprendre pourquoi et de quelle incroyable façon il s'est fait enculer par l'histoire; mais, justement, par définition il a perdu la vue' (39).

Whether a historically induced phenomenon, as in Aquin's novel, or a desirable state, as in Cohen's, memory-loss is in both inscribed in similar paradigms – pornography and blasphemy – and associated with two parts of the body – the ass and the eye. The loss of memory and vision is a result of the same old aggression – an 'enculade' is the rape perpetrated, for a change, on a male subject. Maybe what Aquin himself is saying by sharing Cohen's carnivalesque conflation of the two body-parts is a challenge to Quebec: 'je me souviens... mon cul,' or 'mon oeil': by recuperating his 'trou,' admitting the falseness of the claim to memory, he will regain his vision. The 'trou de mémoire' thus becomes the 'trou de Q,' the Québécois version of the 'rosy sphinx hole,' whose unblocking is a precondition for disentangling the 'caractères' and establishing a Québécois identity. In both cases the hole is the potential locus of insight and truth, whose restoration can only be accomplished by emptying it of false representations – the colonizer's history – and replacing them, in Cohen's case with the ideal of pure being, in Aquin's case with the requisite understanding which will absolve the conquered – make him a 'conquis absolu' – of his alterity. The latter accomplishes this by filling the hole created by the appropriation of the colonized's self-representation with an aesthetic mirror – a novel – in which the distorted 'perspective violente' of the colonizer can be restored.

While the two first texts in my corpus thus converge in their use of the mystery of conjunction and their shared concern with anamorphic vision, as well as in their privileging of the ontological over the political, it could be argued that, in spite of their locating the truth in the same place, their attitudes towards the 'trou de mémoire' differ. To Aquin, the postcolonial writer, alterity is not a desirable state; it can only be remedied through the active assumption and revisioning of the past; to Cohen, the postmodernist, alterity becomes a metaphor for a desired human condition, for which memory loss is a prerequisite. In both, however, the state of alterity – the loss of self – is in the end redeemed by the resurrection of the author.

CHAPTER FOUR

The New Ancestors
The Writer as Sacrifice

Michael Burdener arrives in Lost Coast from England to work as a biology teacher at Workman's University College in 1960. He eventually marries a former student, Ama Harding Awotchwi, with whom he has one son and two daughters. Through Ama's brother, Gamaliel Harding, and her half-brother, First Samuels (often referred to as FS), both active in The Freedom People's Party which, under President Kruman, rules the former British colony, Michael gets involved in local politics. His career falls into decline, his son Cricket dies of sleeping sickness, after which Michael takes a trip to Mopti in Mali with Gamaliel and Samuels. After a short return to London Michael accepts an invitation from First Samuels, who has turned against his earlier party and its leader, to return to Lost Coast and teach at People's Night College where he becomes involved with the counter-revolutionary 'Core.' Several of its members are killed when they try to sabotage Kruman's showpiece, the Kruba dam project. First Samuels suspects Gamaliel of betraying them and kills him; he is himself later found dead. Michael's story in Lost Coast is one of gradual decay and demotion from the better schools to the worst, as his initial admiration for Kruman and the revolution turns into disillusionment and, finally, to revolt, until at last he is deported, whether on suspicion for murder is not clear. It is a story of growing madness, alcoholism, and disregard for his family.

The political turmoil in Lost Coast is reflected in the family life of Michael and Ama. His father missing in the war, Michael grows up in a convent, where he witnesses the rape of his teacher, sister Marcella. When he is six, his father returns but eventually goes mad and spends the rest of his life in an asylum. Ama's story is similar: her mother, the daughter of a native woman and a Canadian sailor, goes mad after having abandoned her first husband – the father of Ama, Gamaliel, and First Samuels – because of his infidelity, and married Hastings Awotchwi, a wealthy entrepreneur who is imprisoned after the revolution. Ama tries to buy her stepfather's freedom by becoming Kruman's mistress. After her marriage Awotchwi pleads with her to refuse Michael her bed to force him to intercede on Awotchwi's behalf with First Samuels, who is close to the dictator. Ama refuses, and her stepfather goes back to jail.

In a manner similar to that of the two texts discussed before, the novel consists of two 'private' narratives telling what is basically the same story from complementary points of view, one Western and one African. The two are further complemented by a third narration which recounts the 'public' version of the story. In the difficult but crucial next section of the novel, 'In the Fifth City,' the murder of an American agent, Rod Rusk, is acted out repeatedly in a number of different ways. The chapter can be seen as a *mise en abyme* of the whole novel, although not in quite so rigorous a fashion as the 'Semi-finale' in Aquin's book.

The text is framed by a prologue and an epilogue. Like Olympe's letter, the prologue in Godfrey's novel introduces the main actors and events. The epilogue in both novels operates a fusion of fictional and historical time and coincides approximately with the time of writing. There are numerous references to real historical events.

The novel is divided into six parts and, with the exception of 'In the Fifth City,' there is rarely any doubt about the identity of the narrators and, unlike *Trou de mémoire*, their narrations are not contradictory. The prologue, dated 5 February 1966, consists of two first-person narratives, the first belonging to Geoffrey Firebank, the British Council man in the Lost Coast city of Silla, and the second to his librarian, Hastings Ayitteh, a native of Silla and cousin of Ama Burdener. The prologue focuses on the imminent expulsion from the country of Michael Burdener. The main events of the story told in the rest of the novel are alluded to through Geoffrey's interior monologue and his reading of local newspapers, which all present various interpretations of the facts, including the murder of Gamaliel Harding, the killing of the Kruba dam plotters, and the death of First Samuels. At the end of the prologue, Michael's personal papers are sent to his address in England. Some of these papers presumably form the next section, 'The London Notebook,' dated 'summer 1965.' Narrated in the first person, with occasional ironical lapses into the third person, it is largely analeptic, centring on Michael's life: his childhood at the convent; his first stay in Africa; his marriage; and his relationship with his father, his African in-laws, colleagues, political allies, and enemies. The death of the son plays a central role. 'The London Notebook' ends with Michael's determination to accept

First Samuels' invitation to return to Lost Coast and, in a cryptic reference, 'go through Mopti' (85/108).[1]

The third section belongs to Ama. Entitled 'A Child of Delicacy,' it is dated the same day as the prologue with which it merges in the final pages when, instead of her disappeared husband, Hastings Ayitteh arrives at her house with the news of Michael's deportation. Ama's section consists of her long interior monologue while waiting for the visit of a childhood friend, who has married and lived in Europe for many years. Many of the events and relationships she ponders are the same as those recounted by Michael in 'The London Notebook.' The two narratives complement each other: here we get the story of Ama's childhood and youth, her marriage to Michael, and her version of the death of their son. The political discourse that occupied a large portion of Michael's story is in Ama's present as background and only to the extent that it affects her own life.

The fourth section of the novel is entitled 'Freedom People's Party' and covers the period from February 1965 to February 1966. It represents the public and political sphere that provided the background to the two 'private' narrations. The point of view shifts between various narrators but centres on First Samuels, whose family ties with Gamaliel Harding and Ama are secondary to his political involvement. The shift from the private to the public sphere means that the characters, whose first-hand accounts have already been read, are now seen through the eyes of others. The section begins on the day of Father Skelly's durbar which, we are told in the prologue, was planned for a few days after 5 February, the day of Michael's departure. A large portion of the chapter, however, is analeptic and focuses on the political intrigues in Lost Coast, particularly on the activities of the 'Core' members and First Samuels' murder of Gamaliel.

The complex fifth section has caused critics the most problems. 'In the Fifth City' is usually interpreted as the dream mentioned by Michael – though it may be more like the nightmare referred to in the prologue's epigraph – in the succeeding chapter or as a drug-induced hallucination, an interpretation presumably corroborated by the poppy-shaped ideogram which accompanies it. It recounts the story of a trip up the river Niger undertaken by four characters who seem to have a lot in common with Michael, Gamaliel, First Samuels, and the American agent Rod Rusk, whose name has been mentioned in the prologue, and who has played a rather mysterious role throughout the rest of the novel. The narration focuses on the murder of Rusk, which is acted out several times in different ways, and vacillates between the first and third person, with occasional intrusions of the first person plural and a generalized 'one.' While the identity of many of the narrative voices is unclear, a definite authorial presence is felt here in the form of a slightly ironic omniscient narrator.

The final section, which constitutes the epilogue, belongs to Michael. Written partly in the form of interior monologue and partly as a journal and letters to Ama, 'The Agada Notebook' is in many ways a mirror image of 'The London Notebook.' Dated 'Harmattan 1966,' its entries ranging from 17 to 20 January, it comprises the time a few weeks before Michael's departure. 'The Agada Notebook' is formally a *mise en abyme* of the book as a whole: it contains a prologue, a notebook and letters, and an epilogue, all in Michael's voice.

Superseding the individual narrations is an authorial presence, revealing itself clearly in such editorial devices as epigraphs, chapter headings, and various typographical interventions: certain passages are printed in italics, and each section (except the prologue) is headed by an ideogram. The relationship of inversion between 'The London Notebook' and 'The Agada Notebook' is reflected in the ideograms heading the two, which are mirror images of each other. The text thus appears circular, with the two notebooks closing the circle, and leaving only the prologue outside.

The text is framed by a number of dedications which include names belonging to the fiction itself, as well as to several writers, some from Africa and Canada. The frame also contains two maps, which, like the dedications, seem to serve the reality effect. The first is a faithful reproduction of Ghana, with all place names changed into those of the fictional Lost Coast. The second depicts the location of the 'Fifth City' section and is an unadulterated reproduction of Mali and the river Niger. Thus, the real Ghana, whose history is at the centre of the novel, is disguised, while Mali, the location of the most 'unrealistic' part of the fiction, is depicted 'realistically,' without distortions of any kind.

Each individual section is preceded by an epigraph resumed in part at the beginning of the book, thus forming part of the frame. The only part again remaining outside the 'circle' is the prologue, whose epigraph, 'Dullness after all, is the garment of nightmare,' is not included in the frame. The epigraphs illustrate some of the basic symbolic and ideological intertexts of the various sections and will be discussed in connection with their respective roles in the whole.

Metamorphosis

The fact that the professional role of Michael Burdener provides the basic metaphoric and symbolic codes in the novel points to a close link between him and the implied author. While it is difficult to define one specific formal paradigm in the novel that would be a direct equivalent to the anamorphosis in *Trou de mémoire*, the form is organized around notions of metamorphosis and transformation, actualized metaphorically in specific processes, such as *cell division*, which is mentioned explicitly on three occasions. Michael's project is revealed, by another character, as the writing of a 'synthesis of biology and social history' (142–3/171). Rejecting the Marxist view of revolution, the implied author of the novel adopts the views of Max Born, who provides the epigraph to 'Freedom People's Party': 'Marxism teaches that the communist economy is a historical necessity and derives its fanaticism from this belief. This idea comes from physical determinism, which itself arises from Newton's celestial mechanics. But, in fact, physics abandoned this theory about thirty years ago. Instead it has worked out a statistical interpretation of natural laws which corresponds better to reality and in the light of which the communist belief that Marxist predictions will necessarily be realized appears grotesque' (159/189). A number of prominent metaphors pertaining to the transformation of energy are provided by quantum physics, which William New defines as 'a scientific theory of uncertainty that underlies the constant metamorphosis of energy forces' ('Canadian Literature and Commonwealth Responses' 20). The thematic introduction of new forces in the political situation is described metaphorically in terms of biological or physical processes. 'There is no action in the world which is ever accidental,' says Michael (59/79): biological processes and the transformation of energy are highly predictable and inevitable phenomena, whose uncertainty lies in their outcome. Heisenberg's uncertainty principle which states the impossibility of accurately measuring both position and momentum at the same time will prove particularly visible in 'In The Fifth City,' and quantum mechanics as a science describing alternative possible happenings has replaced the determinism of Newtonian science in this very science-influenced text.

The fundamental opposition structuring the novel is that between the West and Africa. Modern science would seem to pertain to the West and to Michael who, as a scientist, is the typical Westerner. However, the crucial notion of force is also central to African consciousness, according to which everything is force, not substance: 'Man is a force, all things are forces, place and time are forces, and the "modalities" are forces' (Jahn 100). This is not unlike the idea of *mana*, as explained by Ernst Cassirer, who makes a distinction between a 'mythical' and a 'scientific' idea of force: 'In general, the mythical concept of force differs from the scientific concept in that it never looks on force as a dynamic *relation*, the expression for a sum of causal relations, but always as a material substance' (*Mythical Thought* 57). The distinction between the two views of force can be seen in the different concepts of metamorphosis; according to Cassirer, mythical metamorphosis 'is always the record of an individual event – a change from one individual and concrete material form to another' (*Mythical Thought* 47), while metamorphosis as a scientific term always implies something that happens according to natural law. The distinction between force as substance and force as a matter of relations is analogous to that between the mythological/territorial view of meaning as naming – the word is the thing – and as semiosis – meaning inheres in the relations between words or things.

Kruman's Lost Coast is described as one in a series of repetitions of a general political pattern, tantamount to a natural law, of neocolonialism. While the Lost Coast experience is quite specific, it is at the same time almost exemplary, not only of African neocolonialism, but also of decadent Western civilization; analogies are drawn to the contemporary American experience in Vietnam, the exploitation of the native Indians in North America, and the Second World War. The Jew is described as the archetypal scapegoat.

As in *Trou de mémoire*, the play of the 'double past' confuses the distinctions between colonizers and colonized, victimizers and victims, and 'civilized' and 'primitive' societies; African tribalism is frequently illustrated in terms reminiscent of the discourse of neocolonialism. The tensions that govern the public arena are reflected in the private sphere, with the family compound constituting a microcosm in which is mirrored the macrocosm of the public life of the nation. The adoption or rejection of ideological 'ancestors' in the political world is paralleled in the relationship between family members and particularly in the movement between family compounds. The theme of colonization is expressed through a historical intertext of slavery and exploitation paralleled in the relationship between Michael and Ama. While the African women, represented mainly by the market vendors, enjoy a high degree of independence, Ama is at the mercy of her Western husband, and the theme of slavery is particularly noticeable in her monologue. The marginalization of women in the political arena, which is as obvious here as in *Trou de mémoire*, is thus not an African phenomenon but is imposed by the 'new ancestors.'

Ancestor worship, which provides Geoffrey with such a perfect metaphor for colonialism, is a central aspect of the African religion in the novel. As Ernst Cassirer points out, 'Where this ancestor cult prevails, the individual not only feels himself bound to his ancestors by the continuous process of generation but knows himself to be identical with them. The souls of his ancestors are not dead: they exist and are; they will be embodied in his grandchildren and they will forever be renewed in the generations to come' (*Mythical Thought* 176). Identity in the African sense, then, is clearly defined by genealogy; it is when ancestors are rejected that identity becomes problematic and disorder ensues.

Within the family, the division between male and female parallels the split between public and private in a dichotomy explainable by Ghanaian tradition, according to which the 'spirit-clan' is patrilineal, while the 'blood-clan' is matrilineal (Debrunner 5). Thus, the spiritual, or ideological, ancestry is carried by the man, while family ties are the responsibility of the woman. The continuity of the family and the spiritual survival of the ancestors are reflected in the custom of naming children after their grandparents. In highly mythological fashion, the name carries the essence of the person. The division is reflected in Michael and Ama's marriage in the fact that the female children are named after their maternal grandmother and their mother, while the male child is given a name which is a parodic reflection of the ideological heritage handed down by the father/colonizer: his name is 'Cricket,' which also places him in a parodic code of game-playing which becomes a metaphor of colonization. The division between male and female and its analogy, public and private, is further illustrated by the fact that Ama's daughters stay close to their mother, while the son is sent to a public school. Ama's only participation in the public domain is a result of her relationship with the president, which is an indirect consequence of her stepfather's political convictions; her actions in the public sphere are motivated by her obligations in the private and they submit her to the particularly feminine variant of colonization, sexual exploitation. Godfrey's novel seems to confirm the same pattern as the earlier ones: sexual relations are increasingly becoming the fundamental paradigm of colonization.

The relationship between Michael and Ama thus subsumes a whole series of dualities that structure the novel. Godfrey's genderization of the colonization paradigm is even more pervasive than Cohen's and Aquin's and becomes an almost parodic enlargement of the Manichean allegory: on the one side are the colonized, women, and the private sphere; on the other, the colonizer, men, and the public arena. Godfrey's text provides an almost paradigmatic illustration of the allegorical branching of the private on the public, which becomes equally illustrative of the enlarged Oedipus identified by Deleuze. It might be argued that this is not necessarily a result of the postcolonial situation, but rather a facet of African culture.

The almost stereotypically Canadian theme of orphanhood returns in the ancestor paradigm, where it is treated in the conventional allegorical equation

– no father = no fatherland – and hence as an expression of extraterritoriality. The dominant theme of the loss of the father is first actualized in Michael's childhood when he is believed to be an orphan; his mother is unknown and his father missing at war. Although the father returns he is eventually rejected by his son who, on at least one occasion, replaces him with a fiction. Ama's father has been supplanted by a stepfather, a 'new ancestor,' who is also eventually repudiated. Like Michael's father, his wife's mother is mad and is rejected by the daughter. With the possible exception of Ama and her young daughters, relationships between parents and children are hostile or fearful. This is particularly true of fathers and sons; Michael indirectly causes Cricket's death; Gamaliel Harding, himself rejected by his father, abuses his son, prompting the young Kwame to cry out 'm'agya' ('my father') – the cry of symbolic orphanhood that echoes throughout the novel – and eventually to leave the family compound. Ama's and Gamaliel's half-brother, First Samuels, is disowned by his father and in turn rejects his stepfather. Ama attributes Michael's misfortunes to his disavowal of the father, wondering: 'What is a man without elders, without ancestors?' (145/173), and she implies that it is science that has made him deny his ancestry. In other words, the rejection of the father is a corollary of Western imperialism.

The place of the absent, negligent, or rejected, father is assumed, in accordance with African family patterns, by the maternal uncle, who is the spiritual guide and initiator of his sister's children. Through his marriage to Ama, Michael becomes Gamaliel's son's uncle, and the relationship between brothers-in-law is always relative to their being uncles of each other's children. Michael's avuncular role is underlined by the fact that he is also Kwame's teacher, underscoring the link between uncles and teachers. Through his dual role Michael represents the fusion of the private and the public, and the school system occupies an important intermediary position between family and state. Michael's decline in his family as well as in his public context is reflected in his movements between schools, which is further paralleled in the young Ama's movements between family compounds. Metaphors pertaining to ancestry and family relationships often underscore the analogy between public and private territories. Thus, for instance, the Minister of Defence, Obatala, in tracking down the counter-revolutionaries, thinks of them as misguided 'nephews' and of himself as 'some uncle who knew he was going to fail' (287/330).

The repudiation of paternal authority is also that of ancestral values and is an index of extraterritoriality comparable to orphanhood in *Beautiful Losers* and *Trou de mémoire*: Michael abandons his country and his religion in favour of Africa and science; Gamaliel betrays his public and political role in Lost Coast by travelling to the United States, where his traditional drumming becomes corrupted in the typical trajectory from margin to centre and back; First Samuels rejects a series of ancestors, from his stepfather to Kruman.

As in *Beautiful Losers* metamorphoses are often linked to the theme of initiation and are imbued with the more mysterious or mythical aspects of African culture. Traditional initiation, according to Mircea Eliade, implies becoming another, and initiatory ritual often involves a symbolic death and resurrection, themes that recur on the different levels of the text almost as pervasively as in *Trou de mémoire*. Akin to the sacrificial crisis, it implies a momentary deterritorialization and a kind of metamorphosis or transformation of identity. The tension between the two cultures becomes a reciprocal initiation.

The first explicit scene of initiation in the novel is the rape, in this case witnessed by the child Michael. The paradigmatic, almost mythical status of the incident is emphasized through the literal actualization of the cliché of the rape of innocence – the victim is a nun. Not only does this incident constitute the end of Michael's childhood, but the initiatory value of the scene is ironically illustrated in Michael's metamorphic becoming another by giving himself a new alias, *Michael Bumdinger* (16/42). According to Cassirer, 'In rites of initiation a man is given a new name because what he receives in the rite is a new self' (*Mythical Thought* 41). Eliade's definition of initiation also involves a real, or symbolic, 'forgetting the past' (31) and after witnessing the rape, Michael loses his memory. As in *Trou de mémoire*, rape and amnesia are related, with the difference that in Godfrey's novel it is the witness who, through a metonymic identification with the victim, suffers the loss of memory. Before the rape, Michael is described as 'Definitely poor in science and mathematics, but interested in poetry' (28/34), but the loss of memory makes him turn to science. The analogy between memory and poetry – and, by implication, orality – is thus established at the same time as the opposition between science and memory. The allegorical function of the rape, as stereotypical here as in the other two novels I have discussed is made quite explicit when Michael accuses Hastings Awotchwi of 'raping the nation' (99/122).

Initiation is linked to exploration, first alluded to in Geoffrey Firebank's comparison of his situation in Lost Coast to 'that of a first century Greek expatriate spreading his ideas and wisdom not in Rome but in some distant province' (7/21). The next reference, also made by Firebank in the prologue, is to the Phoenicians and is prompted by the presence of a great number of potential economic exploiters. (One may think of Robert Kroetsch's 'Sad

Phoenician' as an emblematic extraterritorial.) Exploration returns in the epilogue in Michael's mention of Bougainville, a name we have encountered already in *Trou de mémoire*, and which serves as a link between Michael and the mysterious Rusk, both of whom are familiar with the famous figure, not as explorer but as the 'General and the Man of Letter [*sic*]' (386/437). In fact, Bougainville's travels never brought him to northwest Africa, and in Aquin's novel he obviously plays a different role in a political context. Could it be that Bougainville, in his double capacity as military strategist and explorer, is the predecessor of the mercenary agent, exemplified in the novel by Rusk? Bougainville also authored a treatise on calculus, a fact which places him within the discourse of science and the search for laws and formulas, which is presumably Michael's.

The most typical exploration intertext is that of 'General Stanley,' the title of a school play from First Samuels' and Gamaliel's youth. Stanley is played by Gamaliel, who becomes the object of Samuels' jealousy: the brothers are competing for the favours of Laurna Hasley-Cayford. The incident becomes a catalyst in First Samuels' political career; the day after the play he leaves the school full of rage, haunted by Gamaliel's betrayal in playing the role of a white explorer and potential exploiter of Africa. Laurna's ancestors, we are told, were slave traders, the worst betrayers of their own brothers. She belongs to the 'roi nègre' type so frequent in *Trou de mémoire*, and First Samuels' attraction to her is an example of the fascination of the colonized for the victimizer, a phenomenon described in depth by Fanon and Memmi.

The rape of Marcella returns implicitly in Ama's narrative, when she compares a sexual encounter with Michael to a rape and fantasizes about 'some Scattergood teacher raped by three Hausas' (113/138). Marcella's rapists were also three in number and are referred to by Michael as having 'Woloff face[s]' (25/42). (Both Hausas and Woloffs are inferior tribes in the Lost Coast hierarchy.) The equation between Ama and sister Marcella is further emphasized when Ama says: 'like a nun I was through that though until almost the end' (113/138). Through this analogical repetition of the initiatory rape scene, at which he was a spectator, Michael is identified with the rapist(s) of Ama/Marcella in a way reminiscent of Olympe's repeating Magnant's rape of RR. The metamorphic tripartition of Michael, metaphorically implied in the analogy with the 'three Hausas,' foreshadows 'In the Fifth City.'

After the initiation into sex and violence comes that into the mystery of death which, for Michael, is another instance of violated innocence – the horror of seeing his young son die. The death is described in a way that makes it another variant of the rejection of the father: Cricket in his sick-room is crying for his mother when his father enters. The initiatory value of the scene is not as immediately obvious as the earlier rape, but its significance is revealed through its repetition. The theme of becoming another is reflected in Michael's narration of the death scene, when, from being the observer, he becomes the participant: 'He replaced the netting. I replaced the netting. He left his son. I left my son' (32/49). Michael, through this harrowing initiation, momentarily overcomes alterity and becomes himself, and the incident foreshadows the breakdown between observer and observed in 'In the Fifth City.'

Another traumatic initiation is experienced by Michael when he goes with Gamaliel who, by way of Cricket, is an uncle and consequently an initiator, to the shrine at Ntofro. The incident is foreshadowed in the early episode with the mad Denongo women, where Michael first meets Kry Kanarem, the Lebanese trader. The significance of this seemingly irrelevant incident is foregrounded by its position in Michael's narrative immediately after Cricket's death. The encounter with Kanarem and the madwomen is de-scribed in a typical metaphor as one of 'those encounters that at once predict the future by their events and influence them by the introduction of novel forces' (32/49). Michael's account of the Denongo incident includes a de-scription of schizophrenia in terms that will turn out to be significant for the 'Fifth City' section. His definition of it involves 'ideas of reference, change of personality and disintegration thereof, the gift of tongues, guilt hysteria, delusions etc.' (34/51). Michael's familiarity with the subject is obviously related to his father's illness. His encounter with his father in the insane asylum also has an initiatory value, underlined by the fact that Michael has assumed a new name, and that his father does not recognize him.

At the Ntofro shrine, Michael is accosted and ridiculed by a woman who has come to be cured of witchcraft. She accuses him of being syphilitic and mad, like her first husband. The incident troubles Michael, who violently denounces her. She calls him names, and she is the first of many characters to cry 'm'agya,' illustrating the link between madness and the loss of the father/ancestor. When Gamaliel eventually reveals that the woman is his mother, Delicacy – Michael's own mother-in-law and grandmother of his children – he experiences a terrible feeling of betrayal. The revelation is described almost as a murder, as 'poison.' The initiatory nature of the episode is expressed in the mock ritual to which Gamaliel subjects Michael, a parodic repetition of the purification of the witches at the shrine. It is anticipated, however, in Michael's reference to the old woman as 'guider to the diamonds and gold of old Mali' (67/87–8). Mali will prove to be the site of the final initiation/transformation and Delicacy is one of several shamanic guides Michael encounters on the way.

The madness of two of the ancestors of Michael's children – his father, Ama's mother – provides another focus for the conflict between the two cultures, as Western medicine – particularly psychiatry – is juxtaposed with witchcraft or fetishism. The fundamental difference opposing Western and African medicine lies in the total separation in the former between medicine and religion, or between body and soul, while the African fusion of the two is illustrated clearly in the shrines that perform a medical as well as a religious function.

Witchcraft is implicitly linked to the discourse of colonialism. As Debrunner has pointed out, the rise of belief in witchcraft is the African counterpart of the post-war amorality and criminality experienced in Western society (65). It is a result of colonialism which, by ending tribal wars, dissolves the close links between family members and tribal groups, redirecting individual energy and creating alienation and mental problems. The madness that is interpreted as witchcraft is thus indirectly a result of the split between *Gemeinschaft* and *Gesellschaft*, or the change from a high synergy (territorial) to a low synergy (non-territorial) type of society in the terms of Ruth Benedict, to whom Godfrey refers admiringly in an interview (Cameron 2:40–1).

Religion and medicine, or pharmacology, are linked to the *pharmakos* or scapegoat symbolism introduced early on by Michael when he presents himself in 'The London Notebook': he believes that others see him as 'Pharmakos' (16/32). The term is subsequently foregrounded by frequent repetition. It becomes clear that Michael does, in fact, assume this role himself by taking on the white man's burden of guilt in Africa, as he shows by adopting the alias Burdener. As instances of self-naming, both 'Pharmakos' and 'Burdener' may be read as indicative of Michael's specular identity.

The *pharmakos* symbolism returns in several instances within the political context of colonization, in a way which brings to mind *Beautiful Losers*. In its most general actualization, *pharmakos* is simply the innocent victim and, in keeping with the genderization inherent in the paradigmatic rape metaphor, most victims are women. Marcella is the first; Ama is another victim, not only by analogy but because of her husband's infidelity, just as her mother was before her. Delicacy is openly referred to as providing a '*pharmakos* break from the serious business of the shrine' (64/84), thus establishing a connection between madness and victimization. Cricket seems to be yet another *pharmakos*; Ama reveals, rather cryptically, that Michael has named his son after 'his first dead man ... in order to bring himself peace' (146/

175). Whether Michael was the cause of the original death or not, the atonement inherent in the naming of his son is an example of the projection of guilt onto an innocent victim. In the same way, Gamaliel, in abusing Kwame, projects his own frustration over his hypocrisy on his son.

Michael's central role as *pharmakos* is foregrounded explicitly through the frequent repetition of the term in his narration. He finally acts out his predestined fate when he metaphorically becomes both black (as jet) and a Jew and is deported in Kruman's 'Jet Chamber' in a reference to the 'final solution' (4/18), but before becoming Jew, he has already become woman by putting on Peggy Neal's wig in 'The Agada Notebook.' Eliade has shown how initiation rites often involve a symbolic transformation into the other sex, and the incident illustrates the initiatory value of the assumption of the *pharmakos* role. Not only does Michael become woman, but he rejoins Marcella, the 'angel of the earth' (23/40) by choosing, among Peggy's three wigs, 'the silvery, angel hair one' (392/443). Marcella is, as we have seen, linked to Ama by way of the rape analogy. Ama, in turn, becomes ironically angelic in her identification with the heroine of the romances she reads: she becomes 'Angélique of Barbary, Angélique of Lost Coast' (149/178). In a mystic fusion of the two sides of the sacred, witches and angels converge in madness when, encountering the madwomen at Denongo, Michael thinks of 'witch Marcella' (34/52). Michael's own angelic status is also reflected in his name.

As we saw in *Beautiful Losers* the *pharmakos* performs a function that is healing and expiating. Like the drug or *pharmakon*, the scapegoat is both beneficial and evil: it represents the borderline between same and other, inside and outside, holy and damned, thus incorporating the opposite senses of the sacred. In Derrida's definition:

> La cérémonie du *pharmakos* se joue donc à la limite du dedans et du dehors qu'elle a pour fonction de tracer et retracer sans cesse. *Intra muros/extra muros*. Origine de la différence et du partage, le *pharmakos* représente le mal introjeté et projeté. Bienfaisant en tant qu'il guérit – et par là vénéré, entouré de soins – , malfaisant en tant qu'il incarne les puissances du mal – et par là redouté, entouré de précautions. Angoissant et apaisant. Sacré et maudit. La conjonction, la *coincidentia oppositorum* se défait sans cesse par la passage [*sic*], la décision, la crise. L'expulsion du mal et de la folie restaure la *sophrosunè*. ('Pharmacie de Platon' 153)

Derrida's situating of the *pharmakos* at the origin of difference comes from

René Girard, who traces to it not only all religious behaviour but all of human consciousness: 'le mécanisme même de la pensée humaine, le processus de "symbolisation" s'enracine lui-même dans la victime émissaire' (*Violence* 425).[2] The *pharmakos* ritual is the explusion of the spontaneous violence which threatens any society and risks triggering an unending chain of murder, by projecting it onto a victim whose sacrifice will not provoke revenge. The role of the pharmakos is metamorphic and restorative, transforming what Girard calls 'impure' violence into healing and order-restoring violence. The simultaneous abhorrence and veneration to which he is subject are explained by this dual role. The sacrificial ritual is a brief and terrifying 'union des contraires' (*Violence* 164), through which difference and, consequently, order are restored: 'le rite n'est là que pour restaurer et consolider la différence après l'effacement terrible de la crise' (*Violence* 165). The *pharmakos* is thus a catalyst in the process of acculturation: deserving neither blame nor credit to any greater or lesser extent than those who expel him, his expulsion assures their safety. The sacrificial rite is analogous to the carnival and the *pharmakos* is the archetypal extraterritorial: his necessary deterritorialization guarantees the territoriality of the community from which he is ostracized. In this he personifies the sacred: belonging to the 'au-delà' he assures the in-homeness of the *Gemeinschaft*. Like Derrida, Girard emphasizes the marginal position of the *pharmakos*: he must be neither a stranger nor a fully integrated member of the community in order to become the recipient of the projected violence of which everyone is guilty. As such, he is, at least in Godfrey's eyes, the very image of alterity and marginalization.

The symbolic significance of the *pharmakos* ritual is, according to Cassirer, a later development. Originally the rite of expulsion was based on the belief in the actual transference of substance, a belief linked to the mythological idea of force as substance. In this respect, the sacrificial rite of atonement is similar to the alchemical process: 'All alchemic operations, regardless of their individual types, have at their base the fundamental idea of the transferability and material detachability of attributes and states – the same idea which is disclosed at a more naive and primitive stage in such notions as that of the "scapegoat"' (*Mythical Thought* 66–7). The fundamental difference between the two phenomena resides in their opposite ends. Where the ultimate goal of the *magnum opus* is the conjunction of opposites, the ritual of atonement goes further towards the re-establishment of difference and the restoration of hierarchies. Godfrey's use of the theme is clearly related to the African concept of the transferability of force, which is carried specifically in the name and is a fundamentally territorial phenomenon but, as we shall see, the restorative project remains unaccomplished.

Quinta Essentia

The crucial section of the novel, 'In the Fifth City,' is built around the generic conventions of exploration, with the voyage up the river providing the narrative thread. The allusions to Joseph Conrad's *Heart of Darkness*, the archetypal narrative of colonialism, are so overt that there is never any doubt that the exploration is at the same time one of a continent, of the mechanism of colonization, and of the human mind.

'In the Fifth City' appears to be the culmination of the 'quantum uncertainties' which structure the diegesis. Formally as well as diegetically, however, it occupies a place somewhat apart from the rest of the text. It is possible to read it, as Robert Margeson suggests, as the dream mentioned by Michael in the immediately following 'Agada Notebook.' If the rest of the text is regarded as the dream material, it can indeed be demonstrated that the section uses the strategies governing the dreamwork identified by Freud – condensation and displacement – to produce its strange effects. The most striking aspect of 'In the Fifth City,' however, is the reversal of traditional narrative structures. Although fragmented and uncertain, the narrative can, at least in part, be reconstructed as describing a voyage up the river Niger into Mali, but it is told backwards: the journey's end is the beginning and the journey's beginning the end of the story. Rather than being the result of a conventional analeptic narration, such as that encountered in the earlier sections, the form produces an effect more like watching a film backwards. The narrative structure thus resembles the temporal structure of *Trou de mémoire*. The section can be seen as a loose *mise en abyme* of the bulk of the text in the same manner as the 'Semi-finale' in Aquin's novel. If regarded as such, it indicates that the novel should be read backwards, a possibility pointing to the primacy of the fifth part, which, without doubt, contains the *quinta essentia* of the novel, both literally and metaphorically. This means that it is at the same time the *prima materia*, that of which the text as a whole constitutes the transmutation. 'In the Fifth City' is thus the matrix of the text or, to use the appropriate metaphor, the mother cell which has split into the preceding parts. Rather than identifying 'In the Fifth City' as reflecting the text, I prefer to see the rest of the novel as a disseminated *mise en abyme* of this crucial section. It can be argued that the movement of the text is the opposite of that of *Trou de mémoire*; where Aquin's author splits into five only finally to be resurrected – through the various conjunctive strategies – as the prime mover of the text, Godfrey's authorial presence is disseminated through the disjunction in this section, and its subsequent restoration in the epilogue is even more ironic and illusory than, for instance, Cohen's with which it would seem to have a lot in common.

The temporal position of the events recounted in 'In the Fifth City' within the diegesis is uncertain. Two journeys to Mopti have been mentioned: Michael's determination to 'go through Mopti' (85/108) is dated in the summer of 1965, and would seem to have something to do with an earlier trip he took with Gamaliel and First Samuels on 'that evil Christmas' (146/174) after Cricket's death in 1964. Certain allusions, such as to the predominant fashion – the Nehru jacket – seems to place it in the early stages of the revolution, that is, before Michael's return to Lost Coast in late 1965. This uncertainty is characteristic of the mode of the chapter, and the only temporal markers refer to the trip as beginning in November and ending in 'harmattan,' thus emphasizing the movement away from Western chronology to African 'naturetime' and corroborating the mythical quality of the journey into the heart of darkness. A similar uncertainty pertains to the identities of the travellers, who are introduced as Sir Peter Burr or Pierre Burd, Effez, El Amaliel, and Rusk. They are apparent doubles or transformations of the main characters, with the exception of the American, whose name remains the same, while his identity is described in several contradictory ways.

The formal paradigms of metamorphosis and division, or splitting, are more obvious in 'In the Fifth City' than in the rest of the novel and pervade all levels of the text. The four men have come to Mali to prospect for uranium or to relocate and claim an ore deposit found on an earlier trip. Uranium atoms have the property of being capable of splitting and releasing tremendous amounts of energy; the theme thus brings together two of the central metaphors of the novel: force and division. The diegetic *ore* becomes the disjunctive rhetorical *or* which fragments the narrative and splits the central incident, the murder of Rusk, into a number of simultaneous, though mutually exclusive, possibilities.

One central actualization of division is the recurring split between the self as subject and object, or as observer and observed. This particular aspect of alterity also pertains to the theme of initiation; it occurs explicitly the first time after the rape of Marcella, when Michael says: 'I can feel it in my bones now, the distancing of my knowing self from the moment of knowing which seems forever gone' (24/41). The split is foregrounded in the frequent occurrence of expressions of the type 'I see myself, running' (51/71 e.g.) in Michael's narrative, but which also appear occasionally – though less overtly – in Ama's: 'There is a grown woman lying on my bed' (118–19/144). Michael's role as observer is emphasized in the rest of the novel and the split is often illustrated in images pertaining to film and photography. At one point he sees himself as a 'human Leica' (57–76) in a metaphor returning in 'The Agada Notebook,' where he refers to childhood as the time when 'you were creating your camera and could not yet be both cameraman and subject. You were still attempting to be something more than a wide screen for the projections of others' (382/432). The movie metaphor here rejoins the *pharmakos* symbolism.

The photography code plays an important auto-referential role. Sudden authorial intrusions warn the reader that 'this photograph is blurred' (327/373) or blame some of the narrative uncertainties on the failure of the light meter on Effez' camera. The narrative is turned into a series of pictures by way of different photographic and cinematic techniques such as slow motion, close-ups, and freeze-frames. The voyeuristic nature of film is emphasized in the diegetic use of hidden photographic devices, as well as in frequent metaphoric equations of camera lenses and peep-holes, bringing to mind the analogy between voyeurism and anamorphic techniques. The camera is also part of the parody of the conventions of the secret agent genre, introduced by Richard Bewsher in the prologue. Rusk is secretly filming the erotic encounter between Donalda Pedro and the *Cameroon* girl, a cliché of the conventional spy novel – where such a film would be used for purposes of blackmail – when he is shot by Donalda in a scene in the same film.

The cinematic technique reveals itself formally in a montage of what could be called scenes and vignettes. The main story is narrated in a series of scenes which – although disconnected and fragmentary – can be reconstructed as a temporally and causally logical chain of events. The vignettes interspersed in the story are different, insofar as they seem completely detached from the narrative. The central event in the section is the murder of Rusk, which is acted out in a number of disjointed scenes, each of which creates its own generic context.

Not all of the murder scenes pertain to vignettes occurring in 'In the Fifth City'; some are displaced repetitions of events happening in the other sections. The killing of Rusk by a grenade disguised as a pineapple is an acting out of the 'pineapple coup de grâce' anticipated by Michael in his confrontation with the Denongo women (32/50). It also echoes the real attempt on Nkrumah's life, which is hinted at in the novel and which had such fateful consequences for Judge Korsah, who plays a role in the novel.[3] The different versions of the murder of Rusk are foreshadowed in the prologue, where Geoffrey Firebank reads several discordant newspaper accounts of the events that eventually lead to Michael's deportation.

At first glance, the split between subject and object seems even more obvious in the 'Fifth City' section than in the rest of the novel. Already in the first paragraph, we read: 'one can see oneself imagining ... one can regard one's mind observing ... one can see one's brain write out ...' (304/348). This second degree distancing is accompanied by the introduction of the generalized 'one,' a feature which, together with the hypothetical auxiliary 'can,' creates a narrative mode that is both less individual and more uncertain than in the earlier sections. The distantiation here is, however, different from the split within one narrator as observing himself or herself. Rather, it points to the superimposition of a new authorial voice which has several characteristics – notably its arrogance and irony – in common with Michael's. Considering the view of 'In the Fifth City' as the matrix of the text, it is perhaps more appropriate to say that Michael has a lot in common with the implied author.[4]

In the rest of the text, the separation of the observation of the mind from the mind itself is described as a survival strategy, but, when remembering the rape scene, Michael predicts: 'I die with the fifth use of the trick' (24/41). There are indications in 'In the Fifth City' that we are indeed witnessing the fifth trick, where the split finally breaks down. The trauma can no longer be repressed, memory resurfaces with fatal results, in the same way as Rusk enters the film he is shooting and is consequently shot himself: 'Once the observer becomes part of the system he observes, his every measurement distorts that system slightly, and renders his data invalid for a second point of time, a second determination of energy or mass' (310/366). It is the breakdown of the split between subject and object that creates the uncertainties in this section, which can justly be called post-Einsteinian. Split and distancing are still present, but their position has changed: the narrative voice is no longer that of a character/observer observing himself or herself but belongs to a speculative scientist hypothesizing about all the possible outcomes of the various collisions of forces. The third person narration of the general 'one' splits into a multiplicity of voices reflected in a proliferation of personal pronouns. There are a number of unidentified first-person narrators, and there is a 'we' which is sometimes a variant of the 'one,' but which on other occasions refers more specifically to the 'I' and 'you' of implied author and reader. The author sometimes addresses the reader directly: 'We have heard this description already, or would you like it repeated now? I think not' (339–40/387).

The camera metaphor as an actualization of the split between subject and object, and of its eventual breakdown, is brought into conjunction with the analogy between the diegetic *ore* and the formal, disjunctive *or* through a passing remark, foregrounded by its position in a central paragraph dealing with energy transmission and entropy: 'The effect of light in loosening the bonds between the atoms of chlorine and silver (a phenomenon utilized in photography) is a case in point' (307/351). The 'final solution' to the split pertaining to the status of the narrator as subject and object is revealed in 'The Agada Notebook,' where Michael, as we saw earlier, indirectly refers to himself as a 'screen for the projections of others.' Putting on Peggy's silver wig, he becomes the silver screen in a metamorphosis reminiscent of that of Cohen's narrator in *Beautiful Losers* and which fuses the camera code with that of the *pharmakos*, whose function is just that: to become the screen on which are projected the sins of others.

Whether read as a dream or as a drug-induced hallucination, 'In the Fifth City' is often seen as a return to myth and as the culmination of Michael's progressive Africanization. Both explanations corroborate the assumption that Africa represents the territorial movement of what, following Lotman and Uspenskij, I have called the mythological consciousness. Yet the formal aspects of the section, with its disjunctive structure, its diegetic inversions, its proliferation of narrative voices, and the high frequency of shifters, all combine to refute the claim to myth. The hypothetical nature of the text, reflected not only in the alternative possibilities and the use of auxiliaries like 'can' and 'might,' but also in a number of recurring adverbs of uncertainty, such as 'probably,' 'likely,' 'perhaps,' etc., is generically alien to myth, which is ruled by the conjunctive *and* and the absolute.

Nevertheless, myth plays a central – albeit parodic – role in the section. The voyage up the Niger is a symbolic journey into the heart of darkness and to a mythic origin in a way similar to the imaginary trip up the same river in *Trou de mémoire*. The mythical character is emphasized in the near absence of temporal markers, which distinguishes 'In the Fifth City' from the other parts of the novel. Mali used to be the ancient kingdom of Ghana and the cradle of culture in northwest Africa, centred in the holy city of Timbuctoo. The journey into darkness and becoming another, reflected in the name changes of the characters, are mythical features and essential ingredients of initiation. Mali is also referred to in the novel as a place of purification; hence the ritual aspect of the trip.

The parodic treatment of myth is clearest in the treatment of the central event (the murder of Rusk, the archetypal new ancestor), which becomes a re-enactment of Freud's version of the arch-oedipal myth on which civilization is built, the killing of the totemic father. 'Civilization began here and here it must be rebuilt,' says Michael to his students in Lost Coast (134/161). It is significant that the geographical area of 'In the Fifth City' has yielded some of the earliest evidence of human habitation in the world: the skull that becomes an object of worship is at the same time Rusk's and the original father's; history is thus brought into the service of myth. The loss of the father has been revealed throughout the novel as a rejection, a symbolic murder, and the rest of the text abounds with repetitions of the original myth enacted in the 'Fifth City.'

African religious lore plays a central role in the section through the *kambu* ritual, which has been carefully explained by Jane Leney, with the help of Horace Miner's account of native customs in Timbuctoo. According to Miner, the *kambu* is a fetish that can be used for various purposes, whether oracular or protective, as well as to cast spells or inflict death. Its basic ingredient is a pair of tongs made of silver, copper, or iron, depending on the objective of the ritual. The tongs are wound with four cords – red, white, black, and yellow – and a written charm is placed upside down between its legs. They are then wrapped in the shroud of a saint. The fetish is sewn into the stomach of a sacrificial white cock, called the *bono dyongu*, an expression recurring on a number of occasions in the text. The dead bird with the *kambu* inside is then spreadeagled, and spokes are driven through its wings. Blood from lambs or cocks must be poured on it every ten days for forty days, and chewed kola nuts must be offered. At the end of this period the tongs are removed from the bird, and the fetish can be put to use as soon as it has been placed in the sun and 'moved into' the shade three times. The sorcerer can then make the *kambu* speak, or act, by winding one of the cords around the charm and uttering the secret formula. When the *kambu* is used to cast spells or to kill, the metal used for the tongs and the colour of the cord depend on the profession and race of the intended victim.

The *kambu* ritual is situated at the point of origin of a range of intertexts and events disseminated through the text. Rod Rusk's role as scapegoat becomes quite explicit when, in a crucial passage, he takes the place of the *bono dyongu*, becoming the 'white cock,' thus parodically acting out the sexual allusions implicit in his first name. The role of 'white cock,' both as a sexual pun and as *pharmakos* (here, the sacrificial bird) has been played in the rest of the novel by Michael *Burd*ener, whose function is now displaced on Rusk. The American agent's role as the father to be killed is anticipated in El Amaliel's rambling speech, in which he addresses Rusk as 'Big Daddy' (357–60/406–10). And Rusk recounts his own sacrifice in terms translating the mythical parricide into *kambu* code: 'Who would have thought that they would have chosen such a moment, my own sons? ... They slit my throat. I who had seen them through so far. They removed my bowels and intestines as though I were no more than a chicken ... Like that I lay for forty days with the copper tongs deep inside me, the iron lying there impermeable while I watched as my body rotted ... Yellow cords. Black cords. Red cords. When they took the silver and copper tongs from that cavity in my soul. When they stretched out my arms for the iron spears' (361/410–11). This parricide, whose emblematic character is seen in the simultaneous presence of all the various metals and colours, representing the racial diversity of the new ancestors, is immediately repeated in a specific actualization when Burr crucifies his own father, with emphasis laid on the magic of 'the words that Burr speaks as he drives the two spears through the arms of his father to spreadeagle him in the burning sun' (362/411).

The saint who provides the shroud in which the *kambu* is to be wrapped seems to be Kruman, who presumably has sent the four travellers to Mali to perform the sacrifice. The ritual also implies the murder of the Freedom People's Party, whose emblem is a white chicken, and thus, metonymically, of Kruman himself (actualized in Samuels' assassination of Gamaliel, the party spokesman who is the stereotypical chicken and yes-man). The sacrificial cock thus brings together the various levels of the narrative and performs the function of illustrating Deleuze and Guattari's view of the all-encompassing nature of the oedipal drama in the minority situation.

Rusk, as the *bono dyongu* and the archetypal new ancestor, is the ultimate *pharmakos*. The Christian symbolism inherent in the *kambu* ritual is implicit both in images of crucifixion and in other parallels to Christ's passion – the *carême* of *Trou de mémoire*: the forty days of waiting and the symbolic three days before the *kambu* is resurrected. The correspondence between the white cock and Christ is thus obvious. Passion week is in Ghana the most celebrated of holidays; it is a time for going home, thus a time of returning to source, but also one of revolutions, of *coups d'état* as well as *coups de grâce*, as we may see, for instance, in Ayi Kwei Armah's *The Beautyful Ones Are Not Yet Born*.

Heteroglossia

The New Ancestors is more heteroglot than even *Beautiful Losers*; there is a greater proliferation of discourses, idiolects, and natural languages, as well as typographic devices. The linguistic and thematic diversity is reflected in the many epigraphs that comprise African poetry, an Akan song, Max Born's refutation of Marx, the *Bhagavad Gita*, and an African legend, together representing three languages: English, Akan, and French. The relationship between epigraph and text reflects the status of the different discourses, as well as the relation between discourse and language. Thus, for instance,

'The London Notebook' is framed by an extract from a poem by Felix Tchicaya U'Tamsi, probably translated from the French and illustrating an African interpretation of Western religion, foreshadowing the *kambu*. Introducing the personal mode of Michael's narrative as an instance of the overriding conflicts that structure the novel and presenting the theme of betrayal, which in the book is closely related to revolution and colonialism, the epigraph here functions according to convention.

Ama's narrative is prefaced by an untranslated Akan song, which places her in the realm of Africa, orality, and – because of the reader's unfamiliarity with the language – the sacred. Unlike Michael, the Westerner, Ama does not write but talks, or thinks, her text. The 'Freedom People's Party' section is framed by Max Born's refutation of Marxism and American pragmatism and his claim that physics is better equipped to explain both history and 'the spiritual evolution of man' (159/189). Marxism provides the political paradigm of the novel, while physics provides the metaphors. Born's attitude belongs, as we have seen, to Michael, and the presence of this epigraph in a third person narration points to his affinity with the implied author.

The epigraphs for the two last sections seem to have changed places: the legend of Samba Gana and the serpent is interwoven into 'In the Fifth City,' while the virtues of meditation, extolled in the *Bhagavad Gita* epigraph, pertains rather to 'The Agada Notebook.' It is compatible with the structure of the narrative that the epigraph here becomes epilogue. The belonging of the Samba Gana legend to 'In the Fifth City' is further indicated by the fact that it is told in French, a language far more prevalent in Mali than in Agada.

Despite the linguistic diversity, the ironic mode which dominates all narratives, together with the prevalence of metaphors borrowed from biology and physics points to Michael's privileged status. This unifying presence is also found in typographical and stylistic devices, which recur in all the narrations, including 'In the Fifth City.' Thus, for instance, the novel as a whole favours repetition, tautology, and adjectival triads. There is a certain formal complementarity between Ama's and Michael's narrations, as in the parallel between her account of the relationship with Kruman as a parody of *Angélique and the King* (149 ff/178 ff) and Michael's 'Contessa' fantasy (49–50/67–9). Both pertain to the generic discourse of romance and soft porn which is predominant in 'In the Fifth City,' where the presence of the implied author has been established beyond doubt. Within this heteroglossia, however, the fundamental polarity of Western and African can be seen at work on the level of language.

The first idiolect encountered in the novel is that of Geoffrey Firebank, whose Britishness, revealed in paternalistic comments about the natives and references to cricket, is parodied. Firebank's paternalism is related to class rather than race: he is as condescending towards the new generation of foreign service personnel, including his boss, as he is towards the Africans. British class structure becomes another analogy of political hierarchization, but it is not restricted to the English. Hastings Ayitteh looks down on John Yaro as much as Firebank does on him. Clearly intending to humiliate the boy, Ayitteh adopts John's pidgin when speaking to him. Pidgin is the indigenous class marker, a language adopted in speaking to inferiors. Kry Kanarem speaks it to his black driver, and First Samuels uses it almost as a weapon when communicating with his young assistant at the Ewe village incident, which represents the culmination of tribalism. Although British English is primarily represented by the speech of the upper class, of which Michael's is an ironic version, there is also an indigenous British 'pidgin,' seen in Michael's reported (and probably imaginary) conversation with the peasants at Coldwater.

American English, which is less frequent, shows fewer class distinctions. It represents pragmatism and a naive self-confidence, most bitingly parodied in the character of Ricky Goldman, the innocent Peace Corps volunteer. That it is treated with the same irony as the upper-class British is illustrated in the phony folksiness of the American ambassador's speech at Bishop Adisa School, which is as full of clichés as the account of local heroism presented by the Chinese emissary in an exaggerated Chenglish. In American English, class is replaced by race, and pidgin by Black English, which forms part of the cultural baggage imported from the United States by Gamaliel. The irony of importing black speech from America is yet another instance of new ancestry reflecting Godfrey's critique of American cultural imperialism. Because it is filtered through Michael's eyes in his narration, and through the implied author's equally ironic vision in the rest of the novel, the American, like most other discourses, is distorted and exaggerated.

The African linguistic presence is more striking and puzzling because of its unfamiliarity to Western readers. Instances of African language occur without translation in two important contexts: the proverbs heading the chapters in 'Freedom People's Party' and the song that frames Ama's narration. In both cases the African passages are foregrounded by being set apart typographically, above the text and in italics. As we have seen, the function of proverbs, as carriers of wisdom and knowledge, has been thematized throughout the text well before 'Freedom People's Party.' Proverbs, which are generally part of the vernacular, are here – because of their incomprehensibility – elevated to a sacred status. An analysis and translation of the proverbs, undertaken by Robert Margeson, reveal that they are sometimes used ironically. A clear example of this is seen in the last chapter, where one of the two proverbs, according to Margeson (who follows J.B. Danquah), translates as 'If the king's breast is full of milk, it belongs to all the world' (289/332; Margeson 108). In this chapter Gamaliel tries to bribe the market women by distributing cans of Carnation evaporated milk. The sacredness of the proverb is here perverted by its literal translation and consequent parodic actualization. The proverbs which, in the earlier sections, and particularly in Ama's monologue, pertain to the vernacular, are thus sacralized by being returned to their language of origin, only to be perverted through the critic's translation. The relationship between proverb and text here involves a transposition from one register to another, from the sacred to the profane, a perversion operated through translation from the original Akan into English. This indicates again the affinity between African languages and the sacred, as opposed to English, the language of profanity, and introduces the by now familiar allegorical equation of translation and perversion. The actualization of the analogy is similar to that of *Beautiful Losers*, with Akan taking the place of Greek.

Ama's song remains untranslated, and its connection with her interior monologue is less precise. It is apparently an invocation chanted as libation is offered to dead ancestors, and it translates approximately as follows: 'Conqueror of Water, Nana Kusi, who watches over us, we give this to you. Creator, I am cleaning my backyard, and people say I should be sold into slavery. Even when I am moulding a pot and it is not very straight, they say I should be sold into slavery. It rained and rained. I am going fishing. This is an Odo; all fresh fish are not the same ...' (87/109).[5] The Creator is also metaphorically referred to in the song as 'hen' or 'rooster' (who covers the flock with his wings), another allusion to the prevalent chicken symbol. The translation here reveals a conventional relationship between epigraph and text, fusing themes central to Ama – ancestor worship and slavery – and it in no way perverts the original 'sacred' signification of the song. Like proverbs, songs are part of an oral tradition; it is only by way of inscription that the oral element can be made, through translation, to pervert its original function but, at the same time, as in *Beautiful Losers*, it is by way of inscription that its sacred nature can be saved. Unlike 'Freedom People's Party' and its spokesmen, FS and Gamaliel (whose perversion of drumming is also a form of translation), removed from the political, Ama in her role as original or mythic Africa is immune to perversion.

Scattered African terms also appear in Michael's narration, most significantly in the context of madness and in the symbolic realm of the loss of the father, with the recurring refrain 'm'agya.' These words are set apart only through italicization, and their meaning is made clear through repetition or paraphrase rather than translation proper. Considering that Africa is seen as the realm of the sacred, the preservation of the African terms foregrounds the linking of the sacred with madness and wisdom. A small number of African terms is fully integrated into the text, the most frequent one being 'harmattan,' the wind which heralds the dry season that is also the time of 'In the Fifth City.' The integration of the African term indicates that the temporal dimension of the novel pertains to Africa and a cyclical concept of time. The term 'harmattan' is exotic, but it roots the text in an African territory, in contrast to the defamiliarization inherent in Geoffrey Firebank's – the extraterritorial's – to a northern ear odd-sounding reference to 'a very hot February day' (1/15), which mirrors his own estrangement.

'Translation is an exemplary case of metamorphosis,' says George Steiner (*After Babel* 260), and the theme of metamorphosis is clearly carried through translation in this text. On the one hand, certain African elements are left untranslated, as in *Beautiful Losers*, to retain their full mythic or sacred value. On the other hand, translation transforms, or perverts, the sacred, as in the case of the Akan proverbs. And in yet another ironic inversion, the Western scientific formulas that appear on two occasions in 'In the Fifth City' take on a sacred value, appearing without explanation in the text and thus fulfilling a role similar to the ideograms and Ama's song. The use of the Akan proverbs in 'Freedom People's Party' can be seen as a metacommentary on the problematics of translation, but one that is only recuperable to the very diligent critic or the reader familiar with both English and Akan.

There is a great deal of linguistic uncertainty in the novel. Is Ama's interior monologue 'originally' in English, or is it translated from the Akan? In the beginning, translation is only clearly implied in the realm of proverbs. Thus, for instance, when Michael is listening to the hypocritical speeches, he interprets them (in italics) in terms of native wisdom: '*No melon-peddlar [sic] cries: bitter melons. No wine-dealer sings: sour wine*' (42/60). Later, in Ama's narration, translated proverbs abound, most often attributed to Mercredi, who is herself a 'translated' person in a double sense: she is a Europeanized African and her utterances are only imagined by Ama; she never appears in person. It is not until the proverbs begin to be used ironically in 'Freedom People's Party' that they are left untranslated. Because of the strong link established in the first two parts of the novel between proverbs and wisdom/madness, their ironic use is not immediately apparent, even for a reader familiar with the language. There is thus a kind of second degree deterritorialization at work here – a self-conscious subversion of a territorial pattern painstakingly erected throughout the rest of the novel.

This tension between a thematics of linguistic territoriality and a highly deterritorialized use of language (particularly in 'In the Fifth City') pervades the whole text.

Translation at times appears implicit in dialogue, and it is also implied in the borrowing into English of African stylistic devices, such as the use of repetition for intensity: when Gamaliel beats Kwame into submission, he mockingly describes Kruman as 'Our kingkingking the Redeemer ... the money-money man who can only steal from us' (81/103). Repetition features most explicitly in the madness passages, in Delicacy's prayers, and in rhythmic refrains like 'm'agya, m'agya, m'agya' (62/83 and 82/104 e.g.) and 'mnere dane, dane; mnere dane, dane' (62/83), which translate respectively as 'my father' and 'times change.' The loss of the father is thus linked with 'naturetime,' madness, and repetition. Another variant of translation occurs frequently in 'In the Fifth City,' the section set in Mali, where the colonial language forms a link to the Honeywell of Michael's childhood where Marcella taught him French. The French in Mali shows the same hierarchical structure as the English in Lost Coast: there is a pidgin variant, which is curiously similar to the French of Canada at the point of assimilation. Thus, for instance, it is reported that 'les français sont départés' (336/384), a seemingly innocuous phrase that may well allude to the deportations that occur in the novel. Translation from French is implicit when Kry Kanarem refers to prostitutes as 'hens' (29/46) (perhaps concealing yet another ironic allusion to the FPP and its adherents), a result of a literal (mis)reading of the figurative 'poule.'

A more important instance of bilingual wordplay is at work in what seems like a fusion of sixties jargon and the political discourse of Lost Coast. In a passage that could be borrowed from *Beautiful Losers*, Michael addresses the reader: 'Pretend for a moment that you are plugged into my cosmic lusts and hates ... Plug into the high voltage of Africa' (59/79). The 'high voltage' is not only the psychedelic turning-on of the sixties, but an implicit allusion to 'Haute Volta,' or Upper Volta, the former French colony through which one must travel to reach Mali. The voltage is also that of the Kruba dam, the fictional version of Nkrumah's Volta project, which plays an important role in the narrative and which links the private and the public spheres of the protagonists. The dam project is thus, diegetically and linguistically, disseminated through the text, providing a symbol of power and corruption. The metaphoric code centring on force and energy – introduced by Michael – comes into play in this context and is foregrounded by several bilingual puns, including one that plays on the two meanings of power. Punning on the verbs 'see' and 'voir,' First Samuels ponders: 'The reservoir of power.

The power reservoir. The reservoir of power. To resee power. You resee power. I resee power. We resee power' (293/336). The destruction of the dam and the power reservoir is metonymically related to the destruction of the keeper of power, Kruman.

The implied translation becomes more crucial in 'In the Fifth City,' where the tongs that play such a central role in the *kambu* ritual and which become the identifying attribute of Sir Peter Burr, are described as being 'like a goldsmith's or a radiologist's' (375/426). The 'or' and 'ore' discussed above are joined by the French word for gold, *or*, which is further put in conjunction with uranium in such a way as to link past and present. The pre-independence name of Ghana, the referent of Lost Coast, was the Gold Coast, 'la Côte de l'or.'

Much as in *Beautiful Losers*, translation is also intralinguistic, involving transpositions between styles, genres, or even media. Ama's parodic version of her relationship with Kruman is one example of generic translation. And again translation operates a deterritorialization or a distantiation; in Ama's case it is clearly a displacement strategy which allows something that is repressed to surface. In a movement opposed to the desacralization of the proverbs, Ama's translation of her affair into romance divests it of its sordid aspects and, as it were, sacralizes it. The transformation can be defined as anamorphic, in the Lacanian sense of the term.

More complex are the translations between media, of which the most frequent, not surprisingly, is the transposition of the oral into print. Dr Champs' recording of Delicacy's prayers involves a double translation: from Akan to English, and from speech into writing. The auditory nature of Delicacy's hallucinations is lost in its transference into the mute medium of print. In the process, witchcraft, which is wisdom plus madness, is desacralized into schizophrenia, a diagnosable Western disease. The perversion involved in intermedia translation is perhaps most clearly demonstrated in the transformation of oral chant and the rhythm of drumming into the newspaper columns that Gamaliel writes as chief propagandist for 'the Redeemer.' In traditional Ghanian society, the drummer holds an almost sacred office, both as messenger and as master of ritual. Gamaliel has abandoned the drum for print, but his written, as well as his spoken style retains the beat of the music, seen in such features as repetition and pitch – translated typographically in italics, parentheses, capitalization, and punctuation. Gamaliel's editorial column is the result of yet another double translation: from music to chant to print. The perversion of the sacred role of the drummer into that of the hypocritical propagandist is again the doing of the new ancestors; Gamaliel studied drumming in the United States.

Intermedia translation is most obvious, however, in 'In the Fifth City,' where, in addition to the many instances of interlinguistic and intergeneric translation, the transpositions from film to writing structure the whole section, and where, in the final instance, like Cohen's beautiful loser, Michael as *pharmakos* becomes the silver screen on which the drama of history is acted out. There is a generic analogy to this intermedia transposition: myth, an essentially oral and absolute genre, is displaced into a cinematic version of the relativist genre par excellence, the *nouveau roman*.

Names – Intertexts

Proper names in *The New Ancestors* are frequently carriers of intertextual connotations in a way similar to those analysed in *Trou de mémoire*. A large number of the names pertain to the political situation in Ghana at the time and remain largely impenetrable to the uninformed reader. Exceptions are Kruman and the FPP, whose affinity with Nkrumah and his Convention People's Party is perhaps not as parodic as it may seem, judging from contemporary accounts of the period. The ideological and historical intertext can be found in the writings of several of the politicians around Nkrumah, as well as in his own autobiography, *Revolutionary Path*. Central events and circumstances of the Nkrumah regime are fairly easy to trace: the Preventive Detention Act, the Volta dam project, the Kulungugu assassination attempt, and the machinations of 'the Circle,' which becomes 'the Core' in the book. Several of the ministers mentioned have historical referents, as well as Judge Korsah and a number of other figures: the Kanarems are based on the Karem family, the Hasley-Cayfords on the pro-British Caseley-Hayfords, etc. Many of the schools and institutions also have their referential counterparts. The political discourse is thus firmly anchored in a specific territory, allegorized and hence universalized through its transposition into the mythical Lost Coast.

The Western/male versus African/female polarity is mirrored in the proper names. Considering the description of Africa as the locus of myth, the mythological type of naming would be expected to be more prevalent among Africans. We have seen the theme of ancestor worship in Ama's naming of her daughters as a way to ensure the survival of the ancestor's 'spirit-soul.' Naming is crucial in African society: 'Le prénom notamment, qualifie la personne par une phrase condensée et symbolique. Il est la conduite du portrait' (Thomas and Luneau 29). Although Ama's name carries no obvious connotations, it is, to a Western reader, connected with love and motherhood. It is significant also that it is palindromic, or circular. 'Amma' is, in

African culture, 'the great begetter,' the original creator who begot the world through the seed of the word (Jahn 105, 126) – the counterpart of Isis, perhaps. The word-magic seen, for instance, in the naming of children according to their birthday may seem purely conventional to a Westerner, but, rather than being non-mythological, it reflects the belief that children born at the same moment in 'naturetime' share the same characteristics. The force which is being transferred thus resides in the name. This mythological tradition is perverted, or desacralized, in the translated person of 'Mercredi.' Having been given an African day-name, presumably, she is subsequently translated into French, the language of her adopted Western country. She is in many respects the opposite of Ama who, though married to a European, has been confined to Africa and imprisoned by its political and cultural system. In the translation of Mercredi's name, the mythological aspect of day-naming is lost and deterritorialized.

Other similarly translated names are 'Delicacy,' 'Patience,' and 'Comfort.' Delicacy's name used to be 'Awula Kordai' (285/328) before she married and became translated into the oxymoronic 'Delicacy Harding.' The romantic view of translation as a marriage of two tongues is here inverted – marriage involves translation and, by necessity, perversion. It can be assumed that the names of the two prostitutes, Patience and Comfort, are also translated, but according to the mythological imperative; they are what they are called. They do indeed enjoy more individuality than the two 'Roses' with whom Ricky Goldman is set up and whose interchangeability is underlined by the fact that their pimp is called simply 'The Man' (37/54). Rose is a meta-mythological name, in Western literature ever since Shakespeare always associated with the kind of 'coarse naming' that overlooks difference, and against which F. – pace Gertrude Stein – warns in *Beautiful Losers*.

We have seen how Michael Burdener names himself on a number of occasions. The Babelian self-naming discussed in chapter 1 is quite common in the novel and its anti-oedipal character is manifested in its close link to the rejection of the father. The most glaring example of this is First Samuels, whose frequent name-changes demonstrate an awareness of the power of the word in his society. Although his real name is 'Adijamissikah' (188/ 221), his school alias was 'Sammy Jones,' a name presumably in keeping with the colonial ideology. After leaving school, he goes, as Sammy Jones, with his stepfather to empty latrines and has a humiliating encounter with Hastings Awotchwi, his half-sister Ama's stepfather. It is unclear when he changes his name to First Samuels, but his rise in the social hierarchy constitutes the acting out of the maxim 'The last shall be the first.' The expression does not occur explicitly in Samuels' narration but in Ama's, where it seems to be the locus of an intertextual convergence characteristic of the displacement strategies so frequent in the novel. Ama remembers seeing the slogan on a sign on her stepfather's lorry, a symbol of the wealth that earns him Samuels' hatred; it foreshadows his decline, which coincides with Samuels' rise after the revolution.[6] The maxim is equally applicable to First Samuels' self-naming: it is the first name, Sammy, that becomes the last as he himself becomes 'First.' On the whole, the cliché reflects in an ironic manner the ideological intertext of the permanent revolution.

First Samuels continues to show the same mythological mentality in his renamings. As a member of the clandestine 'Core,' he adopts the most anonymous of names, 'Charlie,' but as the killer of his brother – as Cain in the biblical intertext actualized in Ama's interior monologue – he becomes 'Samuels Boshkohene' (292/335), for the first time assuming an African name. The name is translated as 'master of the boshko,' the murder weapon consisting of two spheres of metal which, when put together, become lethal. The description recalls the mention of 'the two stones of my brain' in the epigraph of 'The London Notebook,' indicating that the two poles, Africa and the West, myth and science, always coexist, but that their split involves an alterity resulting in madness in the private sphere and political disaster in the public. First Samuels also partakes of the biblical intertext, not only through the fratricide but also as Samuel, the kingmaker fighting the Philistines. Like his biblical namesake, he is two-tongued in his simultaneous profession of loyalty for Kruman and his clandestine allegiance to the 'Core.' Most susceptible to corruption is no doubt Gamaliel Harding, whose name contains another link to his American allegiance; Gamaliel was the middle name of American president (and renowned rhetorician) Warren Harding, whose government became synonymous with corruption and who, ironically, was rumoured to have black blood (a fact picked up in Ishmael Reed's *Mumbo Jumbo*). Like an inverted version of his namesake, a white man in black mask, Gamaliel is the ultimate traitor, and the centrality of the Harding family indicates the paradigmatic position of the United States as the locus of imperialism and corruption, symptomatic of the time of writing.

Mythological naming is not restricted to the African sphere, however. Many of the parodically mythological or allegorical names that occur in the novel are probably the invention of Michael or the implied author. Most of them appear in Michael's narration: there is the British headmaster Norman Bucketful, who plays host to the equally ironically named American ambassador, Hathaway, the representative of pragmatism. And there is Ricky Goldman, the 'golden boy' of the Peace Corps. There is no doubt that Michael has assumed the name Burdener; his name used to be Buxton, and he has preserved the initials he shares with Max Born (initials are fore-grounded in the novel through FS' frequent use of them). Having been momentarily 'Bumbledour' and 'Bumdinger,' Michael assumes the burden of the white man's guilt, acting out his self-imposed *pharmakos* destiny. In Judaic tradition, Michael is the archangel who fights the evil forces of Rome. We have seen how he has acted out his angelic quality by putting on Peggy's wig, and he is deported on an 'Alitalia flight via Rome' (4/18). As guardian of the formulas by which heaven and earth are established, Michael is the intermediary between God and Moses on Mount Sinai: Michael Burdener is constantly handing down laws, to himself as well as to his students. In what could be a parody of the missionary endeavour, Michael is also the keeper of the records of who is to be saved; as such he is a kind of scribe.

The enigmatic Rod Rusk shares many characteristics with his equally ambiguous counterpart, RR, in *Trou de mémoire*. He is the unknown force and catalyst, whose entry into the system changes and polarizes the forces. Like 'Ruskin,' the name 'Rusk' alludes to Russian and thus implicitly casts doubt on Rusk's true allegiance – he may well be a double agent. His status is as puzzling as that of his anagrammatic intertextual forebear, Conrad's Kurtz, and his special status is indicated by the fact that he alone is allowed to keep his name undistorted in 'In the Fifth City.' We have seen how Rusk acts out the sexual connotations of his first name by becoming the 'white cock' in a ritual of sex and violence, but as the ultimate *pharmakos*, he is also the lightning *rod* which attracts the clashing forces of energy. The coincidence of his last name with that of the then American Secretary of State emphasizes the specific historico-political context and foregrounds his role in the political allegory of American imperialism.

A Proustian intertext, shared with *Trou de mémoire*, may be hidden in sister Marcella, whose role as memory is evident. Robert Lecker has pointed to the predominance of 'recollective vision' in the novel and its structural similarities with *A la recherche du temps perdu*. The time of memory reflects the fusion of the Western sense of time as chronology, represented above all by Michael, and the African sense of 'naturetime' as cyclical. *Chronos* and *kairos* converge in the analeptic narration. The main representative of *kairos* is Delicacy. Ama is incapable of reading Warden's *History of Lost Coast* because 'she couldn't get beyond her own mother. Delicacy was time. Delicacy was a long, high wall against time' (137/165). The rhythm of time as the cycle of generations is incompatible with the sense of time as history. Delicacy's sense of poetry, revealed in her mad prayers, forms yet another link with Marcella and memory. With her mixture of obscenity and prayer, and her orality, Delicacy embodies the profane and the sacred.

Ama's mother is, as we have seen, the guide to Mali, the source of Africa, which is also the realm of madness, among whose features Michael has listed 'the gift of tongues' (34/51). The heteroglossia noted in 'In the Fifth City' extends to another feature of madness, the 'change of personality and disintegration thereof' (34/51). Michael disintegrates into a trinity of identities representing the languages of the colonizers of Mali: Sir Peter Burr, Pierre Burd, and Don [sic] Joao Pedro. In Italian Peter Burr translates approximately into Pietro Spina, the disguised revolutionary of *Bread and Wine*.[7] The eucharistic symbolism shared with Silone, as well as with Cohen and Aquin, is present only as parody in *The New Ancestors*. Sir Peter translates into Spanish as Don Pedro, who appears as the Portuguese consul (in a kind of condensation of old new ancestors, former colonizers), the counterpart of Geoffrey Firebank, carrier of another intertextual connotation: Godfrey at one point defines his novel as 'what's happening outside of Geoffrey's world,' referring to Malcolm Lowry's *Under the Volcano* (Gibson 174). A double displacement is again taking place, whereby the original Geoffrey's occupation is given to his namesake in the prologue and then transferred onto Don Pedro in 'In the Fifth City.' Geoffrey Firmin's personality and fate, however, are displaced on Michael Burderner, whose humiliation and rejection of redemption are as complete as those of Lowry's protagonist. Joao Pedro's wife is Donalda, the Dona Alda, the other of Lady Ama, who in the nightmare takes on the characteristics of Lowry's Yvonne Firmin. Donalda also recalls Michael's childhood landlady, 'the Maltese woman' (20/36), whose physical affinity with 'Circe' (20/36) is transferred on to the consul's wife who turns men into metaphoric swine. The courtyard, where she watches her lover die a painful death from poisoning, may be that of *La Maison de rendezvous*, whose Lady Ava she becomes.[8] Robbe-Grillet is perhaps the most insistent intertextual presence in 'In the Fifth City,' both implicitly and explicitly, also through passing allusions to *Le Voyeur* and *La Jalousie*.

The author has alluded to the existence of a voodoo intertext for *The New Ancestors* (Cameron 36). The consul has a namesake in the voodoo pantheon, where Don Pedro, or Jean Pétro (named after a Spanish slave who rebelled against the whites), is worshipped as a symbol of black power and a protector of revolutionaries. The beautiful and extravagant 'Ezili,' who has a lot in common with Donalda, is one of his loves. Another of Ezili's lovers is Damballah, the loa of fertility, whose name is derived from 'Dan,' which means snake, and 'Allada,' an old kingdom in southern Dahomey. The cult of Damballah worships the rainbow, the 'snake of heaven.' Damballah, Dan-Allada (or Donalda?), is connected with St Peter or St

Patrick (Jahn 43). The legend of Samba Gana would seem to be related to voodoo mythology, and if Donalda is another transformation of St Peter, she represents yet another of Michael Burdener's metamorphoses. The populous voodoo pantheon also contains a loa called 'Papa Loko,' sometimes apparently addressed as 'Miguel' (Laguerre 91), who is the guardian of vegetation, but also of pharmacology and healing, a role that Michael, as biologist and *pharmakos*, would seem to carry. The madness alluded to in the loa's name also points to an affinity with Michael (as well as his mad father). The disintegration of identity thus seems to end in complete entropic undifferentiation; the characters are metamorphosed into each other.

Michael's metamorphosis into St Peter/Pierre/Pedro may indicate that he has fulfilled Gamaliel's plea: 'We need saints' (283/325). There is, as we have seen, a certain affinity between Michael/Peter and the implied author, not unlike that between F. and Cohen or Magnant and Aquin. The parallel between St Peter as implied author in Godfrey's novel and his namesake in *Trou de mémoire* is underscored in the heteroglossia and the emphasis placed on the 'gift of tongues,' actualized homonymically in the essential role played by the 'tongs' in the ritual. The religious sentiment that seems to inspire both Cohen and Aquin, however, is in Godfrey's text turned into irony and Michael's 'sainthood' is a great deal more parodic than that of Cohen's beautiful loser. As seen in the discussion of translation, the 'gift of tongues' is a sign of madness and Babelian perversion rather than pentecostal transcendence. Writing here separates the sacred from the profane, or rather operates an inversion/perversion of their relationship. While in *Trou de mémoire* writing makes possible the convergence of opposites, in *The New Ancestors*, notwithstanding its oxymoronic title, it prevents their fusion.

The thematic metamorphosis is, as I have tried to show, linguistically realized in strategies of uncertainty and undifferentiation, but the process remains unaccomplished, and no new order is restored. The breaking down of the boundaries of identity and difference characteristic of schizophrenia is, as Deleuze and Guattari have shown, a phenomenon of deterritorialization. The sacrifice is here ultimately futile; there is no indication that the crisis leading to the dissolution of identity and difference will be resolved through the expulsion of the *pharmakos*. Thus, only the first phase of the metamorphic process is realized, and the result is entropy. This is the opposite of the *coincidentia oppositorum*: instead of convergence, there is dissipation. Although Michael's and hence the implied author's voice returns in the end, the resurrection is different from that in either Aquin's or Cohen's novels. The dissolution of identity in *Beautiful Losers*, though expressed in codes similar to the ones used by Godfrey, is, in the final analysis, conjunctive: three identities merge into one, and out of that emerges the author. In *The New Ancestors* the movement is reversed: the protagonist is split or dissolved, only to be resurrected as other than he was but as fundamentally isolated, ending where Cohen's 'I' begins.

The absoluteness of the word, thematically related to the mythological territory of Africa as well as to its opposite, science, is on the level of *énonciation* replaced by relativity, and in the final analysis *The New Ancestors* would seem to occupy a place on the territorial spectrum opposite that of *Trou de mémoire*. When the permanent revolution is a law of physics, there is no escape – *point de fuite* – but where there is a religious *parti pris*, the vanishing point – *point de fuite* – is found in transubstantiation, the *mysterium coniunctionis*. If the *pharmakos* is the specular identity of the writer in Godfrey's novel, his sacrifice is insufficient to restore order. On the other hand, when the writer is the Holy Ghost and writing the *pharmakon*, as it seems to be to Cohen and Aquin, his work becomes a sacrament.

CHAPTER FIVE

L'Elan d'Amérique
The Novel as
Echo Chamber

The same themes of colonization and the collision between cultures that provided the ideological paradigms for the novels analysed in the preceding chapters recur in a more specifically indigenous Canadian context in André Langevin's *L'Elan d'Amérique* and Robert Kroetsch's *Gone Indian*, published in 1972 and 1973 respectively. Both novels deal explicitly with the relationship between Quebec, or Canada, on the one hand, and the United States on the other. As in *Beautiful Losers* the inclusion of the Indian completes the triangle. Although very dissimilar in style, Langevin's and Kroetsch's novels both set up a clear distinction between their own culture and the American, using the Indian as catalyst and symbol of a certain continuity. Like *Trou de Mémoire* and *The New Ancestors*, the two create a relationship of close affinity between the private and public spheres, the latter represented in *L'Elan d'Amérique* by big business and in *Gone Indian* by academia.

L'Elan d'Amérique is the most explicitly allegorical of all the novels in my corpus, and constitutes a clear break with the author's earlier work which placed him in the realm of social and psychological realism, most successfully in the acclaimed *Poussière sur la ville* (1953). When *L'Elan d'Amérique* was published, sixteen years after the author's previous novel, it was therefore greeted with considerable surprise, because of both its unique position in Langevin's oeuvre and its novelty in Quebec literature as a whole. Most critics welcomed it as the first *nouveau roman* to come out of the province.[1]

It can be argued that Robert Kroetsch's *Gone Indian* also occupies a unique place in its author's oeuvre, although for different reasons. Constituting the last part of his 'Out West' triptych, after *The Words of My Roaring* (1966) and *The Studhorse Man* (1970), it passed largely unnoticed by the critics at the time of publication. Perhaps overshadowed by the success of its immediate predecessor, it remains, together with the more recent *Alibi* (1983), with which it shares a number of features, the least studied of the author's novels. While in the case of *L'Elan d'Amérique* it was the unexpected formal complexity that attracted critical attention, the apparent simplicity of *Gone Indian* seems to have puzzled critics expecting the overt formal game-playing of the author's earlier novels.

Kroetsch was one of the most influential of the Canadian writers who, in the sixties and seventies, began to subscribe to an aesthetics of postmodernism, sharing Hubert Aquin's admiration for Vladimir Nabokov and showing an interest in American writers like Gass, Pynchon, and Barth. His self-conscious stance towards his craft takes on an added dimension through the awareness he shares with many of his Canadian colleagues, of the alterity inherent in the 'colonized' Canadian language: 'The Canadian writer's particular predicament is that he works with a language, within a literature, that appears to be authentically his own, and not a borrowing. But just as there was in the Latin word a concealed Greek experience, so there is in the Canadian word a concealed other experience, sometimes British, sometimes American' ('Unhiding the Hidden' 43). Like Langevin, who lived for some time on Cape Cod, Kroetsch lived the experience of 'exile' in the United States when he taught for several years at SUNY, Binghamton, where he wrote *Gone Indian*. The situation of writing thus in both novels bears a resemblance to the textual universe in a way which, as in the case of the texts discussed earlier, invites an inquiry into the authors' own position vis-à-vis – or within – their fictions.

In *L'Elan d'Amérique*, Claire is the daughter of Rose Greenwood, née Boisvert, a Québécoise whose family emigrated to New England to 'weaver,' but who ends up as a prostitute until she marries Bruce Smith. Claire grows up in a dingy apartment in Boston but eventually moves with her mother and stepfather to Suoco Pool, a company town and seaside resort. Determined to make a lady out of her daughter, Rose sends Claire to college, where she falls in love with a Yale student who, on a visit to Suoco Pool, rapes her in the lighthouse that becomes her refuge. Allan, the rapist, gives Claire his watch, and for a long time she repeats the rape by taking any man she meets to the lighthouse and exacting his watch as the price of her sexual favours. After the death of Rose and Bruce in a car accident, Claire stays on in their house, watched over by Stephen Peabody, vice-president of the United States Pulp and Paper Company and a good friend of her stepfather. One summer she falls in love with David, a graduate student from Virginia, who spends the summer in Suoco Pool. After a tentative courtship that reveals David and Claire as near twins in their innocence and vulnerability, there is a climactic love scene in the lighthouse. David finds the watches and realizes that what he has heard about Claire's past is true and, deeply hurt, he leaves without waiting for an explanation. He drowns trying to swim back to the mainland.

After David's death, for which she blames herself, Claire falls into a deep depression, during which Peabody subjects her to a sleeping cure and forces her to abort the child she is expecting by David. She eventually marries Peabody in a convenient arrangement that makes her an heiress. Peabody is impotent, and their relationship is more reminiscent of a father-daughter one than a marriage. A year after David's death, Peabody brings her to a company-owned forest in northern Quebec, where she meets his hunting companions, an Indian guide and Antoine, a middle-aged *coureur des bois* employed by the company. Antoine, who dislikes Claire, has had a number of encounters with a moose of mythical proportions, which to him represents the virginal and timeless Quebec wilderness. When Claire tries to shoot the animal, and wounds it, Antoine hits her and sets out to track it down. He catches up with the moose at the moment when it is mustering its last strength to mate with a female. As Antoine watches the pathetic scene, the moose is shot from an airplane by Peabody's semi-automatic rifle. Disgusted, Antoine fires at the airplane, decapitates the dead animal and, disregarding the Indian's objections, carries off the moose head in his canoe on an infernal journey to the chalet, where he presents it to Claire. Almost dying from a stroke, Antoine makes love to Claire in a scene which is neither a rape nor a love scene, but resembles an expiation. Feverish and hallucinating, Antoine reveals his love for Maria, a Peruvian exotic dancer he has met in a Montreal night club. In Claire's mind, Maria merges with a figure from a movie she has been watching on television, and with whom she herself identifies in a tragic Cinderella story.

When Peabody returns to the chalet, Claire stops him from handing over Antoine to the authorities. On the way back to Suoco Pool, she jumps out of the plane with the moose head and drowns in the lake, while the Indian carries the dying Antoine off to his village in the far north, away from civilization.

Although the actual time of telling in the novel is limited to one day in late October, the bulk of the narration is analeptic. It is, with one small exception, narrated in the third person but limited to one point of view at a time: the story is told through the minds of Claire and Antoine, with the end – the coincidence of told time with telling time – left to the Indian.[2]

Metaphor

The thematic bipolarity seen in *The New Ancestors* has a spatial counterpart in *L'Elan d'Amérique*, which revolves around two geographical and metaphoric territories pertaining to the two characters from whose points of view the story is told. On the one hand, there is the New England seaside resort which is Claire's territory, centring on the sea, the beach, and the promontory of the 'maison gris ardoise' where she lives. The opposite pole is the northern Quebec wilderness which is the territory of Antoine, the *coureur des bois*, and which is organized around a parallel tripartite topology: the lake, the forest, and the company-owned chalet. The two territories comprise a series of opposites characterizing the protagonists, and each is governed by a central symbol: the lighthouse in the sea and the moose in the forest.

The symbolic value of the time and space of telling, which is one October day in the Quebec forest, is expressed in a number of images of transition reminiscent of the *carence* of *Trou de mémoire*. The time is 'Un affaissement entre deux saisons' (15), and it converges with space – '*entre* deux pans de paysage qui s'écroulent, *entre* deux saisons qui se chevauchent' (110 emphasis added) – the two landscapes and seasons representing Claire and Antoine – the sea and the forest, summer and winter – between whom the narration oscillates. The transition between the two seasons is 'l'été des sauvages' (69), and it is the Indian who prevails over the change, and who carries the text to its conclusion.

The abandoned lighthouse is introduced on the very first page of the novel when the narrator notes that 'La chambre éolienne qui capte toutes les voix de la mer pour les amplifier, vibre au moindre souffle' (7). The symbolic centre of her space, the 'chambre éolienne' becomes Claire's alter ego. The diegetic importance of the lighthouse is obvious: it is the site both of the crucial rape scene which determines Claire's identity, or rather lack of identity, and the fatal encounter with David, when all hope of redemption is lost. Always described as transparent and vibrant, the lighthouse is a still space in which the surrounding turbulence of waves and tides is reflected and amplified. In the same way, Claire is an echo chamber: completely transparent herself, she vibrates in answer to any wave that hits her. Claire is water and air. Many metaphors relating to water seem to refer to her: she is like the 'eau [qui] se colore des rives qu'elle touche' (27). And it is no coincidence that she is singing 'Any way the wind blows' as she begins her narration (29, 30, 50). As a conventional phallic symbol, the lighthouse also reflects the way in which Claire's identity is determined by the men in her life. David's importance for her and his link to the lighthouse are foreshadowed in a play on the polysemy of the word 'phare': their first encounter takes place 'dans la faible lueur des phares' (9), when his car has been stopped in the fog. David's effect on Claire's life is further reflected in an image of resonance: when he talks to her on this first occasion, 'chaque mot éveille en elle une vibration profonde' (10).

The characters and their relationships to each other are often described in similar images of resonance and vibrancy. There are two categories of people in the novel: those whose voices are resonant and those whose are not. David is linked to Claire both by his voice and by his gaze: 'La vibration de sa voix, comme la lumière de son regard, établit entre eux un lien' (147). Claire's voice is very resonant; she often sings and at times is 'toute vibrante de colère et d'humiliation' (83). David speaks with a voice 'qui résonne avec un timbre chaud et frémissant' (170), until the fatal moment when he discovers the truth about Claire's past, and his voice becomes 'blanche' (173). This adjective also describes Claire's own voice on two occasions: after her lovemaking with Antoine (40), and when she talks to her husband after preventing him from handing over the *coureur des bois* to the authorities (232). The climactic scene between Claire and Antoine is a ritual confirmation of the loss of innocence, and Antoine's voice on the same occasion 'perd ... son timbre' (40), when he discovers that she is not a real American, but that she speaks his own language. It is in the encounter with Antoine that Claire regains her lost identity, and it is significant that the revelation takes place far away from the sea – locus of transparency and vibration – in the forest where she senses 'une plénitude qui avale toute vibration' (51).

Maria also belongs to the vibrant. Antoine is fascinated by 'la sonorité ... de sa voix' (190). She is the opposite of his wife Blanche, whose name indicates her opacity and lack of vibrancy. While Maria dances and Claire plays the guitar, instrument of resonance par excellence, Blanche constantly plays the same, worn-out lullaby on a player piano. In Antoine's mind, 'les bulles de piano se transforment en balles de mitrailleuse' (59) in an auditory association between his wife and Stephen Peabody. As the impotent male who has to resort to technology to kill the symbol of regenerative power, Peabody is as representative as the frigid Blanche of the mentality of what Antoine defines as the 'femelles.' The American capitalist 'parl[e] de cette voix sans timbre' (15), and his voice is described as 'éteinte' (32) and 'feutrée' (215). This links Peabody in Claire's mind to the movie director who, in a voice 'sans timbre' (14) narrates the film she is watching.

In Claire's mind there are always 'trois notes de guitare' accompanying the painful memory of David's death (13, 14, 177). She often plays the guitar in the lighthouse, where the music resonates against the stone walls. As David's daughter Sandra remarks on her visit to 'la chambre sonore du phare' (12), 'il y a toujours quelqu'un qui répond' (161). There are two references to 'la conque du phare' (169, 173), showing it as a microcosm of the surrounding ocean. The echoing is thus both internal and external, reflecting sounds and movements coming both from the outside and the inside. Through the analogy established metaphorically between the sea and Claire, the relationship of identity between her and the echo chamber of the lighthouse becomes even more explicit.

The echo is also an important diegetic and structural device in the novel and can be seen as a kind of auditory counterpart to the specular repetitions in *Trou de mémoire*, stressing the emphasis on orality rather than vision. Thus, for instance, Claire's suicide is an echo of, or a reply to, David's, and both are corollaries of the original rape which reverberates in the novel through its multiple repetitions. More important, however, the rape scene is echoed in its reversal – the love scene with David – and in the final, quasi-ritual encounter between Claire and Antoine, which will turn out to be its final resolution. The blow Claire gives her husband to prevent him from turning Antoine in echoes the one she received from Antoine, which in turn 'répondait à celle qu'elle n'avait pu retenir' (50). In the same way, Claire's shot, which injures the moose, is the first of many, 'tous multipliés par l'écho, sauf ceux de la radio' (50). The shots heard through the radio emanate from the drama which Claire can only guess at.

Considering Claire's metaphorical connection with resonance and vibrancy, it is not surprising that her narrative abounds with images and structures revolving around echoes. However, although located far from the sea in the silent forest, Antoine's narrative territory is permeated with the same formal and diegetic strategies, thus revealing a unity of form which points to an overriding authorial presence.

In the same way as 'la chambre éolienne' identifies Claire and, physically and symbolically, dominates her territory, Antoine's symbolic alter ego is the moose, which figures ironically and ambiguously in the title of the novel. The word 'élan d'Amérique' does not occur in the book until the very last page, when the author has Antoine reflect on what is taught in the schools in his country: 'L'Indien a passé quelques mois à l'école anglaise du gouvernement, au poste de la Compagnie de la Baie d'Hudson. Il a appris des tas de choses. Autant que son garçon à lui, qui n'a pas craint, un jour, de lui enseigner que l'orignal, en réalité, s'appelait l'élan d'Amérique. L'élan d'Amérique!' (239). Implicit in this quotation is an opposition between the 'réalité,' which is the presumed realm of the 'élan d'Amérique,' and something else, which is that of the 'orignal.' The moose that Antoine encounters and identifies with is a beast of mythic proportions, whose death signifies the end of an era, that of the *coureur des bois*, and the taking over of the 'élan d'Amérique' – American capital and know-how. It is in fact the latter, the 'élan,' as represented by Stephen Peabody, that kills the myth, the 'orignal.'

The ambiguity of the title engenders a series of implicit bilingual puns on the word 'élan.' The moose, as Antoine sees it, is the original life force which, he believes, cannot be vanquished by modern technology: 'Parce qu'elle était la vie dans son élan créateur, foisonnante et imprévisible, sauvage et impétueuse, un torrent aux crues subites qui emportait toutes les prévisions des hommes, charriait tous les âges dans son cours, depuis la source du temps' (124). The wordplay is carried on in the emphasis put on the moose's magnificent 'panache' (82, 121, 125, 222, 227), a word which is related to 'élan,' metonymically in French and synonymically in both English and French.

The punning culminates in the translation of the name of the animal, introduced when Antoine tells the Indian that he has heard an American refer to the latter as a 'buck,' 'comme pour le mâle de l'orignal. Et leur maudite piastre!' (65). The translated word fuses the two: 'l'orignal,' with its connotations of animal sexuality, and 'l'élan d'Amérique,' with its political and economic ones. If the 'buck,' in the sense of capital, or 'leur maudite piastre,' is represented by Stephen Peabody, the other side of the coin, so to speak, is the young American 'buck' who rapes Claire, and who lies at the origin of her tragic life and death. On the allegorical level, Allan (whose name is as close to the word 'élan' as possible), is the personification of American arrogance and power, which are raping the virgin forest of Quebec. The parallels with the rape as an allegorical motif in *Beautiful Losers* and *The New Ancestors* are obvious. The dichotomy between the two sides of the 'buck' is complex and perhaps reflective of the author's fatalism. Whereas Allan – the 'buck' – deprives Claire of her identity, Antoine – 'l'orignal' – restores it. It is in the embrace of Antoine, the original Quebec and her mother's country, and with the revelation that she speaks French that Claire stops being an echo chamber and begins acting, rather than simply reacting. The tragic irony of the fate of Quebec at the same time condemns her to extinction. It is, indirectly, the return to a mythical origin that kills Claire. The return to source means death, because the source is 'tarie,' in a metaphor that recurs several times in different contexts. The political allegory is emphasized by the parallel drawn to the white man's suppression of Indian culture through the equation between the moose and another animal of mythic proportions, 'Une bête d'un autre âge, comme le bison. Le *buck* légendaire des Indiens qui chargeait les ours, secouait les loups de ses flancs comme des mouches' (122).

Diegetically, Antoine's identification with the moose is clear. The last action performed by the injured buck is his attempt to mate. By making love to Claire just before he suffers his stroke, Antoine not only becomes the moose but, by the same token, restores Claire to her mythic origin by turning her figuratively into the female of the 'orignal.' And, like the moose, Antoine is 'decapitated' when the stroke cuts off the blood supply between his head and his body. The reference to the legendary buck shaking off the wolves also echoes Antoine's journey to the chalet with his trophy.

Antoine explicitly identifies with the moose in his mind. Claire's shot that injures the animal 'hits' him: 'Ce qu'il ne s'avoue pas avec des mots, mais qu'il sait avec certitude, et qui a tout déclenché, c'est que la première balle lui a déchiré les entrailles, et que c'est pour ne pas mourir qu'il a frappé du pied, de toutes ses forces, la carabine de la fendue, qui a volé à dix pieds de là, en éjaculant une derniére balle' (77). The sexual connotations foreshadow the final drama of both Antoine and the moose. The *coureur des bois* addresses the moose as 'vieux frère' (187), forming a link between the animal and his older brother, Hercule, who, as a small farmer forced from his land, belongs to yet another species doomed to extinction. At one point, Antoine refers to the moose as 'son père, et le père de son père' (124), an identification strengthened by Maria's calling him 'abuelo' (86). Just as David and Claire are near twins, Antoine and Maria are kindred spirits: they both represent an original America. Maria has élan and comes from 'une Amérique torride et vibrante' (85). The opposite of Claire, who is connected to water and who, as a child, 'a toujours retenu ses élans' (164), Maria is linked to fire and heat. Antoine often refers to her magnificent hair as her 'écume noire' (85) or 'crinière' (86), which swirls around her face when she dances. Both Maria and Antoine carry their own kind of 'panache': in Antoine's case it is the barrier to the blood supply to his brain, 'l'étau qui lui broie les os du crâne, sous la chape de plomb' (57).

In a much less overt manner than in *Trou de mémoire* an equation is made between blood and ink, indicating perhaps a sacramental view of writing and pointing to the congruity of the implicit metacommentary and the diegesis which, as we shall see, plays with the idea of sacrifice. Thus, the bloody moose head is on two occasions likened to a frozen squid: 'l'encre noire projetée par un poulpe velu aux tentacules rigides, échoué à des centaines de milles de la mer' (235). The unexpected metaphor, appearing when Antoine throws the 'panache' at Claire, echoes an earlier incident, when John Marshall, Claire's third rapist, threw a squid at her, 'poulpe spongieux qui a bien survécu au coup reçu deux ans plus tôt' (44). Again there is a triad of echoes, and John foreshadows both Antoine and the moose. After having sex with him, Claire hits him with a rock and leaves him 'le crâne moussant de sang' (44), an image resembling the descriptions of the dying Antoine and the moose.

The identification continues when Maria calls Antoine 'el toro' (74, 87). This also equates him with his brother, who acts out the identity hidden in his name by turning into a bull, first in the 'corrida' (140) of the nightclub and later, when he is surrounded by the troops in another bullring. Hercule's identification with the trapped and injured animal is obvious in both instances, but he also understands Antoine's feelings for the moose and foresees their common fate: 'C'est pas à toi, la forêt, c'est à la Compagnie, et la Compagnie parle pas ta langue, puis un *chevreuil* comme toi, ça lui sert plus à grand-chose. Quasiment de Montréal à la baie d'Hudson, c'est le pays de la Compagnie, les villes aussi avec leurs usines. Et pour que ça rapporte, il faut de la machine et des Anglais instruits. T'es comme le maudit *buck* dont tu parles tout le temps, un géant que tu dis. Eh bien, ton *buck* est fini lui aussi, mort. Il sert à rien lui non plus, et la forêt lui appartient pas' (132–3).

The buck thus serves as a *point de fuite* – much like Saint Catherine in *Beautiful Losers* – where the various perspectives – the personal, the mythological, and the historico-political – converge. It also serves as the counterpoint to the lighthouse. Where Antoine is earth and origin, in the form of the 'orignal,' Claire is water and echo. It is the opposition and interaction between those two principles that structure the novel.

It is not surprising to find that one of the central images in the novel is that of *waves*, which pervades Claire's symbolic and narrative space in particular. It recurs, however, in Antoine's narration, together with a specific variant – the pebble thrown into still water, creating rings spreading and receding. Both of these metaphorical matrices govern the formal structure of the novel, where Claire's and Antoine's narrations are interwoven in the manner of waves: Antoine's *récit* constitutes the *ressac* to Claire's. The result is like 'les vagues qui s'entrechoquent et se défont en tous sens' (148). The rings on the water are present formally primarily through the strategy of *enchâssement*, whereby the narration recedes ever outward from a present centre, through a recent to a more distant past, as indicated in the motif introduced from the beginning: 'plus loin encore,' 'plus loin,' 'très loin' (7, 8).

Although both sound- and light-waves are frequent, and the wave image is closely related to the echo, it is water that is the dominant element, in an imagery sometimes reminiscent of Aquin's style in the more poetic passages of *Trou de mémoire*. While the ocean totally dominates Claire's territory, it is also the pervading metaphoric domain superseding both Claire's and Antoine's narrations. Thus, Antoine frequently likens the forest to the ocean, which it is unlikely he has ever seen.

The allegorical analogy between people and their elements or territories is reflected in a variety of elemental images that establish a relationship of microcosm versus macrocosm between the internal and the external world of the characters. Thus, for instance, the flow of blood in Antoine's body is like the movement of the waves: 'Un sang léger et doux irrigue son grand corps, un flux et un reflux réguliers, qui ne s'emballe pas aux passages étroits de ses tempes' (69), and for a moment he forgets his disease, the pebble that threatens to disturb the calmness of the waters, 'ce caillou qui n'en finit pas de tomber dans son eau intérieure, de la troubler' (69). Yet other elemental images liken the flux and reflux of blood to the tides of the sea, as well as to the rising dew.

Water imagery spans a symbolic spectrum from the sea to the 'pool' of the company town. The sea is Claire, symbol of transparency but also of virginity: 'la mer conserve la virginité des premiers âges' (175). The lake, on the other hand, is anathema to Claire, who feels herself in prison 'au continent sec et à l'eau douce' in Quebec (32). The lake is above all the territory of the Indian, while Antoine, who is earth and forest, has trouble on the water. His canoe constantly gets tangled in the roots of water-lilies, which makes it easier for the wolves to catch up with him. This is another instance of his identification with the moose, which is attracted by the sweet taste of the lilies and gets caught in the same way, in one of Antoine's imaginary reconstructions of its life. Suoco Pool, with its smell of sulphur, is the locus of Stephen Peabody and the United States Pulp and Paper Company. It is not insignificant that the company airplane is painted 'jaune soufre' (210). In his impotence, Peabody is a stagnant pool, representing the opposite of the source of life which, as Claire painfully discovers, is dried out.

Repetition

While it occupies a fairly small place in the space of the text, the rape, positioned almost in the centre of the book, plays a role which reveals it to be at least as crucial as its counterpart in *Trou de mémoire*.[3] The fact that it is the first event that takes place in the lighthouse, whose central role is established from the very beginning, indicates its importance. The rape is the pebble thrown into the still water; its reverberations constitute the waves of the narration and determine the vicissitudes of Claire's adult life. The identity between Claire and the lighthouse is first explicitly established immediately after the rape, when her stepfather names the island on which it stands 'Claire Island' (152). Ironically, Bruce Smith names her 'Master Claire' (98) when he sees her dump the rapists in the water, thus corroborating the initiatory value of the incident. Only through this harrowing initiation which confirms Claire's role as perpetual victim or scapegoat does she paradoxically establish her territory and become 'Master' of herself. At the same time she – her territory, her body – becomes 'Federal Property' as the sign outside the lighthouse reminds us (152).

Claire's retelling of the rape clearly stresses its ritualistic character. After Allan, together with his friend, has raped her, he recites a poem over her naked body and drops the two watches on her, saying: 'time is dead ... She is a woman now. Two more hearts will help her to suffer. God bless you! Oh, three-hearted woman!' (94–5). Time does stop for Claire at the moment of the rape, and she is caught in repetition, as Allan anticipates in his choice of lines from Tennyson's *In Memoriam* as the requiem over her lost innocence: 'But, for the unquiet heart and brain / A use in measured language lies: / The sad mechanic exercise, / Like dull narcotics, numbing pain' (94). Although the poem is ironically ambiguous (Allan has introduced Claire to drugs), the sacramental nature of the event is underscored by the description of the room: 'Elle voit des pépites d'or dans le rais de lumière qui tombe comme d'un vitrail. Et la voix d'Allan qui a des sonorités d'église' (94). The lighthouse room – the echo chamber – is a sacred space; David on his first visit tells her: 'Vos cheveux méritent cette lumière de cathédrale' (161). Although the link between the rape and amnesia is not as explicitly stated as in *Trou de mémoire* and *The New Ancestors*, Claire's compulsion to repeat indicates her repression of the memory. Freud speculates that the compulsion to repeat an unpleasant experience may be the result of an instinct for mastery; the repetition of the neurotic trauma is an attempt to develop retroactively the anxiety whose absence caused the trauma in the first instance ('Beyond the Pleasure Principle'). Claire was not afraid of Allan; she was totally unprepared for his brutality and the shattering of her dream. It is the 'cérémonie d'expiation' with Antoine (34), the conscious re-enactment of the original scene, which finally allows the repressed to surface and which triggers Claire's retelling of the trauma. Through her repetition compulsion Claire has assumed, though passively, the role of *pharmakos*: 'elle n'a pas douté d'un instant qu' [Antoine] avait ce droit, et tous les autres, qu'elle devait s'en remettre entièrement à sa volonté, parce qu'il était l'officiant depuis toujours désigné d'un rite qui préscrivait qu'elle serait l'offrande expiatoire' (31).

Next to David's desertion and the loss of the hope of redemption, the original rape is the most painful event with which Claire's reborn memory has to come to terms. Her retelling of the incident is separated in the novel from that of the love scene by a lengthy section narrated by Antoine, and it is immediately preceded by a remembrance of a childhood incident which carried the seed to her future. As a child of six, Claire inadvertently squeezes her canary to death in an excess of love. On this occasion her mother utters two phrases that are eventually revealed as instances of accusation/nomination: 'Tu tues tout ce que tu touches' and 'She does not even cry' (91). The first of these echoes in Claire's mind after David's desertion, and the second recurs, whether uttered by one of the perpetrators or in her own imagination, after the rape. The death of the bird, the rape, and David's flight are the main links of the chain of naming that seals Claire's fate.

If it is true that Claire is doomed, through her mother's accusation and David's death, which constitutes its confirmation, to kill everything she touches, it is equally true that she will kill herself, as she alone is to realize: 'Elle brise tout ce qu'elle touche, et tout ce qui la touche la tue un peu plus' (92). And what touches her most profoundly is David, her symbolic twin. Connected physically by the beach, with its connotations of whiteness and 'virginité' (13), which links their two houses, they are both – in spite of their past – innocent and vulnerable. Claire's identity with the virginal sea has been established, and David comes, not coincidentally, from Virginia. Their eventual drownings, which are both corollaries of the rape, are fore-shadowed in frequent images of their drowning in each other's eyes. 'Je me suis tout de suite perdu dans la mer de tes yeux' (170), says David, and his look at Claire 'rend son corps si transparent qu'il n'existe plus' (149). Al-though the love scene is not described in as explicitly sacrificial terms as the rape and the final scene with Antoine, what is left after David's departure is his sweater 'aux manches étendues en croix' (145).

The relationship between myth, symbolized by 'l'orignal,' and reality, symbolized by 'l'élan d'Amérique,' is reflected in the dual time perspective introduced through the rape – similar to that brought on by the murder in *Trou de mémoire* and *Macbeth* – when Claire's broken heart is replaced by clockwork and the dull mechanics of repetition. The first mention of the watches in Claire's narration refers to their 'tic-tac assourdissant' (12), show-ing her repetition compulsion as an attempt to immerse herself in the 'dull narcotics' of *chronos*. If, as Allan says, two more hearts will help her suffer, ten will help more.

When David and Claire make love, the fact that they are 'deux coeurs battant en des corps étrangers' (169) indicates that Claire's heart has been restored to her. When David discovers the watches, he asks, in a voice that has lost its resonance: 'Je n'ai jamais porté de montre. Tu ne veux quand même pas que je laisse mon coeur dans le coffre. C'est tout ce qui bat chez moi' (174). The watches have long since stopped ticking, but when he picks one up, it starts again. Time as *kairos*, which came back to Claire when she fell in love with David and saw the possibility of redemption, dies again at that moment, and Claire confirms the replacement of her heart by clockwork by naming herself 'ten-hearted woman' (177). And with her heart dies her memory, until the act of expiation with Antoine a year later: 'Claire Peabody, en juillet, noyait sa mémoire à ces invisibles ailes. La nuit se meurt. Et Claire renaît, battant des ailes contre sa mémoire' (8). The nature of her encounter with Antoine becomes clear when Claire believes him dead, until 'elle a entendu le battement de sa montre' (46), with the word 'montre' taking the place of the expected 'coeur.' Reversing, and thus undoing, the rape, Claire metaphorically gives Antoine a watch for a heart.

Kairos, or memory-time, is metaphorically related to Claire's element, water. She begins her narration under the shower; it is here that memory returns, and she discards the false identities imposed on her by discarding her last names. The water thus performs a baptismal function, restoring Claire to her true identity.

The *chronos-kairos* distinction relates to the characters in the same way as voice and resonance. Claire, David, and Maria, who are all close to nature, have resonant voices and wear neither shoes nor watches. Time, when it is measured in the text, is so according to chronology, but there are a number of references to a time which cannot be measured. Thus, for instance, when David has left Claire, she waits and goes after him only 'Après un long temps qu'aucune des montres dans le coffre ne peut compter' (175). And when Antoine returns to the chalet with the moose head, he and Claire look at each other 'Un temps sans mesure possible' (23). Maria can stay in the air for 'un temps prodigieux' when she is dancing (57). Dancing, like music, represents time as rhythm rather than pure succession.

Chronos is time without resonance, as opposed to the waves and vibrations of *kairos*. The most obvious representative of this mechanical time is Stephen Peabody who, impotent in himself, possesses power through his relationship with modern technology. There are two overt references to clockwork in the novel: the first is Claire's characterization of the director in the television movie as 'cet impassible horloger d'un destin' (15). The director is, by way of his flat voice, a double of Peabody, and through her identification with Maria in the film – the barefoot dancer turned into a star by the director – Claire's relationship with Peabody becomes clear. The other clockwork allusion is more directly linked to power. It occurs when Hercule is surrounded by the soldiers in Montreal, whose movement is 'réglé comme un mécanisme d'horlogerie' (201). The clockwork people are those who possess power, and they are also foreigners: the troops are English Canadians, who speak to Hercule in a language he does not understand, and Peabody and the director are Americans.

Intertexts

As a Quebec exile in New England, Claire's mother, Rose Greenwood represents what has become an indigenous literary stereotype, particularly since the appearance of Honoré Beaugrand's *Jeanne la fileuse* (1878) and the better known classic, Ringuet's *Trente arpents* (1938). Like the orphan Jeanne, presumably fleeing a life of poverty, Rose's family comes to the Boston area to work in the textile industry. Unlike her virtuous predecessor, however, Rose ends up as a symbol of the conventional equation of exile and prostitution. Born and raised in the United States, where she learns French at college, with a negligent mother and an unknown absent father, Claire has no roots in either culture. Her tragic fate is resolved in the return to her ancestral origins in Quebec, but she is just as much in exile there as in New England. As she points out to her husband: 'Nous ne sommes pas chez nous, Mr Peabody,' to which he retorts: 'C'est le territoire de la Compagnie, Claire' (232). By virtue of his power, Peabody is at home anywhere.

Antoine is an exile in his own country. Told that he will not be needed in the forest any longer, he is effectively shut out from the only home he has ever known. His wife's refusal to let him stay in their bungalow in the company town after he has performed his necessary duties as guarantor of her motherhood also turns him into an outcast. But it is in Montreal that the feeling of exile is most obvious, as Hercule realizes: 'Même tes mots ne te servent plus à rien, parce qu'on te comprend pas. Ils parlent étranger. T'es en exil. Toi aussi Antoine, c'est fini' (132). The October crisis is the culmination of this alienation, and Antoine thinks of the troops in Montreal as a reversal of the tourist invasion at Expo 67: 'Tous ces étrangers qui, par millions, trois ans plus tôt, avaient nagé dans le bonheur et la gentillesse, dans les îles créées de toute pièce au milieu du fleuve, revenaient casqués d'acier, avec armes et blindés, le visage impassible, rouages tous semblables et terriblement efficaces d'une chose énorme qui ne pouvait porter qu'un nom: *l'étranger* ...' (202-3). The clockwork people do not speak the language of the country yet they hold the power. There is an implicit parallel drawn between the invasion of the federal troops in Quebec and the Americans in Vietnam (an intertext shared with *The New Ancestors*) when Peabody's shooting of the defenceless moose from the airplane is likened to pilots in Vietnam shooting at any trace of life.

It is in Montreal that Antoine meets Maria who, coming from an America that has not yet been violated by 'l'élan d'Amérique,' is the only one of the exiles who can choose to go home. Unlike Rose, Maria happily and freely gives of herself, but she is equally stereotyped. Fingering her rosary, when she is not dancing or making love, Maria is the madonna-whore. She is the opposite of Antoine's wife Blanche, the frigid, self-sacrificing, and tyrannical 'mère poule,' who rejects her husband and smothers her children, in what amounts to a caricature of the archetypal French-Canadian mother. Putting all her energy into mothering, before she settles down 'à l'ombre du clocher et du curé' (120), Blanche turns her daughter into a nun and her son into an example of Deleuze and Guattari's vision of the Canadian potential for 'la reterritorialisation la plus réactionnaire, la plus oedipienne, oh maman, ah ma patrie, ma cabane, ollé, ollé' (*Kafka* 45), another Québécois stereotype at the time: 'Lui qui chantait la forêt sans jamais avoir abattu un arbre, les humbles qu'il avait toujours fuis, un peuple sans voix, dont il n'avait jamais parlé la langue, avait, depuis longtemps, émigré à Montréal où il avait épousé, un an auparavant, une grande fille brune aussi instruite que son philosophe ...' (119).

Several critics regard Claire's orphanhood as the cause of her fate. At the same time, however, there is almost general agreement that Claire is not really an orphan, but that Stephen Peabody is her father, as indeed she seems to believe herself. At one point she asks her husband about her ancestry: '– Je n'ai jamais tiré un coup de fusil de ma vie. – La fille de Bruce Smith, je ne suis pas inquiet. – La fille de qui Mr Peabody?' (48). The question is never answered, but Claire continues to think of her husband as 'Un vrai père' (49). The only allusion to Peabody's age is the revelation that he is 'quinquagénaire' (32), while Claire is twenty-four, which puts her date of birth at 1946 or 1947. Peabody's injury, which rendered him impotent, is generally interpreted as stemming from the Korean war. However, the only mention of his war experience is a reference to his having 'fauché du Japonais durant la guerre' (144), a comment that clearly alludes to the Second World War, when he could have been in his twenties. If this is the case, he could hardly have fathered Claire.[4] Whatever the truth of the matter, the equation between no father and no fatherland is a common allegorical convention, as we have seen in both *Trou de mémoire* and *The New Ancestors*.

As so often in the literatures of both Quebec and Canada, and as we have seen in the earlier novels, fatherhood is rarely a successful enterprise. Antoine is a father who, much like Michael Burdener, has been refused his own children: the opposite of an orphan, he is an 'orphaned' father. Bruce Smith is a stepfather, and Stephen Peabody is, if my reading is correct, not a father but a husband deprived of both wife and children. Hercule is certainly a father but in another stereotypical way: he has so many children that he cannot remember their names, a not uncommon phenomenon among rural Quebec families if we are to believe Marie-Claire Blais' *Une saison dans la vie d'Emmanuel* (1965). Ironically, the only 'real' father is David, who only sees his daughter occasionally and who, by drowning, makes her an orphan, and whose other potential child is aborted. Claire's role is quite paradoxical. She is 'une orpheline, ou une héritière' (150). Deprived of a country and a father, she figuratively inherits both. Raped by the American buck, she inherits it and becomes the new ancestor of 'l'élan d'Amérique.'

Besides the ideological discourse of colonization, actualized specifically in the October crisis and the many literary clichés, the indigenous intertexts of the novel pertain mostly to the realm of myth and legend relating to Antoine's territory. The *coureur des bois* is in himself representative of a whole cultural tradition, 'la légende du coureur des bois qui croyait trouver la liberté dans la démesure même de son effort' (75). Among the references to the mythology surrounding the legendary figure is an allusion to Antoine's 'canot d'enfer' (226), from the legend of the 'chasse-galerie.'[5]

On his infernal journey Antoine is pursued by wolves, next to the moose the most frequent of many participants in the vast network of animals linked to the elemental imagery. One aspect of the wolf that is particularly stressed is its sophisticated hunting pattern. Wolves, which always hunt in packs, have a highly developed strategy of communication working according to a relay system, by which they encircle their prey and take turns leading the pursuit. The circular pattern is taken up by the Indians who, we are told, defeated Custer by using the method. The circle of wolves surrounding Antoine on his journey is made to recede momentarily by his shots, which echo the image of the pebble creating rings in the water. The worst figurative wolves, in Antoine's eyes, are Peabody's company: 'Une compagnie, ça a toujours faim. Ou c'est comme les loups, ça peut dévorer sans avoir faim' (105). Antoine, on the other hand, is a 'lone wolf' (211, 224, 225), and Claire at one point sees herself as a 'louve' (235) for having 'devoured' David's child, or having submitted to an abortion. David, for his part, reassures Claire, after inviting her to his cottage for the first time, that he is 'Trop âgé pour jouer au Chaperon Rouge' (163). Through the fairy-tale intertext he identifies himself as the opposite of the big bad wolf, the other side of America.

Although not quite to the same extent as the moose, the wolf is foregrounded, both through frequent repetition and through translation, in the expression 'lone wolf,' which is twice italicized. The translation points to the possibility of a bilingual pun, in the vein of Aquin's 'entre ce chien de Montcalm et Wolfe.' While the defeated general's presence may be indirectly looming over the ideological intertext, another 'wolf' exerts a strong formal influence. The many references to virginity, particularly in David's geographical origin, and the obvious coincidences in the symbolism – notably the lighthouse and the waves – point to Virginia Woolf. Thematic similarities such as suicide by drowning and the implications of androgyny in the relationship between David and Claire corroborate this. The multiple perspectives and interweaving of the streams of consciousness are reminiscent of *The Waves*. Gérard Bessette, who likens *L'Elan d'Amérique* to the *nouveau roman*, also points out its likeness to *Mrs Dalloway*, whose first name, incidentally, is Clarissa (29) (possibly sharing a common intertext in Richardson's *Clarissa*).

While an important element in the wolf network, *Little Red Riding Hood* is not the most important fairy-tale serving as an intertext. *Sleeping Beauty* is present most obviously in Claire's sleep cure, but more important is *Cinderella*, introduced explicitly in the context of the television film Claire has been watching, but present indirectly from the beginning in metaphors relating to ashes and linked to 'Claire Peabody, personnage trop bref et d'emprunt, lové sous la cendre d'un seul hiver' (7).

Throughout the text movies constitute a metaphoric and formal code. Rose Greenwood dreams of making Claire 'une sorte de Greta Garbo latine' (43). Claire identifies easily with films, and there is an ironic comment on the power of the cinema – particularly American movies – to create this kind of identification. The reference is to the Indian, 'Cris devenu Sioux depuis que la Compagnie de la Baie d'Hudson lui offre le cinéma' (223). The auto-referential aspect of the movie code becomes clear in Claire's narration, as she anticipates the return of the men from the hunt to find Antoine on her bed: 'Mr Peabody, le pilote et l'Indien, quand ils reviendront dans le soleil, le trouveront ainsi, nu sous la couverture, prisonnier de la nuit, éclaboussé d'un sang inconnu, sans réponse possible aux questions précoces qu'elle ne peut poser parce qu'elle ne sait pas, et elle devra, elle, raconter un film plein de noirs qu'elle ne peut comprendre parce que les bobines coupées n'ont projeté que des images inintelligibles, sans rapport aucun avec la trame sonore ininterrompue' (179–80). The importance of 'sonorité' has been stressed in connection with metaphors of vibrancy. Formally, the text is generated through sonority: abounding with assonance, alliteration, and internal rhyme, it is an example of the *roman-poème*. But it is also the 'trame sonore,' rather than actions or events, that holds the story together in Claire's mind. In the same way that one fills in the gaps in a defective reel of film, Claire has to try to piece together the events of the day with the help of a few auditory clues or echoes: the shots heard through the radio and Antoine's delirious ramblings.

The film Claire has been watching on television serves as an interpretant for the events of her life, since her encounter with Antoine brought back her memory. It is a modern version of *Cinderella* in which a poor but beautiful dancer, whose name happens to be Maria, is discovered by a Hollywood director, who makes her a star. The reception at the chalet is not the best; the television screen is as full of 'snow' as the air outside Claire's windows, and her reconstruction of the film is as sketchy as the memories of her own life. The central role played by the film, which is introduced on the first page and returns in instalments throughout Claire's narration, is foregrounded through italics. The intertext is Joseph Mankiewicz' *The Barefoot Contessa* from 1954, a melodrama starring, among others, Ava Gardner and Humphrey Bogart.[6] It tells the story of Maria Varga, a Spanish flamenco dancer brought to stardom in Hollywood. In a manner resembling a *mise en abyme* of the form of the novel, the movie is told entirely in flashbacks by three narrators, among whom is Harry, Maria's director and friend, who begins to tell her life story as he is standing in the rain at her funeral.

The first sight of Maria Varga in the film is of 'les pieds nus sous le rideau tiré' (14), and throughout her career she refuses to wear shoes when dancing. Aloof and untouchable, Maria carries on a secret relationship with a cousin, the only remaining link with her past. After years of fame and boredom, she is the guest of a rich admirer, who creates an embarrassing scene from which she is saved by a silent man, who recognizes her as the woman he has seen dancing at a gypsy camp. He turns out to be the count Torlato-Favrini, the last male of his prominent family. Maria finally falls in love and they marry, but on their wedding night the count reveals that he is impotent from a war injury. One day Maria reveals to Harry that she is carrying another man's child, because she wants to help her husband carry on the family name. Suspecting that the count's reaction may be another than the one Maria expects, or pretends to expect, Harry follows her home. He arrives just in time to hear the shots, when the count kills her without waiting for an explanation, after having followed her to Harry's. Harry never tells the count the truth. It is late October when Maria is buried, watched over by her barefoot marble statue and the count's family motto, 'che sarà sarà,' which could be Claire's.

Much of Maria Varga's story echoes both Claire's and the other Maria's. The three identities fuse in Claire's imagination, and the two Marias become projections of herself. As shown in the discussion of clockwork and voices, Claire's identification with the barefoot contessa becomes explicit in the text by way of the equation between the director and Stephen Peabody, who is the 'horloger' of Claire's destiny. As an actor in a play over which she has no control, and prevented from giving birth to her child, Claire is paralleled by the star in the movie intertext. Like Maria, Claire marries an impotent powerful man, and Peabody becomes identified both with the director and the count. Claire's view of the people around her is literally projected onto a screen, in the same way as she herself has never been anything but a projection of others' views.

It is the first name shared by the television figure and the woman in Antoine's ramblings that causes Claire to explain to him: 'Maria ha muerto ... Matada por el amor ...' (37). The equation of love and death, *mise en abyme* in the canary episode, and a frequent theme in the author's other works, is here the subject of yet another bilingual pun, clear to anyone familiar with the intertext. Maria Varga's screen alias in the film, 'd'Amata,' with its connotations of love, is an anagram for 'matada,' 'killed.'

The film intertext underscores the melodramatic nature of the text. American culture, represented on the one hand by movies and rock 'n' roll, is conveyed, on the other hand, by the pseudo-intellectual Allan, who shows off by quoting Tennyson and referring to Claire as 'Ophelia' after the rape (94), thus foreshadowing her death and confirming the rape as the cause of her 'insanity,' the repetition compulsion. The initiatory significance of the rape as an instance of naming is thus corroborated through the Shakespearean intertext. Shakespeare returns in a reference 'au bruit et à la fureur' (54), alluding to the American music to which Claire dances. There is more Faulkner than the original in this reference, however, the Faulknerian mode being echoed in the narrative style as well as in the theme of the dispossession of the land, with the moose as a variant of the better known bear. Less explicit allusions can be traced to Hemingway's hunting and bullfighting stories, particularly to 'Big Two-Hearted River.'

Like the ideological and literary ones, the mythical intertexts are stereotypical. Antoine thinks of the *coureurs des bois* who used to rule the forest as 'marins sans voiles au fond d'un océan sans cartes où les distances se comptaient en journées' (124). When put in context with other allusions, such images are shown to pertain to a mythic intertext. Blanche is at one point called 'Pénélope' (111), and connected with images of 'tissage' and 'coton' (221). (Rose, who in many ways is a complement to Blanche, has also come to New England to 'weaver.') And Antoine's children do not recognize their father when he returns from the forest. Yet another, and perhaps more fundamental, mythic intertext appears overtly only once, when Claire, in another foreshadowing of the fate of the doomed lovers, traces the name 'Tristan' in the sand (150). Like Isolde, Claire is married to the 'king' and, like the legendary couple, the two young lovers die through each other. As a creature of water, Claire is also an 'Ondine,' in a way that brings to mind Giraudoux's modernist rewriting of the legend.[7]

The mythical territory of the text thus ranges from the occidental (Homer, Tristan and Isolde, fairy-tales) to the indigenous (la chasse-galerie); the referential is resolutely modernist (Woolf, Faulkner, Hemingway, Giraudoux) or in the parodic mode, linked to American pop-culture, particularly music and movies, and perversions of the British canon (Shakespeare, Tennyson). As we will see in the following discussion of naming and the relationship between the sacred and vernacular, however, the main thrust of the text is clearly territorial.

Naming

Allegory is, according to Angus Fletcher, related to repetition compulsion by way of the coexistence in it of separate and often contradictory significations. Furthermore, '*The magic of names*, which more than any other linguistic phenomenon dominates the allegorical work, is likewise an essential ingredient in the neurosis' (294). The heightened proper-name-consciousness in the compulsive neurotic is linked by Fletcher to the obsession with ritual and repetition. Implicit in his discussion is an equation similar to that suggested by Derrida in *Glas* between nomination and accusation, which we have seen at work in the instances which determine Claire's destiny: 'Tu tues tout ce que tu touches,' 'big three-hearted woman' – amplified in the echo chamber to 'big ten-hearted woman' – the ironic 'Master Claire,' and 'Ophelia.' Allegorical naming pervades the novel. Claire, who is pure transparency, only loses the names conferred on her by her 'père putatif' (41), Bruce Smith, and her 'paternel époux' (54), Peabody, when she immerses herself in the timelessness of water, or in David's presence. Neither of the two 'noms du père' that presumably identify her is the name of her real father, however, and Claire is orphaned in more ways than one.

Where Claire is transparent, Blanche, Antoine's wife, is her exact opposite, an opaque screen. Giving herself to her husband, 'blanche de soumission' (112) only for the purposes of fulfilling her destiny as a mother, Blanche lives unperturbed by her surroundings in her 'univers laiteux' (113), in another metaphor opposing her to Claire's water. Rose Greenwood, the third woman belonging to the colour code, has a name which is in itself a *mise en abyme* of the political/historical allegory: 'Rose Greenwood, née Boisvert peut-être, petite fille d'un Boisvert venu du Québec un demi-siècle plus tôt pour *weaver*, lui et ses femmes, parce qu'ils filaient un mauvais coton sur leur terre rocheuse du nord où les enfants levaient plus vite que les récoltes, avait compris très jeune qu'il n'y avait pas de salut possible pour les Canucks dociles et soumis dans leurs filatures et leurs écoles paroissiales pour nègres blancs qui égrenaient leur exil sur des chapelets' (42–3). Rose thus incorporates a number of clichés relating to the discourse of exile and colonization. Like the green forest of Quebec, she has to sell herself to the Americans, and her prostitution is reflected in the translation/perversion of her name. As in the case of the prostitute Rose in *The New Ancestors*, her first name can also be seen as a sign of her exchangeability. The ubiquitous 'nègres blancs' (d'Amérique) become the opposite of the 'élan d'Amérique' in the implicit political allegory. The quotation also contains a chain of metaphors and puns generated by the anglicism 'weaver.'

Antoine makes a clear distinction between 'femelles,' represented by his wife, and real 'femmes' like Maria, whose name is determined by diegetic necessity: Claire must make a connection between the heroine of the film and the woman Antoine talks about. Unlike the transparent Claire, Maria is all substance and sensuality. Her integrity is greater than the other characters' because she represents a country that has not yet been destroyed, and her exile is voluntary and temporary. Hercule's wife, the quintessential French-Canadian mother, is also called 'Marie.' Blanche and Antoine's daughter becomes 'Soeur Marie de la Passion' (118) when she takes vows. Maria and 'Soeur Marie' represent the two meanings of the word 'passion,' in a conventional equation between religious fervour and sexuality symbolized by Maria.

Although he has a father who appears in the text, Antoine has no last name: he is symbolically orphaned. While the linguistically homeless women all have names that can be pronounced in either French or English, Antoine's name is exclusively French; it is more territorial and also less stereotypical, containing none of the obvious metaphoric connotations attached to the others.

Stephen Peabody is not only the vice-president of the United States Pulp and Paper Company and the king of Suoco Pool, but he is also metonymically linked to the town, whose name is in itself a near anagram of the name of the company and with which he shares his initials. American business is represented by the company and the smell of sulphur, while American culture is represented by 'pulp' in the form of Hollywood movies. The identification between Peabody and the United States is thus as complete as possible. While it is a plausible New England family name, his last name is also an ironic reflection of his physical shortcomings and his lack of procreative power and implies an almost carnivalesque inversion of the invective 'pea-brain.' (Could it also be a retort to the 'pea-souper' sometimes levelled at French Canadians?)

David, who is Claire's double and potential saviour, has a name with overtones of messianism, royalty, and innocence. Born of the water, as indicated in Claire's comment when she first meets him: 'La mer a vomi' (10) Langevin's David is, like Michelangelo's, a male virginal Venus. In the novel David is connected with music; in the Bible he sings and plays the harp. In the elemental imagery, he becomes the wind which plays the Eolian harp that is Claire.

As indicated in his generic epithet, the Indian plays a more exclusively allegorical role than the other characters. Unlike the others who, as per-formers in a psychological drama, are subject to the conventions of indi-viduation, he belongs to only one level of the text.

The mythological/allegorical character of naming and the central role played by metaphor point to the fundamental territoriality of the text. The allegorical role played by language, seen in the translation of Rose Green-wood's name, is also mirrored in the bastardized speech which reflects her status as exile and prostitute. Claire's orphanhood is emphasized by the fact that she learns her mother's tongue as a foreign language. English as a symbol of the encroachment of American capital and culture is foregrounded on a number of occasions. When Peabody demonstrates his rifle to Antoine, he is scandalized to find that the *coureur des bois* does not speak his language: ' "Don't you speak English!" Comme si vous n'aviez jamais été à l'école, comme si vous le faisiez exprès pour compliquer leur existence. Vous étiez aussitôt rangé parmi les êtres obtus ou nuisibles, ou les deux à la fois. Cela finissait par vous travailler. Une vraie disgrâce héréditaire. Vous vous sentiez amoindri et plein de respect. Vos parents vous avaient joué une belle co-médie. Ils ne possédaient pas le pays, et ils avaient négligé de vous apprendre la langue du propriétaire' (75–6). Antoine's inability to speak English makes him an exile in his own country and is one of the reasons for his dismissal. English is not only the language of the Americans, but it is also increasingly that of his own country. The nightclub in Montreal is 'la *cathédrale* des *étrangers*' (129), the foregrounding of the two words reflecting the substi-tution of rock music imported from abroad for the old religion.

The discourse of colonization is reflected in actualizations of the 'nègres blancs' cliché and its corollary, linguistic alienation. Rose's reaction to the slur 'Canucks' – 'We are all white men' (90) – implies an ironic commentary on the second-degree colonization of women. The linguistic imperative stemming from the cliché is 'Speak white' (with obvious reference to Michèle Lalonde's poem), a command somewhat unexpectedly directed at Spanish-speaking Maria by a drunk in the nightclub. More versed in English than Antoine, Maria gaily complies and translates what she has just told the men: 'You are dogs. Dirty dogs!' (86). Unlike Antoine, Maria asserts her power over the men in assuming their language. Coming from a still unviolated culture, she does not see English as a threat. This is true also of the Indian, who remains aloof to the political turmoil around him. Never corrupted by the world of the 'horlogers,' he remains a seasonal figure completely at home anywhere in the forest, whoever may own it. As guide and interpreter, he is indispensable to the vice-president, and he retains his integrity while participating as much as necessary in both cultures surrounding him. Antoine envies him: 'L'Indien était bilingue, depuis trois cents ans, depuis l'arrivée en Amérique des premiers fusils et des premières croix' (76).

Antoine's sense of language is also seen in his indignation when he hears that Claire has won a bet over his missing finger, a symbol foreshadowing his own downfall at the hands of the company: 'Comment, dans leur langue, pouvaient-ils parler de son corps à lui, de ce qui lui manquait!' (66). When he talks about Maria he uses the few Spanish words that he knows, asking the essential question 'Por qué?' when she leaves, 'comme si l'essentiel ne pouvait plus être dit que dans sa langue à elle' (196). When David asks the same question of Claire, however, even when it is typed on a paper in her dream, it is 'POURQUOI? POURQUOI? POURQUOI?' (216). No trace of translation is visible in the language of any of the anglophone characters, or in Claire's or Antoine's reminiscences.

The primacy of French as the language of the text is evident when Claire is introduced to Sandra as 'Claire, comme la mer' (159), an identification impossible in the language in which it is supposedly made. This instance of linguistic licence reveals clearly the French territoriality of the metaphoric network based on Claire's name. An instance of obvious (literal) translation occurs in Bruce's comment when he sees Claire throwing the two rapists in the water: 'I have seen you drop them in the water. It was a beauty. I kicked the lousy bastards out of here' (98). Bruce's laborious English seems to result from the author's good, but not native command of the language, rather than from the character's own speech. The same can be said for Allan's 'Two more hearts will help her to suffer' (95). The author's striving for verisimilitude instead has the effect of defamiliarizing the presumed language of action and thus inadvertently revealing French as the primary, vernacular territory of the text.

Thus the text's (metropolitan) French is not only Claire's but also that of the implied author. While sharing the basic formal and stylistic characteristics of the text as a whole, Antoine's language, on the other hand, is interspersed with Canadianisms. Although the vocabulary of his territory would be well known to anyone familiar with Canadian French, a number of expressions are italicized: 'faire chantier' (112 e.g.), 'bûcheux' (75 e.g.), 'panache' (121 e.g.), 'chevreuil' (103 e.g.), 'faire du pays' (104), 'été des sauvages' (69). Even an anglicism pertaining to the same semantic field, 'lumber-jack' (130), is similarly foregrounded. Other words, however, are never italicized: for example, 'orignal' (passim), 'quenouilles' (58), and 'brunante' (81). This indicates that Antoine's discourse is naturally territorial in its use of a vocabulary relating to the flora and fauna of the forest, while the authorial foregrounding highlights the territorial mythology upholding the text. With the exception of Rose's speech, dialogue is generally modified to the point where few oral characteristics are left and, even in the conversations between Antoine and Hercule, pronunciation and syntax are basically those of writing rather than speech.

As symbolically linked to the territory, the moose, 'orignal' and 'origine,' is closely connected with language, as seen in the bilingual word-play centring on its various names, which forms a crucial part of the allegory. To Antoine, the moose – in a modernist rather than postmodernist view of the original myth – is a buffer against 'la nouvelle Babel dont l'ombre s'étendait chaque jour davantage' (124). It is not until it is dead that the 'orignal' becomes 'l'élan d'Amérique': as it becomes the property of America, the language belonging to it dies with it. Although Langevin does not use joual, and the language of writing on the whole is less specifically identifiable as Canadian French than, for instance, Aquin's in *Trou de mémoire*, it is the intralingual translation of the vernacular/mythic 'orignal' into the vehicular (metropolitan) 'élan d'Amérique' that symbolizes the final alienation and death of a culture.

In the thematic discussion of communication, language plays another role. The need to communicate is as fatal as the impossibility of doing so, which is not always a result of a natural language barrier. According to David, 'Le besoin de communiquer détruit toujours quelque chose ... L'amour ...' (165). This lifts language out of the political sphere and onto a wider existential plane, which echoes the author's preoccupations in his earlier novels. The auto-referentiality of this discussion becomes explicit on only one occasion in a comment by David: 'Les mots sont fragiles parce qu'ils ont trop servi. Ils s'émiettent au moindre contact comme une aile de papillon séchée. C'est pour cela que tant d'hommes ont tenté de les épingler dans les pages d'un livre' (165). Through an earlier metaphor likening Claire to a butterfly, she implicitly becomes the book, and consequently the view of the novel as echo chamber is conclusively confirmed.

My discussion of sonority and echo has shown the primacy of the auditory in generating content as well as form. In the same way as Claire's waves of consciousness and her reconstruction of events are triggered by auditory stimuli, the text is generated to a large extent according to principles of sonority; that is, according to poetic, rather than narrative, conventions. Words and sounds echo and resonate throughout the text, traversing the two narrative perspectives and creating a unity based on auditory, and not primarily diegetic, coherence. The narrative parts are often written in very long sentences that vibrate with alliteration, internal rhyme, and assonance, strategies already encountered in the central 'Tu tues tout ce que tu touches,' but even more obvious in descriptions: 'C'était en octobre, dans une ultime lumière miellée qui vibrait ainsi qu'un adieu silencieux entre mer et ciel, et prêtait au vol plané des mouettes, à contre-soleil, une éblouissante douceur' (15). Intensity is achieved through several poetic devices, seen, for example, in the following passage describing the love scene between Claire and David:

> Et c'est le délirant, le blanc, le liquide ballet de leurs deux bouches, de
> leurs souffles, leurs mains, leurs corps emmêlés, noyés l'un dans l'autre
> en une tendre et douce marée qui ne les portera jamais assez haut, une
> poudreuse et tiède clarté qui les irradie jusqu'à l'âme, la quête acharnée
> et oppressante de l'autre, une neigeuse brûlure que leur désir de se
> fondre avive, un torrent moelleux de lait qui les emporte, les fait s'en-
> trechoquer sous les vagues de velours, s'épancher l'un dans l'autre dans
> une soif toujours plus vive, qui les laisse pantelants au coeur d'une
> tempête pourpre et or qui charrie dans leurs veines une rosée vermeille
> plus enivrante qu'aucun soleil, qui les cloue l'un à l'autre en une flam-
> boyante crucifixion.   (169)

We notice in this climactic passage a number of tropes that bring to mind the discussion of *Trou de mémoire*, notably oxymorons ('poudreuse clarté,' 'neigeuse brûlure,' 'vagues de velours'). The conjunction of opposites, which can perhaps be aptly described as the successful outcome of 'la quête acharnée et oppressante de l'autre,' results in the transformation of the 'entre' of alterity into the, at least momentary, convergence and reciprocity implicit in 's'entrechoquer.' And the final crucifixion, where the one seems to be superimposed on the other, offers at least a possibility of redemption. Again, as in Aquin's text, the conjunction, which is mystery and passion, is inscribed in water imagery; it takes place in a 'liquide ballet,' a kind of pas de deux where two finally become one.

Another instance of territorial, poetic, and intranslatable language generation is seen in the almost surreal 'rosée vermeille,' a blood metaphor triggered perhaps by the 'pourpre' and playing on the polysemy of 'ros(é)e.' The poetic charge carried by the preponderance of prepositive adjectives (very common throughout the text) would, of course, also be lost in translation. It is hardly surprising that this is the only one of Langevin's novels whose challenge has not been taken up by a translator.

More than anything else, it is the poetic character of the text, together with its narrative structure, that has led critics to link it with the expressionist variant of the *nouveau roman*, as represented in particular by Claude Simon.[8] As Brochu remarks, however, *L'Elan d'Amérique* is quite a traditional novel in that it does not question the unity of the subject nor negate the powers of language to represent the world (258–9). In this it reflects an earlier tradition than both *Trou de mémoire* and *The New Ancestors*. It has, indeed, more in common with the traditional 'roman du pays' (Brochu 259). While sharing the allegorical mode of Godfrey's novel, Langevin lacks the irony marking the distance of the author from his text. The explicitly thematized deterritorialization is offset by clearly territorial strategies of signification, most notably mythological naming and conjunctive metaphor, culminating in the oxymoron, as well as by the signifier-oriented, auditory text generation. The allegorical equation between translation and perversion, which is more overt than in *The New Ancestors*, underscores the theme of the territoriality of language, and rather than emphasizing a linguistic homelessness, the bilingual wordplay on *élan* and *buck* closely links the text to its geographical and cultural territory, Franco-America.

While the congruity between the form of the novel and its symbolism can be seen in the *mise en abyme* function of the echo chamber, there is a certain incongruity between the main themes of identity loss and cultural and linguistic alienation and the language of writing, whose highly territorial character has been demonstrated. The deterritorialization depicted diegetically is counteracted in the reterritorializing of language seen in the authorial foregrounding of indigenous myth and vocabulary and, more significantly, in the identification of word and thing, of name and identity. *L'Elan d'Amérique* may be a good illustration of postcolonial allegory in its obvious branching of the personal onto the political. While it is certainly melodramatic on the psychodramatic level and can hardly be accused of being either anti-oedipal or non-territorial, it does, I would argue, demonstrate the postcolonial necessity for referential grounding. Its political force may, in fact, cast doubt on the analogy between radical extraterritoriality and political effectiveness implicit in the theories of Deleuze and Guattari, and I will return to this problem in my conclusion.

CHAPTER SIX

Gone Indian
The Novel as Rebus

Jeremy Sadness, a graduate student of English at SUNY, Binghamton, is sent by his thesis director and spiritual father, Professor Madham, to a job interview in Edmonton in the middle of winter. At the Edmonton airport, he finds himself in possession of the wrong suitcase, one that looks exactly like his own but which belongs to Roger Dorck of Notikeewin. Intending to find the rightful owner and possibly retrieve his own lost luggage, Jeremy gets a lift to the little town. In Dorck's office he meets Jill Sunderman, who informs him that Dorck has had a snowmobile accident and is unconscious in hospital. Driven by curiosity, Jeremy visits the hospital and meets Dorck's mistress who, it is later revealed, is Jill's mother, Bea Sunderman. She tells him a strange story of how, twenty years earlier, her husband Robert disappeared and has been presumed dead by everyone but herself. She insists that her husband phoned her after supposedly falling through the ice and drowning in Elkhart pond.

In a series of bizarre events involving many cases of mistaken identity, in one of which he is forced to take Dorck's place as master of ceremonies in the winter festival, Jeremy tries to fulfil his childhood dream of becoming Grey Owl or 'going Indian.' In the process he has affairs, first with Jill, then with Bea, who at one point seems to mistake him for her lost husband. Dorck eventually wakes up from his coma but suffers from amnesia and, believing Jill to be her mother, resumes the love affair with the daughter. After witnessing Dorck's awakening, Jeremy seeks refuge in Bea's bed. She receives a phone call – we are not told from whom but are led to believe it is from the hospital. Saying 'He's alive,' she flees into the night with Jeremy. They are never heard of again, but their snowmobile is found, smashed by a collision with a train, and Jeremy's cassette recorder is found hanging on the railway bridge. Although their bodies are never retrieved, it is generally believed that they fell to their deaths.

Such are the main events that make up what is usually interpreted as a tale of a young man's search for himself. The authority behind the story is dubious. Dated six months after the main events, it is told by Professor Madham, who has reconstructed it on the basis of tapes Jeremy sent him. In the beginning of the book, the narration alternates between Jeremy's first-hand account, transcribed verbatim by Madham, and the professor's own commentary as he edits some of the tapes and tells Jeremy's story in the third person. As in *Trou de mémoire*, we are confronted by an editor who gradually reveals his own involvement in the story he pretends simply to recount, but the two discourses – Jeremy's confessional one and Madham's editorial one – are not clearly set apart. Contrary to Jeremy's wishes, or so he pretends, the editor has destroyed the original tapes, and the whole of the text is therefore subject only to his authority. Madham's implication in Jeremy's story is not limited to his role as supervisor, correspondent, and spiritual father, but is complicated by the fact that he is having an affair with Jeremy's wife, Carol. More important, however, is the fact that Madham himself was born in the Canadian Northwest, in the very place Jeremy visits, and that Jeremy's adventures evoke in him memories of his own youth. This fact, which Madham confides to the reader, is apparently unknown to Jeremy.

The narration is thus triple-layered: there is the first-person account by Jeremy, presumably untampered with by Madham; the critical discourse of Madham's editorial persona; and Madham's own first-person account, which reveals both his own understanding of Jeremy's experience and his increasingly personal involvement in the adventures, all of which belie his presumed scholarly detachment. Both the complex narrative structure and the foregrounding of the editorial process resemble those of *Trou de mémoire*, and both novels recall that seminal work of postmodernism, *Pale Fire*, which Kroetsch sees as a 'paradigmatic text' (Neuman and Wilson 59).

The novel opens with a letter addressed to Jill Sunderman in Edmonton and signed by Madham in Binghamton. Laid out completely in italics, it is set apart from the bulk of the text. Although it is positioned as a prologue, it is in fact a postscript to the long letter which constitutes the narrative. As there are two first person narrators, there are two addressees: the 'you' to Jeremy's 'I' is Madham, while the 'you' to Madham's 'I' is Jill. The primary addressee of the text is thus Jill, a crucial fact that has been overlooked in most critical readings. As in *Beautiful Losers*, the reader is made to read a letter adressed to a character, and the diegetic situation of communication mirrors that between text and reader. The narrative beginning thus precedes the formal beginning, while the latter constitutes the narrative end. Such circularity is common in Kroetsch's novels, not only in their structure and formal patterns but also in the spatio-temporal imagery which is symptomatic of the author's vision of the prairies, where the absence of reference points in space and time often causes a confusion in the perception of ends and beginnings. It is significant that Kroetsch's fictions are sometimes defined as preposterous, a term originally related to time, meaning putting first (pre-) that which should come after (post-) or vice versa.

The prologue/postscript apparently frames the text. It is headed by an address, which occupies the place normally reserved for chapter headings. The address, which is that of Madham's private residence, is further foregrounded by being typographically set apart from the rest of his communication, indicating a mimetic distinction between a preprinted letterhead and a typed letter. The information contained in the address seems irrelevant: Madham's address is not pertinent to the text *per se* and it is, furthermore, clear that the addressee, Jill Sunderman, is already familiar with it. Madham's letter is in fact a response to a request from her that he 'explain everything' (1). As is the case with the address heading the letter opening *Trou de mémoire*, this foregrounding has another purpose. Its real referent happens to be the residence of Robert Kroetsch at the time of writing, when he was teaching at SUNY, Binghamton (Thomas 68). In this way the affinity between author and narrator and the blurring of the border between fiction and reality are present, although very covertly, from the beginning.

The discrepancy between the formal opening of the letter, 'Dear Miss Sunderman,' and the informality of the scribbled signature of the sender foregrounds the latter. The handwritten 'Mark,' which ends the prologue, is not Madham's first, but rather his middle name. As the typewritten clarification indicates, his full name is R. Mark Madham. Peter Thomas has pointed out that Mark is 'only a minimal sign, a virtual anonymity' (75). The word signifies nothing but 'signature'; it brings to mind the Xes made under Indian treaties in place of names. Preposterously then, the letter which (and this must be remembered) *is* the whole novel, is signed but, in a way, anonymous. This strategy nicely illustrates Benjamin's view of the novel; the oxymoronic anonymous signature undercuts the presumed intimacy of personal communication. Not alerted to this ironic subversion of the conventions of signing, the reader might interpret the novel as a gospel according to Mark and see the preposterousness in the ironic inversion of the relationship between teacher and disciple. In an interview with Russell Brown,

Kroetsch defines the American voice as prophetic, as opposed to the confessional mode of its Canadian counterpart. Reading 'Mark' as a conventional seal of authenticity would underscore Madham's prophetic role and implicitly emphasize his American, rather than his Canadian identity. This (mis)reading is exactly the one Madham, a highly unreliable narrator, is striving for, as we shall see.

Rebus

The epigraph of the novel, taken from an essay by Frederick Jackson Turner, seems to be the only element of the text which does not form part of the narrative, but frames it in a conventional manner by subsuming the theme of the text: 'For a moment, at the frontier, the bonds of custom are broken and unrestraint is triumphant.' Jeremy's and Madham's locales are both frontiers: Binghamton is not quite east, and Edmonton is not quite west. Jeremy's arrival in Edmonton, in one of many allusions to *Tay John* (74) called 'The Gateway North' (53), coincides with the beginning of the winter carnival in Notikeewin, a time which is indeed one of unrestraint. The carnival occupies a central place in the novel and provides the diegetic justification for the many metamorphoses and role reversals that take place.

The dissolution of the self connected with the carnival is often discussed in Bakhtinian terms by Kroetsch's critics, who emphasize the Rabelaisian aspect of his fictions (e.g. Neuman and Wilson 35–6). The epigraph, insofar as it is applied to the Canadian rather than the American frontier, is already an ironic inversion, considering the myth of the orderly settling of the Canadian West and the absence of a Wild West mythology. The fact that the first person Jeremy encounters on his arrival in Canada is a customs officer could be a comment on the Canadian way of handling frontiers. However, the frontier, whose customs are broken, is more than a symbolic and political barrier, and the epigraph turns out to play a significant role in the puzzle that constitutes the text. Jeremy's adventures begin when he mistakes Roger Dorck's suitcase for his own identical one; it is this error that leads to his being detained by customs. It is when he literally 'breaks the bonds of [c]ustom[s]' by escaping from the law that he enters the realm of unrestraint and carnival, the domain of game-playing.[1] A true postmodernist, Kroetsch is fascinated by games and the playful aspect of fiction-making, and his novels are often described as puzzles. We have already seen this aspect of postmodernism in connection with both *Beautiful Losers* and *Trou de mémoire*, as well as in the interest in the detective genre among postmodernist writers. Just as a handkerchief dropped at the scene of a crime is insignificant outside its proper place in a chain of other signs (clues, motives), the rules of a game are created inside the game itself and have no meaning except in the context of a specific range of possible operations.

The play on the word 'customs' is one of many examples of the uprooting of the signifier which lies behind my characterization of this novel as a 'rebus,' a concept that appeared in chapter 1 in my discussion of the Derridean notion of the dissemination of the proper name in the text. In its general definition, the 'rebus principle,' according to the OED, is the basis of 'logographic script' in which 'a given word is expressed by a clearly recognizable picture of a quite different thing, which has, however, the same phonetic value.' Commonly associated with picture puzzles, hieroglyphs, or pictograms – exemplified in the 'cartouche' of which Holbein gave an example in his hidden signature – which rely on the disassociation of the sign from the referent, this type of writing represents the transition between ideographic writing and syllabic writing. In its verbal form, the rebus principle is dependent on the divisibility of the sign and the consequent transformative power of the signifier, and we have indeed seen examples of this already in connection with *Beautiful Losers* (bale-veil, rei-Ray) and possibly also in *Trou de mémoire* (q-cul). Some rebuses have been so commonly adopted that their original puzzle character has been forgotten (e.g. IOU for I owe you). In an interesting note the *Encyclopedia Britannica* informs us that rebus pictures 'were used to convey names of towns on Greek and Roman coins or names of families in medieval heraldry ... In the Far East, especially in China and Korea, rebus symbols were commonly employed to carry auspicious wishes.' Hence, the rebus incorporates many of the features of postmodernism we have encountered so far: it is the phonetic coincidence of signifiers – as in the cases of homonymy that were so important in *Beautiful Losers* or the polysemic properties of the 'buck' in *L'Elan d'Amérique* – that creates meaning; it also seems to imply the potentially revelatory force of such chance: it could be argued that each toss of the three *I Ching* coins constitutes an auspicious rebus that can only be interpreted within that textual system.

The rebus is the perfect example of a semiotic system or game, insofar as each element in the signifying chain gains its significance only through its (lateral) position *vis-à-vis* the other elements in the system, with no regard to reference, just as the clue in a mystery is only significant in its relation to others within the same system. Making language 'visible,' a desirable endeavour for Kroetsch, as for most postmodernists (see Neuman and Wilson 141), it permits words, sounds, and letters to be uprooted from their 'proper' or conventional meanings in order to take on entirely new significations. Foregrounding the arbitrariness of the sign, the rebus allows for the 'breaking of the bonds of custom' that link signifier and signified and makes possible a a radical process of un- and re-naming. Moreover, a rebus can rarely be read in a simple linear fashion but requires a process of detection, not unlike that pursued by the great literary detectives such as Sherlock Holmes, whereby any one element, or rather any combination of elements, can provide the initial key to the deciphering of the whole. It can be said to constitute the transposition of the detective story onto the level of language; as we shall see it is words themselves that become the suspects, and like the mystery it has only one solution. More obviously than any other game or any other system, the rebus carries its key completely within itself: it is hermetic, self-contained, closed. Like that other image dear to post-modernists, the labyrinth, there is only one way out of a rebus.[2] Completely governed by the signifier, the rebus is the epitome of depthlessness, the ultimate challenge to romantic notions of transcendence. Superficiality or laterality is the main characteristic of the rebus; all its elements pertain to the same horizontal axis and, unlike the modernist structures of a novel like *L'Elan d'Amérique* with its reliance on metaphor, it permits little interpretative freedom; as Holbein's example shows, it is akin to anamorphosis.[3] Kroetsch's novel is an unusually complex example of the phenomenon and we shall see in the following how the hermetic nature of the text is intimately related to the dissemination of the proper name. First, however, an inventory of the salient features of the textual system must be made.

The frequent use of images of the fall, the flood, and the building of the ark in Kroetsch's novels has led critics to discuss his works in apocalyptic terms. Like that of most postmodernists, in my corpus perhaps particularly Cohen's, his world-view is apocalyptic, but in a particular sense of the word. One of the peculiarities characterizing the Albertans about whom he writes is, according to Kroetsch, their sense of being outside time: 'Perhaps I speak as a westerner. In the rhetoric of prairie politics – in the voices of Riel, Tommy Douglas, Aberhart, Diefenbaker – we go from Eden to the apocalypse in one easy leap. They never quite know whether it's the end or the beginning ... There's very little credence given to the notion that we exist in history, in time' (Cameron 1:84). The difficulty in distinguishing between beginnings and endings which, in Kermode's terms, would constitute an inability to distinguish between the 'tick' and the 'tock' of a clock, gives rise to a world of constant and simultaneous genesis and apocalypse, a preposterous notion indeed. This peculiar anhistoricity is linked to the prairie landscape, and time and space are inextricably intertwined in a scenery where space is measured by the 'tick, tick of the telegraph poles' (15).

The double time perspective of *chronos* and *kairos* is in evidence in *Gone Indian* and, as in many of Kroetsch's novels, it is often linked to the male/female dichotomy we have already encountered in *The New Ancestors*. Bea Sunderman is the most obvious example of the rule of *kairos*. Since her husband's disappearance she has been living in memory at 'Worlds End,' the house that was so apocalyptically named probably by him. The suspension of *chronos* in her life is interrupted, as by the knocks on the door in *Trou de mémoire* (and in *Macbeth*) and David's discovery of the watches in *L'Elan d'Amérique*, by the final phone call which prompts her flight with Jeremy, and which echoes the earlier one made by her husband from the 'other side,' the one that stopped time. The connection of the double time perspective with Robert Sunderman's disappearance is obvious in the description of the clocks that Jeremy finds in Bea's bedroom and that, no doubt, used to belong to her husband. The clocks have all been standing still since Robert's disappearance, but when Jeremy reappears, after having witnessed the awakening of Dorck – the intermediary between Robert and himself – the clocks mysteriously start ticking again, and Bea mistakes him for her husband.

Robert Sunderman, who might have been the 'homesteader who couldn't stand the vision of space' (31), and who therefore planted a grove of spruce around Worlds End, seems to have been a victim of *chronos* just as much as Professor Madham, whose home, according to Jeremy, looks curiously like Sunderman's. Thus, when Madham reminisces about the prairies, he remembers the sense of being '*trapped in* the blank indifference of space and timelessness' (124). While *kairos* is the time of openness, women, and the prairies, *chronos* is that of closure, men, and the USA, all symbolized by Madham's adopted territory, American academia. *Chronos* is anathema to memory, whereas *kairos* is always tied to it, and memory in turn is linked to love. As Jeremy points out: 'Memory alone ... converts the ravening of lust into the mystery of love' (83).

Memory plays a complex diegetic role in the novel. Jeremy's story turns out to be a re-enactment of Madham's past, and the professor retreats further into memory, love, and *kairos* as he recounts his disciple's story. When Roger Dorck wakes up from his coma, after having symbolically given birth to the new Jeremy by 'hatching' the American's suitcase under his bed, he lives in the past, embracing in the daughter – Jill – the memory of the mother – Bea. This parallels Bea's response when she mistakes Jeremy for her husband and embraces him.

The perception of time, which, as we have seen, is closely linked to the experience of space, also leads to a problematic perception of motion. Jeremy invokes the image of Zeno's arrow and the famous argument that claims that movement does not exist because, at any given moment, the arrow is in one particular static position. If movement does not exist, you cannot get from here to there, since the space between the two points will have to be divided indefinitely. The image captures the sense of space on the prairies, where the light at the horizon remains at the same distance no matter how fast you travel. It is this seeming futility of movement that prompts Jeremy to contemplate writing his thesis on 'The Forgery of Distance' (113). Where beginnings are ends and vice versa, there is little movement, and Jeremy, like so many of Kroetsch's picaros, is more moved than freely moving. In the races that play a part in the carnival games, for instance, the finish line coincides with the starting point. It is perhaps not purely coincidental that the realm of game-playing is a land of surfaces where no real progress is made and where, as in Alice's chess game in *Through the Looking-Glass*, no matter how fast the game is played, the pawn remains a pawn.

Zeno's arrow is also actualized in the image of the unending leap or the unfinished fall, which occurs in a *mise en abyme* fashion, almost in the exact middle of the book, in the description of a ski-jumper: 'The figure of a man tipped over the edge, onto the slope of the tall wooden ski jump, began to move, began to slip, caught his balance, raised his arms, swept on down the graded slope, took off into the air, soared up at the blinding sun: and then was motionless, flying' (74). The leap or fall is generally depicted in the novel in terms of flying. But, as Jeremy says, 'Flying is easy. The whole, the absolute mastery resides in knowing how to fall' (78). The enigma with which the reader is left at the end of the book is the question of whether Jeremy does or does not master the art of falling.

The fall is actualized in several instances. The first fall in the text, that of Robert Sunderman, is repeated not only by Dorck, but by Jeremy on one occasion before the final and enigmatic flight. Like Dorck, Jeremy, on his first snowmobile ride, flies off his vehicle and lands, head first, in a snowbank. The fall as a kind of rebirth or metamorphosis is clearly foreshadowed in this incident, when Jeremy is brought back to life by Jill, who 'would create him into life' (41), according to Madham. The archetypal leap is represented by the buffalo jump, which occurs in several of Kroetsch's novels as an emblematic Canadian image. The cliff from which Roger Dorck falls is such a jump, the same one that figures in *The Studhorse Man*.

Metamorphosis

The fall and its corollary, metamorphosis, are yet more variants of the by now familiar Orphic descent. The ambiguous title of Jeremy's first, unwritten dissertation is 'Going Down With Orpheus' (62) and, after his first fall, he is transformed into a 'pillar of ice' (41). Not only does the descent remain unaccomplished or incomplete, but it is transposed horizontally. After having won the snowshoe race and been taken for an Indian and beaten up, Jeremy comments: 'As you yourself remarked, Professor, every river is the River Styx' (94). Rather than crossing Styx, however, the race goes *along* the frozen river. This incident constitutes Jeremy's definitive metamorphosis. In keeping with the lateral functioning of the processes of signification in the rebus, the descent is projected horizontally into a constant sliding on surfaces: 'Only the river itself offered a way: you must follow its surface with your feet, almost with the tips of your fingers, in order to see' (78). The metaphoric *mise en abyme* of this sliding on surfaces, as well as of the repetitive nature of the diegesis, is the game of curling. The sliding of the rocks on the ice and the echo of their collisions as they attempt to replace each other at the centre of the target hover over the text and embody what we shall see to be its main formal characteristics: echoes, repetitions, and the absent centre.

Jeremy possesses no fewer than twelve unwritten theses, but the most important is the one entitled 'The Columbus Quest: the Dream, the Journey, the Surprise' (62). The title is another *mise en abyme* of the narrative, hinting at the notion of exploration as missing the mark, getting lost, or believing that you are where you are not. The first and only existing sentence of the thesis reveals the irony of the title of the novel: 'Christopher Columbus, not knowing that he had not come to the Indies, named the inhabitants of that new world ____' (21). This sentence is, in fact, foregrounded through repetition (71, 149). The theme of faulty naming as a result of mistaken identity runs through the text, and it provides a first clue to the true status of the 'characters.' The Columbus intertext renders the notion of 'going Indian' rather ambiguous. This central theme is personified by Grey Owl, whom Jeremy calls his 'pathfinder' (101), in an implicit reference to James Fenimore Cooper and American lore, which indicates that the intertext is used with a certain parodic intent. Grey Owl embodies the narrative paradigms of the novel: he was an English naturalist, Archie Belaney, who, according to Jeremy, 'died into a new life' (62) and was taken for an Indian. He is Jeremy's specular identity, 'the truest Indian of them all' (80). We encounter here a peculiar parallel to the 'becoming other' = 'seeing as the Red Men' equation in *Beautiful Losers*; in both the Indian symbolizes the coincidence of identity and difference – in order to find yourself you have to become other – assume an alias – or see as the other sees.

The problem of identity is linked in the novel to that of narrative authority. Jeremy's first recorded comment, which presumably refers to the suitcase and is directed to the customs officer, is, according to Madham, 'Hey ... this isn't mine' (6). It is instantly followed by the professor's cryptic remark: 'How appropriate that those should be his first words' (6). Jeremy's refutation of ownership is repeated no less than eight times, once in capital letters. The last time it is in reference to his own suitcase, found in Dorck's office. As we have seen in both *Trou de mémoire* and the 'Fifth City' section of *The New Ancestors*, narrative authority is always a complex problem in postmodern texts, and it becomes clear in *Gone Indian* that Madham's remark is a warning to Jill (and consequently to the reader) concerning Jeremy's ownership of his story. Robert Kroetsch has commented on the development from traditional, or even modernist, narrative convention, to postmodernism: 'the conventions that used to apply to the hero in the text, apply instead to the reader. The reader has to be aware of so many ... facets, and certainly he has to be watching where the story is coming from' (Neuman and Wilson 175).

Jeremy is guided on his journey by a number of initiator figures, whom Peter Thomas calls 'shamanic guides' (71), and whom we recognize from *The New Ancestors*. These are familiar characters in Kroetsch's fiction and related to Indian legends of the trickster but they also embody the pathfinder; Jeremy sometimes refers to them as pied pipers. The first of these guides is a transvestite 'grass' smuggler encountered in customs detention at Edmonton airport, who reveals that he used to be a buffalo in an earlier life. Here is another man who claims to have 'died into a new life.' The smuggler refutes ownership of the 'grass' hidden in his false breasts, and his sweatshirt carries another implicit warning about narrative authority: 'Whatsoever is Truth' (8). When Jeremy escapes from Customs and enters the carnival realm of 'unrestraint,' he does so, as he says, 'DISGUISED AS [HIM]SELF' (11), thereby foregrounding the theme of alterity or loss of identity as disguise which runs through the text. It is echoed soon after this first incident, when Jeremy calls Roger Dorck's office: 'I had a voice that sounded exactly like mine' (12). The pattern is already introduced in Madham's epistolary prologue, however, where he quotes Carol as saying: 'Professor Madham ... is being Professor Madham,' to which the professor enigmatically replies: 'Never' (3).

Coming to Notikeewin, the site of the Winter carnival, Jeremy enters a world of metamorphosis, reflecting the theme of identity loss. He is presented as trying to go through the looking-glass on the first morning after his nocturnal arrival: 'And don't ask me why, this morning when I peeked into the splotchy mirror over the basin in a corner of my room, I tried to reach through the glass and touch my own skin' (19).[4] If Jeremy's specular identity, which he appropriately tries to find on the other side of the mirror, is Grey Owl, his totem is the buffalo. His totemic relationship with the animal, which is similar to Antoine's identification with the moose in *L'Elan d'Amérique*, is described in several instances. We have seen how the first of his pathfinders used to be a buffalo. Jeremy first identifies with his totem on his arrival in Notikeewin, where he is greeted by an ice statue: 'An Indian on a galloping horse bore down on a huge and galloping buffalo, leaned over both the buffalo and Jeremy, aimed an arrow of ice at their twinned hearts' (18). Later, in the snowshoe race, which is an important stage in his progressive metamorphosis, Jeremy again identifies with the buffalo:

> I swear I could smell the blood of a buffalo jump: right there in those hills the Cree and the Blackfoot drove the unknown herds to a fatal leap. Over the cliffs the buffalo lunged to the heaped bones below.
> I stumbled.
> There was nothing under my feet that might have tripped me. (85)

The link between the buffalo jump and the leap into a new life has already been touched upon in connection with Roger Dorck's fall.

Jeremy's identification with the buffalo is also indicated in the embarrassing case of sympathetic magic which causes him to be impotent in any position but the upright one. It is Professor Madham who points out the significance of this predicament: '*buffalo make love standing up*' (106). Hence his inability to 'go down' with Orpheus. The importance of the buffalo in the paradigm of metamorphosis is further implied in the fact that Jeremy once possessed three buffalo nickels, in what might also be an allusion to the coins of the *I Ching*. Jeremy achieves his desired communion with his totem when he dreams that he is a buffalo and mates with Buffalo Woman, a beautiful squaw who, according to legend, became a buffalo cow and mated with a bull. Though in an intentionally parodic way, the buffalo plays the same role here as the moose in *L'Elan d'Amérique*. It is, as we have seen, for instance, in the paradigm of the fall, at the origin; it represents the original or primordial Canadian prairie in the same way as the 'orignal' symbolized the Quebec forest.

The affinity between Jeremy and Madham is also revealed through this buffalo code. In the prologue, Madham, in a seemingly redundant anecdote, confesses that he and Carol (Jeremy's wife) like to commune with the buffalo at the Ross Park Zoo in Binghamton. The original buffalo is gone from the prairies, and the only live buffalo that appear in the novel, outside of dreams, are the pathetic couple of transplanted exiles in the zoo, removed, like Madham himself, from the openness of the Canadian prairies to an American enclosure. The buffalo as a link between the professor and his disciple is implicit in another strange incident of mistaken identity, when a stranger takes Jeremy for somebody named 'Ross' (57). Jeremy interprets this as a result of his looking like the arctic explorer who set off to search for the lost Franklin expedition. Franklin is yet another example of the absent corpse, the presumed death, of which there is no evidence. But Ross also echoes the name of the zoo of the transplanted 'fake' buffalo, and the mistake absolves Jeremy from the inauthentic buffalohood that is Madham's.

The distinction between real and fake buffalo is expressed in a dichotomy between bulls and oxen, which in turn is linked to a range of other binary opposites, hinted at in Jeremy's harangue to his professor: 'I should have kept that tape I mailed you, you *dumb-ox*, Professor. Who are you, you pompous *ass*? *Sitting* there in your office in the Library Wing, *chewing your cud*, the *grass* you cropped off the green fields twenty years ago, vomiting it up in your own mouth, chewing it again. And again' (19 emphasis added). Three other 'oxen' appear in the text: Robert Sunderman's father, Sonny; Carol's father (who, in Jeremy's opinion, is 'as stupid as an ox' [45]); and Dorck, who is 'Strong as an ox' (132). All four are father figures, including Dorck, of whom Jill says: 'I thought of him as a *father*' (42). Besides Jeremy, there is only one other 'bull,' Johnnie Backstrom, 'a big bull of a man' (130). Backstrom is the Notikeewin undertaker who, in *The Words of My Roaring*, proved to be a 'bullshitter' of considerable talent. The opposition between bulls and oxen reflects the dichotomy between essence and appearance, between true sexuality and 'MINDFUCK[ING]' (49). Madham's sexuality, like that of the zoo buffalo, is appropriately located in his 'horny forehead' (2), a fact which he proves by catching Carol's panties 'as if with great bruising horns' (3).

The opposition between bulls, or real buffalo, and oxen, or zoo buffalo, is paralleled in the opposition between grass and cud. The Ross Park buffalo are looking in vain for 'the buffalo grass that is not to be found' (3), and they are reduced to chewing their cud. As seen in the passage quoted above, cud-chewing is equivalent to living in the past. Jeremy's first alter ego, the ex-buffalo transvestite, was a smuggler of another kind of grass. The buffalo grass has vanished with the animals, and both represent origin and essence. It is symptomatic that when the buffalo return in Jeremy's dream, they graze on the lawns of Edmonton but chew their cuds on campus. Cud-chewing is a typically academic activity. When Dorck wakes up with amnesia, he too chews the cud by mistaking Jill for Bea. The idea of 'embrac[ing] in each the memory of the other' (43) clearly fascinates Madham.[5]

'Bullshitting' is, in Kroetsch's world, the essence of storytelling on the prairies and a specifically male occupation (e.g. Thomas 103). The phenomenon is actualized in rebus form through a play on the signifiers which form part of the central opposition between speaking and writing. Madham, the ox, is a silent scribe, while Jeremy, the bull, is a compulsive talker, whose twelve unwritten dissertations testify to his inability to put things down in writing. The only time we see Jeremy write is when he – unsuccessfully – tries to grade the contestants in the Winter Queen pageant. As a professor, Madham judges his students' performances, and an equation is established between writing and *mark*ing. It is Madham who suggests that Jeremy take along a tape-recorder, which becomes the modern equivalent of the Wild West hero's gun as problem-solver and creator of order. The recorder turns into a security blanket, to which Jeremy turns in moments of fear, when the alternative seems to be 'shitting himself,' thus establishing an equation between shitting and talking, or telling stories. In an interview Kroetsch says: 'In a sense, we haven't got an identity until somebody tells our story' (Kroetsch, Bacque, Gravel 63). If bullshitting is storytelling, then 'shitting yourself' must be telling your own story, that is, inventing your own identity. Madham hints at this: 'Jeremy – again I quote him – nearly shit himself. A linguistic feat which one wishes might have been translated into mere reality. Thus he would have given himself birth into a more appropriate demise' (143). It is significant that this incident – Jeremy's 'nearly shitting himself' – takes place as he watches Dorck awaken from his coma, since it is Dorck who, in a sense, gives Jeremy his new identity.[6]

In an instance of 'cud-chewing,' Madham ruminates on what Jeremy might have been thinking before setting out on his quest: 'And why, he asks, does man venture into the unknown when he might be safe in his two-room walk-up apartment with beer in his refrigerator, spaghetti on his menu, unread books piled high on his bricks and boards, nooky in his sagging bed? The old conundrum, he tells himself, victim of his own rhetoric: the old shovelful of rice, he complains, but the bull's ass once again nowhere to be seen' (10). The curious reference to the truth as the 'bull's ass' is explained by the wordplay on 'bullshitting.' The impossibility of attaining the goal of the quest is articulated by the second of Jeremy's guides, who gives him a lift to Notikeewin. Referring to the difficulty of getting a drink on Sundays, the driver says: 'Everything along here is closed up tighter than a bull's-ass in fly-time' (15). As we have seen in the falling and flying imagery, it is indeed fly-time in Notikeewin. The theme of looking for the truth in the bull's ass is already foreshadowed in the incident at the airport, when the Customs officer is 'waving the Queen's Own flashlight up [Jeremy's] Royal American' (9). Jeremy's, the bull's, ass is empty; there is no grass to be found. It is obvious that if the story is bullshit, its origin is the bull's ass, which is either nowhere to be found, or which is empty. The target of the quest, with its carnivalesque inversion of the bull's-eye into its opposite, retains the figure of the circle with the unattainable dot in the middle seen on the ice in the curling game. The imagery here is remarkably similar to Cohen's use of this particular part of human anatomy. Jeremy can indeed be said to, however unwittingly, act out 'I's' desire in 'shitting himself,' hence liberating himself from the constipating stronghold of history or academia.

The absent centre is metaphorically analogous to the image of the lost original, which returns in several instances, structurally as well as diegetically. Not only are the original tapes (on which the text presumably is based) destroyed, but the original raison d'être of the whole narrative, Jill's request for a response from Madham, is equally lost. The leaps taken by Dorck and then Jeremy and Bea are nothing but repetitions of the original one taken by Robert Sunderman, the absent centre of the paradigm. This first fall may in turn be seen as a reversed re-enactment of Grey Owl's. It appears to be the lack of any proof – the absence of corpses – of Jeremy's and Bea's deaths that prompts Jill to write to Madham, but it is Robert Sunderman's absent corpse that constitutes the centre of the narrative. This is neither the first nor the last time that an absent corpse is at the origin of one of Kroetsch's fictions, a fact which shows his affinity with Aquin's locating of the origin of literature in the corpse. The pattern is most clearly developed in *What the Crow Said*, but it appears already in the first novel, *But We Are Exiles*.

It is not insignificant that Kroetsch's working title for *Gone Indian* was *Funeral Games*, alluding to book 5 of the *Aeneid*. The Notikeewin carnival is a kind of funeral which has been celebrated every winter since the year after Robert Sunderman's disappearance and in which the corpse is eternally absent. Jeremy participates in the twenty-seventh festival, and Robert Sunderman disappeared twenty-eight years earlier. This can be deduced from the information given about Jill's age: Bea was pregnant with her when Robert disappeared. Jeremy's progressive identification with Sunderman becomes explicit when he, for a moment, takes the place of the absent corpse by climbing into the empty coffin in Johnnie Backstrom's funeral parlour.

The absent corpse and the lost original are both variants of the image of the centreless circle – the figure which is all circumference or margin – on which Kroetsch observes: 'There is a paradoxical notion, which shows up in Beckett, that a circle can exist that has no center. All we will know is its circumference. Now existing on the circumference rather than in the center excites me. It is a way to resist entrapment, to resist endings and completion' (Neuman and Wilson 130). The image of going in circles without ever getting to the centre is, of course, a commonplace of being lost. Jeremy goes in circles and bullshits until, at one cathartic moment, he finds himself in the centre of a circle and understands the truth of 'going Indian.' This happens when he has made the mistake of winning the snowshoe race while looking like an Indian and after having lost his identity by running 'right out of himself' (90) and becoming a *pharmakos*, as he is beaten up by the white men. The real Indian, Daniel Beaver, knows, as he has shown by giving up a sure win in the dogsleigh race, that 'going Indian' means, as we learned from Cohen, knowing how to be a beautiful, that is willing, loser. Jeremy thus takes Daniel's place in the lions' den. And Daniel accurately diagnoses what happens to Jeremy: 'They kicked the shit out of you' (93).

In this moment of truth, Jeremy speaks a language which he remembers but does not understand. It is not bullshit any more but a language of origins, street talk from Little Italy, the place of his childhood: 'Va fa'nculo... Vatte fa' fot'. Va fa'nculo' (92). After the beating, Jeremy is given some of Beaver's old clothes and, more significantly, he is given the Indian's moccasins. (The importance of footwear alludes to the proverbial test of understanding otherness by walking in somebody's moccasins, but it also echoes Cohen's metonymic foot-magic.) His metamorphosis is complete and, in a reversal of Grey Owl's story, he is taken in by the Beavers. (His specular ego took beavers into his cottage and studied their habits.) It is while he is sleeping in the Indians' truck that Jeremy enters Mrs Beaver's dream and goes buffalo.

On the subject of metamorphosis, Robert Kroetsch offers this observation: 'I suppose one of the healing acts that we engage in is the transformational act – metamorphosis –, the way in which you have to move out of yourself into other possibilities ... keep it open ... re/dis/cover' (Neuman and Wilson 173). Jeremy's metamorphosis is achieved by his 'running out of himself' and 'going Indian' (being beaten up and putting on Daniel's clothes). The transformation is accomplished with the help of the Indians, who also heal the injuries he suffered in the beating. The equation between healing and metamorphosis, or rebirth, is evident earlier when Jill's healing hands 'created him into a new life' after his first fall.

The reversal of the relationship between winners and losers is also actualized in a series of animal transformations. When Jeremy first comes to Notikeewin, his cowboy guide takes him for an Indian and talks to him about trapping muskrats and, when he is beaten up, his victimizers turn into muskrats. The most interesting of the animal transformations, however, is an implicit one. In the snowshoe race, which leads to Jeremy's eventual metamorphosis, he is led to the fateful victory by another pied piper, a magpie. It is when he is just about to be beaten by the white men that Jeremy realizes the significance of the bird: 'The magpie looked like *you*, Madham, all dressed up in black and white. The old mad Adam of the original day. The first night, outside the garden. Kee-rist on a crutch. The grief-spinner, horned and horny in his nightmare hope, and even then, that first time, trying to recapture everything that was gone' (91–92). In this way, Jeremy reveals the role of Madham as it is implicit in his name. Jeremy's encounter with Madham's bird incarnation is not his first meeting with a magpie – the bird has appeared carved in ice on the back of the throne where Bea, the bear, judges the imaginary crimes of the citizens rounded up by fake Mounties. This coincidence points to a link between Madham and Bea which will turn out to be crucial to the narrative.

Unnaming

Robert Kroetsch has commented on the notion of character as 'an example of a convention that has gone dead' (Hancock 42), and, as may be expected, that death has entailed the demise of the proper name, which the narrator of *Gone Indian*, the 'mad Adam,' defines as 'that part of identity which is at once so totally real and so totally invented' (51). This double view of the name, which recalls my discussion of the specular identity, is at work in the novel. Jeremy's name is clearly tautological. His story is a jeremiad, or a tale of woe, and his last name is nothing but a repetition of his first: 'Jeremy' is synonymous with 'sadness.' He is given his name by an 'unre-membered father' (48) who, after performing the act of naming, disappears, never to be heard of again, except possibly via an unsigned postcard from Genoa indicating that he has performed a reversal of Columbus' quest, another search for a lost origin. A sailor from Little Italy who performs an act of obviously mistaken naming, he sets off to Columbus' birthplace. The mistake in Jeremy's name lies in the fact that his father, wanting him to become a professor, names him after Jeremy Bentham. Bentham, who figures as an intertextual presence in the novel, thus engenders Jeremy's name – taking the place of the father – and, in an ironically mythological manner, determining his sad fate. Jeremy is a truly preposterous novelistic phenom-enon, a no-name character; not one of his names belongs exclusively to him, and his existence as a separate identity is thus put into question.

Robert Kroetsch has pointed out that he associates the name Jeremy with Tristram. Like Jeremy, Tristram Shandy, the model hero of many postmodern writers, was improperly named, to the great chagrin of his father, whose belief in the power of names is purely mythological: 'His opinion, in this matter, was, That there was a strange kind of magick bias, which good or bad names, as he called them, irresistibly impressed upon our characters and conduct' (Sterne 43). Mr Shandy intends his son to be named Trismegistus after the Greek epithet of Thoth, the god of letters, measure, and wisdom, as well as the patron of alchemy whom we have encountered in *Trou de mémoire*, but a misunderstanding causes him to be christened Tristram and thus be condemned to a sad life. Like the novel *Tristram Shandy*, *Gone Indian* tells the reader a great many things, but in fact very little about what it purports to tell – the story of its hero. Jeremy/Tristram also echoes the legend of Tristan and Isolde, an intertext shared with *L'Elan d'Amérique*, as will become clear in the discussion of the relationships among Jeremy, Madham, and Bea.

Madham's name has already been revealed as a portmanteau word, and its connotations of madness are spelled out when Jeremy calls his professor a 'mad Adam,' an epithet that hints at his possible role as name-giver. It is also almost palindromic, a rare characteristic of proper names and one that reflects circularity (as in the case of Ama in *The New Ancestors*) or the confusion of ends and beginnings. Like their two locales – Edmonton and Binghamton – Madham's and Jeremy's names share an implicit set of suffixes: R. Mark Mad[*ness*]*ham* – Jeremy [Bent*ham*] Sad*ness*. Leaving 'Mark' to its marked unmarkedness discussed above, all the elements in the two closely related names have either a referent, whether real (Jeremy Bentham) or fictive (mad Adam), or a signified (madness, sadness), with the exception of Madham's mysterious first initial, which occurs in two instances in the text, but which is never explained.

The referential aspect of names in the novel becomes clear through an investigation of etymologies. 'I think etymologies are such beautiful things, such storymaking things,' says Robert Kroetsch (Neuman and Wilson 148). This is specifically revealing for the name of the intermediary between Sunderman and Jeremy, Roger Dorck. The *Oxford English Dictionary* informs us that 'dorck' is an old spelling for 'dark,' an appropriate epithet for a king of winter. Dorck thus completes the near synonymous triumvirate of madness, sadness, and darkness. 'Roger' is also, according to the OED, sometimes used antonomastically to refer to boys or young men. Kroetsch has a certain preference for this kind of generic name in other novels too, but the most obvious example in *Gone Indian* is Jill. Although there is no

Jack to complement her, Roger Dorck plays the role by falling down the hill and, both literally and figuratively, as king of the carnival, breaking his crown. 'He looks as if he was scalped,' as Jeremy says (29). 'Roger' is also, in certain systems of communication, an affirmation. This makes an oxymoron of his two names, the first one contradicting the negation of darkness. In this sense, the name reflects his state of being both alive and dead, like the zombies in *Trou de mémoire*. As the jolly Roger, he is also implicitly linked to Jeremy's wife, whose last name is Scull. This connection is related to the Bentham intertext; Carol is depicted as sitting at Madham's feet in the same position as Bentham's skull in his glass case in University College in London. Bentham, as 'his own icon' (51), is the model for the 'disguised as himself' pattern, as well as of the state of suspended animation – being in a state of *carence* or alterity, neither alive nor dead, or both at the same time. The relationship between Madham and Carol is, as so often in Kroetsch's male/female dichotomy, synecdochic: he is the mind to her skull.

Roger Dorck's name also contains a sexual connotation, one which the OED fails to mention. 'Roger' as a euphemism appears, for instance, in *The Secret Diary of William Byrd of Westover* (1709–12), where the writer informs us of the circumstances under which he 'rogers' his wife. As a verb, Roger is a most 'improper' name. The most interesting facet of his name, however, is revealed by the OED, when it informs us that a 'roger' is an obsolete synonym for 'port-manteau.' Considering the by-now established parodically 'mythological' logic of naming strategies in the novel, it is inevitable that Jeremy assumes Roger's identity when he inadvertently steals his suitcase, and that Roger, by the same token, lapses into a coma when his suitcase/identity is taken from him. It is significant that Jeremy, for a moment, forgets his own name when he discovers that the suitcase he is carrying is not his own. And he gets his identity back when Roger wakes up, and Jeremy's suitcase mysteriously appears under Dorck's hospital bed. The OED further tells us that a portmanteau 'opens like a book with hinges in the middle of the back.' Roger Dorck, as the intermediary between Robert Sunderman and Jeremy, occupies the middle of the plot, and he will prove to function much like a double mirror, reflecting both that which comes before and that which goes after him.

Like the ski-jumper who was forever left flying in the middle of the book, Roger remains suspended between the various protagonists, and it is when he finally accomplishes his fall, by returning to the land of the living, that he precipitates the end of the story and the possible fulfilment of Jeremy's quest. If Madham's name is a portmanteau word Roger's *is* a suitcase, and the equation between name and identity is emphasized when Madham tells

Jill, who has found Jeremy's lost luggage in Dorck's office: 'Out of his suitcase you are creating *him*' (20). Roger's and Jeremy's identical suitcases are described as 'Samsonite two-suiter[s]' (20). The two 'suitors' are Samsons, and images of scalping, as opposed to crowning, abound in the text. The academics in the novel, the presumed possessors of the 'balding truth' (35), are the almost bald Madham and Chairman Balding, whose job interview is the ostensible goal of Jeremy's trip. (The chairman of the English department at the University of Alberta at the time was George Baldwin.) But the fickleness of truth has already been pointed out by the first guide, who removes his wig – in yet another image of scalping. Jeremy's long braids contribute to his being mistaken for an Indian. His hair effectively hides the truth, and the opposition between long hair and bald scalps parallels that between bulls and oxen. Bea and Jill together become the Delilahs of both Jeremy and Dorck. (Although Jeremy is never scalped, he gives away the winter queen crown to Jill.) When Jeremy has seen the truth and 'gone Indian,' he dreams the scalping of Edmonton and the return of the buffalo.

The first participant in the repetitious chain of falls, the absent corpse and lost centre of the diegetic circle, Robert Sunderman, remains an enigma. At one point Madham defines the influence of the northern prairies on human definition as 'the diffusion of personality into a complex of possibilities rather than a concluded self' (152). It is this sundering of the self that is reflected in Robert's last name, and he would consequently be a sundered man, a sundering man, or both. Sunderman's first name is one of the few 'proper' names in the book: it does not appear in the OED, and it would appear to be the only name that does not contain any clues to the rebus but seems perfectly neutral. It has, however, already been seen, on the cover of the book, to be that of the author, and it also happens to share the first, mysterious initial with Madham, who, through the address and SUNY connection, is clearly a double of Robert Kroetsch. These coincidences indicate that the professor and Sunderman have more in common than meets the unsuspecting reader's eye. A mad Adam or un-namer would indeed be a sunderer of identity. The narrative repetitions have already been mentioned: Robert Sunderman disappears, leaving Dorck to take his place with Bea. Twenty-eight years later, Dorck leaps into amnesia, leaving Jeremy to take his place with Bea, while he eventually takes Jeremy's place at Jill's side. In the meantime, Madham has an affair with Jeremy's wife. Surprisingly well-informed, Madham points out that Jill and Carol are the same age. The two women are complementary in many ways: one is blond and cool as ice, the other dark and sensuous as fire. The story is beginning to look like a ring-dance (for which the OED gives us 'carol' as a synonym), but there is an incongruity in the seemingly neat circle. There are four men, including Sunderman, but only three women.

Madham, fascinated by the phenomenon of 'arctic hysteria' brought on by the darkness of the prairie winter, on one occasion quotes Shackleton's delusion (124). The explorer apparently believed that his expedition consisted of one person more than could be counted. Shackleton's mistake will turn out to contain an important clue to the reading of the novel when put together with Jeremy Bentham's comments on the trickery of word-magic, which may seem like a rebuttal to Mr Shandy:

> Words – viz. words employed to serve as names – being the only instruments by which, in the absence of the *things*, viz. the *substances* themselves, the ideas of them can be presented to the mind; hence, wheresoever a word is seen, which, to appearance, is employed in the character of a *name*, a natural and abundantly extensive consequence is a propensity and disposition to suppose the existence, the real existence, of a correspondent object – of a correspondent thing, of the thing of which it is the name, of a thing to which it ministers in the character of a name.
>
> Yielded to without a sufficiently attentive caution, this disposition is a frequent source of confusion – of temporary confusion and perplexity; and not only so, but even of permanent error. (Bentham, quoted in Ogden xxxxv)

What Bentham warns against here is exactly the stubborn principle of unique reference that Kroetsch plays with in his text. There is, in fact, one name left over in the diegetic equation, which would only be complete and in keeping with the circular form of the story if Jeremy and Madham changed places and wives; that is, if the professor is Bea's husband and, consequently, Jill's father. If this were the case, Jeremy would also act out the Tristan fate inherent in his name by falling in love with 'king' Mark's wife.[7] Taking Bea's place with Madham, Carol turns out to be, like the beauty queens at the carnival, a copy of a lost original. (It is not coincidental that she works in the Xerox room.)

A number of narrative clues also confirm that Madham is Sunderman's alias.[8] For instance, the professor's reconstruction of Jeremy's first visit to Worlds End in chapter 15 is particularly revealing. His description of the Sunderman home, which he has 'come to love ... as well as if it were [his] own' (154), shows his familiarity with it. Where Jeremy sees only snow-covered stubble, Madham knows that there are 'wheatfields' (31). It is significant, considering the identification of Madham as a 'mad Adam outside the garden,' that the Sunderman house is described as a garden of Eden.

There is also a curious temporal lag between Madham's and Jeremy's respective identification of certain characters, notably Bea and Robert. All through the text, Madham seems to be privy to more information than Jeremy, who supposedly tells the story. At times, Madham interprets Bea's thoughts and motives rather inexplicably, as, for instance, when she first invites Jeremy into her bedroom: 'In fact she was no doubt a little bit astonished at her own behavior, experiencing the lightest regret, and quite possibly already bored' (32). He also quotes Jeremy's comment about Bea being 'the woman you should have married' (30). A number of other minor indices include the hockey subtext referring to the young Sunderman's prospects of playing with the New York Rangers. According to Bea, 'He had the perfect body' (33). Madham reveals that he too played hockey in his youth, and his vanity leads him to quote Jeremy's comment on Carol's attraction to his 'squash-player's perfect figure' (60). Sunderman disappeared in the late fall; Madham tells us he rode the train east 'through a hard winter' (153). As Jeremy gets more involved with the Sunderman women, Madham gets increasingly lost in his own thoughts: 'The forest of my own intent is inhabited by strange creatures, surely. The figure of Roger Dorck for one comes to haunt me. He was a dedicated man who spent his life caring for the family of a drowned friend. I cannot for a moment accept the notion that his 'accident' was motivated by disappointment in love. Accident is part of our daily lives; if not, then all of modern physics is madness. Are not explanations themselves assigned almost at random?' (51). Here it is clear that Madham knows, or suspects, more than Jeremy does about the relationships among the various characters involved in Jeremy's story. The caution against the authority of explanations conceals another warning to the reader concerning the truth of the story and forms part of Madham's self-conscious undermining of the critical endeavour in general.

As Madham takes over as sole narrator towards the end of the novel, he begins to address his correspondent as 'Jill' rather than 'Miss Sunderman' and becomes more obscure and reflective as his obsession with the Sunderman mystery grows: 'It would surely seem impossible that anyone might drown in all that ice and snow. God knows, I shall never forget it. And yet, Robert Sunderman went through the ice. Or knocked a hole in the ice and disappeared ... No, it is just possible. A night in late fall, a thin coat of snow, the ice deserted, darkness ... his child-bride pregnant, the boy-husband alone ...' (155). What exactly is it that Madham will never forget? If we are told the truth about the professor's age, he would have been nineteen at the time of the 'boy-husband's' disappearance. The clue to Madham's involvement in Jeremy's story might be hidden in the latter's passing comment: 'A peculiar experience of time: to encounter, after the act, the thought that was father to the act' (60). It is, after all, Madham who sends Jeremy to Edmonton to look for a job he probably does not have much chance of securing, and it is Madham who points out – sweating as he does so – that the only problem Jeremy has ever taken seriously is the mystery of Grey Owl, 'the man ... who died into a new life' (62). It seems as if Jeremy, in reliving Madham's youth in reverse, answers the professor's questions about his own motives. The complexities of Madham's discourse can then be explained by his dual purpose. On the one hand, he wants to convince Jill of Jeremy's death because, in so doing, he will also implicitly convince her of her father's, of which Jeremy's is nothing but a repetition. In this way he will foreclose any possible recriminations. On the other hand, he seems to feel a need to come to terms with his own guilt. It is most probably to himself he refers when he asks: 'Is it not odd, this impulse in the erring man: this need to divulge, to confess?' (95). The letter to Jill can thus be read either as a defence speech or as a confession; much like Magnant's writing in *Trou de mémoire* this text begins as an alibi, but, as in the earlier case, it ends up uncovering the crime it sets out to cover.

In retrospect, Madham's obscure comment in the prologue that the story will show him 'to be, so to speak, unfallen' (3) becomes clear. He can say, 'I am my own man' (3), because he has not fallen through the ice and drowned but has become the mad Adam of his own creation. If we accept the Grey Owl paradigm as the matrix of the narrative repetitions, then we cannot accept Madham's self-interested contention that Jeremy and Bea are dead. When we last hear of them through Madham, they are falling but unfallen. His comment, 'I made the discreet phonecall' (6) – presumably to arrange Jeremy's job interview – becomes ambiguous. It could refer to the one Bea claims she received from Robert after his disappearance or to the mysterious call that provokes Bea and Jeremy's flight.

In her wisdom, confirmed in her performance as a judge, Bea, the bear, is a Minerva figure. Minerva's owl returns in Sunderman's preposterously named father, Sonny; in Madham, Dorck, and Jeremy, who are all on one occasion metaphorically described as owls – thus forming links both to Bea and Grey Owl. As already noted, the owl has been turned into a magpie on Bea's throne in order to emphasize the link to Madham. A further connection between the two is established implicitly through another mythical intertext centring on Wodin, the Nordic god of darkness, who thus also recalls Dorck. Wodin occasionally transforms himself into a bird. Jeremy sometimes addresses Madham in his role as member of the 'Friday Night Mead Sippers' (43, 88), who meet at 'Ye Olde Valhalla Bar and Grill' (89). It is significant that Jeremy and Bea approach their Valhalla on the undertaker's snowmobile which, according to Madham, is of the non-existent brand 'Sleipnir' (137), named after Wodin's horse.

Because Bea is the possessor of wisdom and truth, the question 'What is truth?' becomes 'How do you woo a bear?' (74). The impossibility of the truth quest is implied in Daniel Beaver's mutilated hand: 'I was setting a bear trap. The trap closed' (99). In spite of his constant grip exercises, Jeremy will never be able really to grasp the 'bear.' As the bull and the bear, Jeremy and Bea will, at least in stock-market terms, cancel each other out.[9] Together they constitute an oxymoron in the same vein as Roger Dorck: they can neither rise nor fall, but are doomed to stay suspended, representing the balance which Kroetsch, in a way similar to Cohen, sees as a typical Canadian temptation (Neuman and Wilson 123–4).

When Jeremy 'goes Indian' in the dream he steals from Mrs Beaver, Poundmaker changes his name to 'Has-Two-Chances' (106), a mythological epithet that clearly indicates that Jeremy indeed dies into a new life and that initiates him into Cohen's pantheon of second chancers, which is beginning to appear as the collective Canadian specular identity. In the dream, his name used to be '*A*ntelope *S*tanding *S*till' (105), acronymically confirming Madham's view of Jeremy as a 'buffalo's ass.' The role played by acronyms in the text is best illustrated in the case of the '*E*nglish *G*raduate *O*rganization' (47), a comment on the pomposity and self-aggrandizement of academia. The affinity between Jill and Jeremy is also reflected through their common initials. Sharing a father – Jill's biological one being Jeremy's spiritual one – they are soul siblings.

This analysis of the names in the novel has shown that the strategies behind their formation are incompatible with 'proper' naming as defined in chapter 1: synonymy, antinomy, and tautology all involve a meta-level of language. Rather than identifying their bearers, the names un-identify or dissolve their separate identities into 'a complex of possibilities.' The names all perform important functions in the rebus, whose scaffolding is constituted by their interrelationships. Robert (Kroetsch?) is the only 'character' in the book who has a proper name and an existence outside the rebus. His Bea(trice), who has entered the text both surreptitiously, via Virgil, and via the implicit Dantesque quality of the Orphic descent, constitutes an imperative: Be a Sunder-man. By subverting the proper function of names as unique and identifying, the mad Adam narrator/author has managed to undermine both the notion of character and that of naming in a signifying structure that reflects the author's own view of the problem of identity. Shirley Neuman at one point tells Robert Kroetsch: 'Your concept of character would certainly contradict the more naive notions of identity, those that say that the self is individual, autonomous, stable. When characters are grammatical elements in the story, they are in fact defined by their relationship to the rest of the "sentence," they're defined by the syntax of the story' (Neuman and Wilson 191). Jeremy's role as victim – *pharmakos* – originates in childhood, when his friends 'name' him the Indian in their cruel games and, consequently, lay the foundations for his later fate. It is not a coincidence that he is introduced to Grey Owl by his neighbour, the tailor: the important identities in the novel are, so to speak, tailor-made to suit their wearers. As we have seen, the many errors in identifying the characters are due to mistaking the clothes for the person or the suitcase for the carrier – in other words, mistaking the surface for the essence. But unlike the traditional comedy of errors, here it is the surface that eventually creates the essence; a misreading of the surface creates a mistaken essence. Ungrounded and freed from any pre-existing meaning, the signifier creates its signified. The ice on the river or on Elkhart pond metaphorically represents the bar dividing the sign into its two components.

The insistence on surfaces, coinciding with the metamorphic potential of the word is, indeed, reminiscent of the movement seen in *Beautiful Losers*, but I would argue that there is a crucial difference. Kroetsch's signifier follows Cohen's recipe for sainthood, riding the ice like the escaped ski in search of balance rather than names, but where Cohen mystically operates the conjunction of surface and essence, by way of the paradoxically lateral transcendence brought about by the 'prayer book,' Kroetsch's metamorphosis prevents the signifier from ever reaching the movement of conjunction. The liquidity or flux that is the element of conjunction is here frozen into the ice on Elkhart pond. The lateral, or sliding, movement that dominates both the diegesis and the form, with its *mise en abyme* in the curling game, shows that nothing happens under the ice; nobody drowns or transcends or ever hits the 'bull's ass.' Unlike Tay John, his mysterious predecessor, neither Sunderman nor any of his followers disappears into the ground in Kroetsch's universe.

Throughout, the ice is described in terms of healing. As exemplified in Jeremy's transformation into 'a pillar of ice,' it makes possible the healing metamorphosis which is the opposite of the proper name. In Kroetsch's own words, 'At one time I considered it the task of the Canadian writer to give names to his experience, to be the namer. I now suspect that, on the contrary, it is his task to un-name' ('Unhiding the Hidden' 43). *Gone Indian* may be Kroetsch's answer to Howard O'Hagan's contention that 'The un-named ... is the darkness unveiled' (*Tay John* 80) but, as in *Beautiful Losers*, whatever unveiling is attempted reveals no essence, only changing shapes. In the syntax established by the rebus, this is tantamount to keeping all movement (of action/signification) above the ice/bar, even if the meta-morphic divison of the sign is also realized on the level of metaphor. The sliding of signification between signifiers recalls Lacan's definition of me-tonymy, to which I will return later, and which is, in fact, close to my, and Kroetsch's, view of metamorphosis. Metonymy/metamorphosis cures (one is tempted to say in this case 'puts ice on') the wound or symptom of metaphor; it heals any breach in the surface.

The metamorphic structures of signification indicate that *Gone Indian* occupies a position far removed from myth on the spectrum of territoriality. Although it is commonplace to point out that Kroetsch is a demythologizer, the extent of this project is not generally recognized. Unnaming, or sun-dering identity, is as far removed from myth as one can come without lapsing into silence. It is perhaps significant that, in several instances in the novel, a name is substituted by a dash, parodying the convention of the unspeakable, as when the customs officer asks Jeremy: 'Then you are not ____' (7). The dash also appears in connection with the 'bull's ass,' when Jeremy suggests that Madham 'stick [his] unwritten dissertation ____' (19). But while Kroetsch situates truth in the same place as does Cohen, the desired emptiness does not have the same significance. There is nothing to receive in *Gone Indian*: no sainthood, no transcendence.

The unnaming is achieved, on the one hand, by covertly debunking the myth of identity in the diegesis and, on the other, by using names 'im-properly,' as signs which gain significance only through their interrelation-ships, and which function on the same level as other marked signs in the text: puns, metaphors, intertexts, etc. *Gone Indian* is an example of the novel as 'godgame' (Neuman and Wilson 68), where Jeremy is the pawn and Madham the game-playing trickster-god. The figure of the pied piper, whose intertextual origin is underscored in the name of the site of Bea's throne, 'Fort Duhamel' (68), is a magus. Fort Duhamel is close to the place where the first guide in the chain of falls or leaps, Robert Sunderman, was last seen. Madham/Sunderman is the magus and pied piper, who uses Jeremy as his 'tool' (17) in his attempt to rediscover his own youthful motivations and the truth behind his dying into a new life. Like 'I' in *Beautiful Losers* and not unlike Claire in *L'Elan d'Amérique*, Jeremy is unwittingly acting in a drama over which he has no control. His role is foreshadowed when Jill, on the occasion of their first meeting, asks him: 'Which – Whom do you represent?' (22). Anticipating the protagonist of Kroetsch's latest novel, *Alibi* (1984), Jeremy is an agent who does not become free until he breaks out of the magic circle drawn by the magus. 'It's all fixed' (120), in the same way as the beauty contest, but the principal participants do not know how or by whom. That Jeremy is playing Madham's role becomes obvious when Sonny Sunderman calls him 'you dumb asshole' (120), an epithet revealing Jeremy's growing, although unwitting, identification with his 'dumb' professor. In the reading game, however, it is the reader who is the pawn and the author the trickster, a role Kroetsch, in fact, admits to perhaps having played too well: 'I almost feel I was unfair to the reader in *Gone Indian*' (Neuman and Wilson 176).

As shown in my discussion in chapter 1, any text exhibiting a marked preference for laterality and horizontal patterns of signification will likely be qualified as metonymic. Kroetsch, like his postmodernist colleagues, is intensely sceptical of metaphor and advocates a movement toward metonymy. His definition of the trope is, as I indicated above, Lacanian, and what he defines as metonymic is what I prefer to see as a metamorphic uprooting and proliferation of the signifier. Metonymy, in the strict rhetorical sense does, however, also play an important role in the text, from the traditional substitution of the crown and the throne for the king or queen, to the synecdochic relationship between men and women. One could also claim that many puns used in the text are metonymic in nature. Thus, for instance, the magpie as 'magus + pied piper' and Madham as 'mad Adam' are portmanteau words – a kind of linguistic actualization of a synecdoche *in presentia*, comprising both container and contained. Roger Dorck would, in this sense, be the ultimate metonymic 'character,' and his relationship to his two pendants, sadness and madness, is equally metonymic. The author remarks: 'I have learned a little bit more clearly that to go from metaphor to metonymy is to go from the temptation of the single to the allure of multiplicity. Instead of the temptations of "origin" we have genealogies that multiply our connections into the past, into the world' (Neuman and Wilson 117).

Kroetsch further reveals that, from having considered Genesis as the most interesting myth, he has come to be fascinated by Babel, 'one of the greatest things that has happened to mankind' (Neuman and Wilson 116), and he sees a connection between this interest in the proliferation of language and the movement towards metonymy. If metonymy equals multiplicity, then it is clearly the appropriate trope for the 'complex of possibilities' that replaces identity on the prairies. Kroetsch also sees a link between metonymy and the possibility of renaming and translation – in the sense of the opposite of 'proper' naming (Neuman and Wilson 18). Renaming is thus also, by definition, the very opposite of mythologizing. As I have indicated, Kroetsch's use of myth is highly parodic: in the same way that he rewrote the *Odyssey* in *The Studhorse Man*, he parodies the *Aeneid* in *Gone Indian*.

It is perhaps significant that Kroetsch likens the prairies to a labyrinth: 'They have been mapped like grids, all those roads, but you can get lost in them so easily' (Neuman and Wilson 80). Getting lost (and confusing beginnings and endings) is to find oneself in a labyrinth, where the point of entry coincides with the point of exit, forever going around the invisible centre occupied by the monster/magus who operates the transformations that take place while you are in the maze. The paradox inherent in the coexistence of the perceived openness and multiplicity of the metonymic strategies and the hermeticism and closure of the rebus, or labyrinth, is at the core of the postmodern dilemma.

In the final analysis, the process of unnaming is reflected in the motif of 'going Indian': '*To go Indian*: an ambiguous phrase: to become released or wild in the carnival sense' (Neuman and Wilson 36). The novel shows, however, that all identity, including the carnivalesque dying into a new life, is an alias. To 'go Indian' is to create one's 'self,' which is never static and certain, by telling one's story. Madham's admission at the end of the text that he has been 'Indian enough' (124) is an implicit confession that the story he has told (about 'going Indian') is his own. 'Going Indian' is thus a false story of creation, a pseudo-genesis which is preposterously apocalyptic in nature: 'A trumpet sounded. Right behind me. I nearly shit myself right there' (112). The trumpet of doom triggers Jeremy's bullshitting, and fear rather than freedom is at the origin of story. *Gone Indian* in many ways anticipates Kroetsch's most recent novel, where language becomes an *Alibi* – the cover-up that Aquin's narrator would like it to be – something that is always elsewhere, rather than 'where the action is.'

The opposition between the United States and Canada, depicted thematically in *L'Elan d'Amérique* as that between capital and nature, is in *Gone Indian* a formal, as well as ontological, distinction between closure and openness, between false identity and 'a complex of possibilities.' The rape of the land, which has been explicit as a metaphor of colonization in all of the novels discussed earlier, is here reversed when Jeremy, in Mrs Beaver's dream, conjures up the lost 'original' and the vengeful return of the buffalo and the Indians to rape and torture the people of Edmonton. In Langevin's novel, the rape, on the allegorical level, reflects the loss of a specific cultural source, while on the psychological level it constitutes the origin of Claire's loss of identity. Quite contrary to the basic assumptions about the status of self and identity in Kroetsch's text, Claire's identity loss is a consequence of the rape; it is both psychologically and symbolically realized. While the lost 'origine/orignal' is associated with a specific culture, Kroetsch's version of it reflects an ontological assumption that gives rise to a particular aesthetics.

Syllepsis

Gone Indian is, in many ways, like *L'Elan d'Amérique*, an echo chamber resonating with historical, mythical, and literary intertexts. The difference between Langevin's and Kroetsch's uses of these echoes lies primarily in the parodic intent of the latter and his constant subversion of referential expectations. In Langevin's case, the authorial strategies work to focus the many strands of the text and project them centrifugally through a metaphoric prism, as it were, onto a political and historical reality. In *Gone Indian*, on the other hand, the narration reduces the story by flattening the text and insisting on lateral, intratextual patterns of signification. The split in Kroetsch's text is not between story and commentary, as many critics would have it, but rather between narrative and narration, with the intricacies of the latter contradicting the former's insistence on character and identity. Quite contrary to the practice in *L'Elan d'Amérique*, puns and names are here used to undermine the authority of the signified and to assert the play of the signifier in a movement of deterritorialization. While Kroetsch does not reject metaphor outright, his subversive use of it (as of naming and myth) gives new meaning to the common view that the Canadian novel is characterized by horizontality, as opposed to the verticality of its Québécois counterpart.

Quite unlike Kroetsch, Langevin sees the Babelian proliferation of language as a threat to the indigenous culture of Quebec and a reterritorialization of its language as the necessary prerequisite to the retrieval of the lost identity. While in Kroetsch's text language is deterritorialized, the signifier 'liberated' from its signified, Langevin's novel depicts the thematic deterritorialization of its characters through a highly territorial language which confirms, by its use of names and metaphors as well as its lyricism, the fundamental unity of the sign. Language transcends the psychological and political constraints of the referential territory of the text, and the double-layered diegesis is unified through the central symbols and the polysemic play on *élan* and *buck*. Governed by the signified, the wordplay in *L'Elan d'Amérique* is primarily metaphoric, while the play of the signifier in *Gone Indian* can be described as sylleptic.

As I have mentioned in passing, syllepsis is a term currently subject to a certain confusion of definition. Derrida, following Dumarsais, uses the term to describe the coexistence in one word or expression of two conflicting meanings, leading to an undecidability of interpretation. It is, in this sense, the figure of the *coincidentia oppositorum* ('*La Pharmacie de Platon*' 249). In my conclusion to chapter 3, however, I claimed that where there is a conjunction of opposites, there is no longer any ambiguity or undecidability. The definition of syllepsis which I am using here is rather that of the *Princeton Encyclopedia of Poetry and Poetics*, according to which it implies the syntagmatic actualization of the different meanings of a word: 'The use of any part of speech comparably related to two other words or phrases, correctly with respect to each taken separately, as to both syntax and meaning, but in different ways, so as to produce a witty effect.' The example commonly given of this figure is from *The Rape of the Lock*: 'Whether the nymph shall ... / Or stain her honor or her new brocade.' The figure is often – mistakenly, according to the *Princeton Encyclopedia* – called 'zeugma.'[10] I prefer to keep the term syllepsis, bearing in mind the distinction between the Princeton definition and that of Dumarsais and Derrida. In this strict sense, then, my view of syllepsis as the opposite of the oxymoron is justified: rather than the conjunction of opposites, it reflects an explicit foregrounding of polysemy and disjunction. The story of *Gone Indian* could, in fact, be paraphrased in a few sylleptic statements: Jeremy goes in circles and finally Indian; falls down and in love; shits himself and a lot of bull; and in the end grasps doorknobs better than the truth.

Because it is located primarily in the verb, syllepsis is, much more clearly than metonymy, realized syntactically, or laterally, in a way opposed to the paradigmatic resonances of the noun-centred metaphors in *L'Elan d'Amérique*. On the one hand, Kroetsch strips figurative expressions of their metaphoric meaning, literalizing them in a manner similar to that described in connection with Kafka and the fantastic. But, on the other hand, he reinscribes them in a new hermetic code constituted in rebus-like fashion within the text. Thus, for instance, 'bullshit,' a common expression for 'tell stories' or 'lie,' is literalized (and nominalized) into something like 'product of the bull's ass.' 'Bull's ass' is turned simultaneously into a metaphor for 'locus of truth' and an alias for Jeremy. Consequently, the generating term of the chain – 'to bullshit' – is turned into its opposite – 'to tell the truth' – and implicitly equated with 'to give Jeremy his identity.' Thus, lying becomes telling the truth, and telling lies becomes identifying, in what amounts to the narrative equivalent of the unnaming and renaming seen in the proper names. But, unlike in *Trou de mémoire*, the paradox is not resolved, and it remains an ironic commentary on the deceptiveness of language, which always says something other than it claims. Both Aquin and Kroetsch are engaged in quests that are fundamentally ontological, but where the former reaches some kind of truth in the mystery of religion, the latter refuses any transcendence, as hermetic signification takes over from meaning, or even reference, and the text creates its own semiotic system. The ice/bar prevents both the liquid *coincidentia oppositorum* and any kind of transcendence; writing can never be the truth but remains an *Alibi*.

CHAPTER SEVEN

Retracing the Map

Looking back over the territory covered, dis-covered, or re-covered through the prism of territoriality, a new configuration takes shape, as the constellation of texts based on thematic and chronological affinity reveals a hidden figure in the ground. Thematic similarity gives way to formal dissimilarity and, as in an anamorphosis, a second image appears. In all of the novels we have witnessed how the quest for identity – whether Canadian or Québécois – has turned into its apparent opposite. In *Beautiful Losers* the metamorphic crisis led through a loss of self which is not so much a dissolution as a conjunction, a fusion of identity and difference, leading in the end to the resurrection of the author. In *The New Ancestors* and *Gone Indian* we saw the dissolution of identity reflected in metamorphic, disjunctive strategies, which in the first case seemed to end in entropic dissemination, in the latter in the – rebus-like – reinscription of the author. In *Trou de mémoire* the author is resurrected, much as in Cohen's text, through the mysterious workings of the Holy Ghost, while in *L'Elan d'Amérique* the thematic transparency of identity is redeemed through its territorial grounding in the vernacular.

While *Beautiful Losers* occupies a space encompassing 'all the polarities,' the four texts discussed in chapters 3 to 6 in themselves seem to constitute a labyrinth where, as in the last novel, the point of entry coincides with the point of exit. The parallels between *Trou de mémoire* and *Gone Indian* can be attributed to the isomorphism between their respective structuring principles, a parallelism not overlooked by Baltrusaitis, who identifies anamorphosis as 'un rébus, un monstre, un prodige' (5). Both figures – the anamorphosis and the rebus – are related to the postmodern labyrinth and are indices of intentionality: we have seen how they constitute the author's 'signature.' As the labyrinth is designed so as to offer only one way out, so the anamorphosis can only be perceived from one angle, determined by its creator, and the decoding of the rebus must follow the same steps as its encoding. In both cases the reader is manipulated into a specific position, although the strategies used are different: *Trou de mémoire* sends the reader outside the text in search of the clues necessary to construct the prism through which the concealed textual pattern can be restored, whereas in *Gone Indian*, as in *Beautiful Losers*, the referential movement is undercut, and the key to the rebus is hidden within the text. While in Aquin's novel the congruity between form and content – the isomorphism of anamorphosis and transubstantiation – may be found without recourse to the intertext, the restoration of the hidden figure remains incomplete without the discovery of the affinity between the fictive narrator and his historical and anagrammatical alter ego, Père Maignan. Thus, while the anamorphic technique in both Cohen's and Aquin's texts is linked to the paradigm of transubstantiation, the former is clearly more hermetic.

The opposition between the directions of the semiosis in *Trou de mémoire* and *Gone Indian* can be seen most clearly in the naming strategies. In both cases, names are highly charged with meaning and in some way 'improper.' But while in *Trou de mémoire* the names gain their significance in the reference, those of *Gone Indian* create their signification inside the text, with the exception of some cases of etymological play which may remain obscure without recourse to the OED, a highly improper source for names. Although 'Ruskin' bears no relation to 'Maignan' outside Aquin's text, the *intra*textual relationship between the Ruskins and Magnant can only be fully appreciated through an investigation of their individual *inter*textual connotations. The significance of the fictional names in Aquin's novel is thus ultimately found in the intertext. The fact that two names refer to the same person explicitly undermines the conventional principles of individuation in both novels (Magnant is synonymous with Mullahy, and Madham with Sunderman). The violation of the rule of unique reference is more radical in *Gone Indian*, however, because the text appears – to a greater extent than its counterpart – to conform to the novelistic convention which stipulates that the referent of the proper name be constituted within the text. And, in contrast to the apparent simplicity of *Gone Indian*, the editorial commentary in *Trou de mémoire* alerts the reader to the possible complexities of individuation and naming. In *Beautiful Losers* names play a much less important role; the 'characters' are clearly presented as positions rather than identities from the outset, and the few names that appear are motivated either allegorically or according to the rebus principle – Mary is the mother/nurse (her last name, Voolnd, remains a mystery except as possibly anagrammatically related to her charge of the V.D. loon, F.); Edith may constitute a self-destructive, auto-erotic command to be consumed – eat it – (and may possibly have some relation to a Greek pronunciation of Isis).

The theme of metamorphosis which is present in all of these three texts is represented by two symbols that would seem fundamentally opposed: the mystery of transubstantiation and the carnival. *Trou de mémoire* and *Beautiful Losers* operate a territorializing conjunction of opposites, reflected in metaphoric and linguistic structures and epitomized in the oxymoron which, I have argued, works in such a way as to transcend the more visible strategies of disjunction in these texts. *Gone Indian*, on the other hand, works in an opposite direction, performing a deterritorialization through sylleptic strategies that reveal the essentially disjunctive properties of language. The dissolution/sundering of identity ends in both of these Canadian novels with the inscription of the author's presence, but the irony of Kroetsch's 'Robert,' posturing as a mad Adam, is the opposite of Cohen's (and Aquin's) mystical assumption of the alias of the Holy Ghost.

The secret of the *mysterium coniunctionis* which rules Aquin's text is revealed in the *Tabula Smaragdina* attributed to Hermes Trismegistus who, as the patron of alchemists, is the ancestor of Magnant and his 'vert parchemin.' Hermes is the Greek counterpart of the Egyptian god Thoth who gave the *pharmakon* of writing to humanity. The legend reports that, when presented with Thoth's invention, Ra – the sun-god and creator – predicted that it would be a poison rather than a cure to memory. To Magnant/Aquin writing is a true *pharmakon*: it kills and heals, covers and dis-covers at the same time. The narrator, whose affinity with his creator has been established, identifies with the sun. In a clearly mythological fashion, there is no distinction between the creator (Ra/Ammon/Aquin) and the scribe (Thoth/Hermes/Magnant); creation and writing are indistinguishable. To Aquin, as to Cohen, the *pharmakon* is embodied in the woman, who thus becomes the sacrificial victim, the scapegoat on whose necessary sacrifice the restoration of order depends, a disturbingly common phenomenon, as Patricia Smart has shown in *Ecrire dans la maison du père*. Isis may be the equivalent of Thoth in *Beautiful Losers*; she is sometimes referred to as the inventor of writing as well as the healer.

In the wintry north of *Gone Indian* the sun is rather conspicuously absent. By way of his relationship with Tristram Shandy, Jeremy Sadness is, we will recall, distantly related to Trismegistus, a fact that further underscores the misnaming (Jeremy cannot write). His own deity is the 'great god Tit' (45). The name of the god, whom we may presume to be a goddess, perhaps symbolized by Bea (forerunner of the more mythologically named 'Tiddy' in *What the Crow Said*), is foregrounded through Madham's repetition of it near the end of the novel (154). As the silent scribe and the presumed bearer of professorial wisdom, Madham is a Thoth-figure. Hermes is also the messenger, and we have seen how Madham uses Jeremy as his 'tool' to convey a coded message to Bea and Jill, his wife and daughter. What Jeremy finds in fleeing Thoth/Madham – the scribe and liar – is Tit/Bea – the 'bear'er of truth.

According to Derrida, the epithet of the sun-god, 'Ammon,' means 'le caché.' Robert Kroetsch's artistic project is, as his short but important 1974 essay indicates, to 'unhide the hidden,' a project not unlike Cohen's quest to lift the veil of Isis. What is concealed behind the word in both novels, however, is not truth but rather the magus/author – whether as a serious Holy Ghost or an ironic mad Adam – playing with the reader. The sylleptic structures of Kroetsch's text reveal the deception inherent in any creation based on language. The view of writing as alibi is implied in both Aquin's and Kroetsch's novels: as Madham's story is a defence speech, to cover an old mistake, so Magnant's writing is an attempt to cover his crime. But while Aquin's presumed covering of his murder becomes an un-covering of a corpse and a re-covering of memory, thus turning what is conceived as an alibi into a revelation of truth, Kroetsch's dis-covery reveals nothing but the capacity of language to be elsewhere. It could be argued that a kind of paradoxical conjunction of opposites occurs in Kroetsch's novel, insofar as Madham, in lying about Jeremy, tells the truth about himself and vice versa (Jeremy by 'bull-shitting' inadvertently reveals the truth about Madham/Sunderman). The parodic mode of the text, however, and the fact that the two narrators always reveal something other than what they claim to talk about, emphasizes the non-coincidence of language with its presumed meaning.

Derrida's contention that Thoth is the god of the *coincidentia oppositorum* and thus, in his definition, of syllepsis, highlights the opposition between his definition of the trope and mine. Considering the separation between creation and writing implicit in the legend of Ra and Thoth and my definition of syllepsis as disjunction, as opposed to (oxymoronic) conjunction, it is preferable to consider him as the god of the former.

The two novels occupying the middle ground in my textual corpus – *The New Ancestors* and *L'Elan d'Amérique* – would also seem to share certain generic features, which reveal their affinity with the *nouveau roman*. The most obvious example of this influence is found in the 'Fifth City' section in Godfrey's text. The novel as a whole straddles several generic territories, however, and the more conventional narrative strategies in the other sections to some extent undercut the effect of the radical experimentation here. There are fewer formal similarities between Ama's interior monologue, for instance, and 'In the Fifth City' than between the former and Claire's stream-of-consciousness in *L'Elan d'Amérique*. And both Ama's and Claire's narratives have more in common with the modernism of a Virginia Woolf than with the *nouveaux romanciers*. Unlike the latter, Langevin does not refute the power of language to represent reality, but the world he describes, both internal and external to the characters, pre-exists his description. Although Langevin's style has been likened to that of Claude Simon, his use of metaphor differs significantly from that of the French writer. To Simon, metaphor always implies a 'comme,' which is a sign of the individual's being 'hors de soi' (*Nouveau roman: hier, aujourd'hui* 82–3). Metaphor is in this view a symptom of alterity. In Langevin's text, however, it performs a territorializing function, aiming at identity rather than difference: it is through metaphor that the coincidence of self and identity – whether solid or transparent – is accomplished.

A mythological type of naming is at work in all the novels but differs according to the degree of ironic intent which, at the extreme, reverses the mythological endeavour. In *L'Elan d'Amérique* it can be argued that certain of the names are stereotypical (the Marias and Hercule, for instance), but the only potentially parodic name is Peabody. *The New Ancestors*, on the other hand, clearly parodies the equation between nomination and accusation which is so central to Langevin's text. Michael seems indeed to be more of a 'Bumdinger' than a Burdener/*pharmakos*: his sacrifice does not lead to any restoration of order. The most obvious inversion of mythological naming, however, is seen in the motif of misnaming and the linguistic play in *Gone Indian*, where the only name exempt from parody is 'Robert.' The mythological equation of name and identity, which governs *L'Elan d'Amérique*, is reversed in *Gone Indian* to the point where diacritical signification replaces all unique reference, with the notable exception of the reference to the author. The two novels discussed in chapters 5 and 6 would thus seem to move towards the opposite poles of the territorial spectrum: *L'Elan d'Amérique* is governed by mythological naming and metaphor, while *Gone Indian* carries the demythologizing endeavour to its extreme through the sylleptic undermining of stable meaning and the preference for lateral, intratextual patterns of signification. This movement is paralleled in *Beautiful Losers*, but is there counteracted by the sacred power of the Greek word which, in the midst of chaos and disjunction, operates the oxymoronic conjunction of the sacred and the profane. The deceptiveness and uncertainty of language are exhibited also in the metamorphic techniques of *The New*

Ancestors. The dissipation of identity in 'In the Fifth City' is a process of unnaming. The syntactic or lateral actualization of the same structures is seen in the use of the disjunctive *or.* The horizontal and intratextual (non-referential) nature of the sylleptic and metamorphic strategies distinguishes the Canadian novels from the verticality of the metaphoric and symbolic resonance and the referential dependence of *L'Elan d'Amérique* and *Trou de mémoire.* Unlike Kroetsch, however, Godfrey realizes only the first phase of the metamorphic process and stops at the stage where the forces of energy have collided in total undifferentiation or entropy. *Beautiful Losers* goes in an opposite direction: the dissolution of the self is described not as the denial of identity but as the potential for a kind of cosmic territorialization – the desiring machine in Cohen's novel has in the end lost all of the political power with which it was imbued by Deleuze and Guattari. The revolution of the second chancers is pre-empted by the author's assumption of control.

The thematic, as well as structural, equation of translation and perversion analysed in *Beautiful Losers, The New Ancestors,* and *L'Elan d'Amérique* would seem to point to a shared view of language as territorial. The central role played by translation in Langevin's allegory (crystallized in the transformation of Boisvert to Greenwood) also serves to situate the novel in its geographical and cultural territory, Franco-America. Its thematic function is thus a territorializing one emphasizing the link between language and its territory, between bastardized language and exile. The heteroglossia of Godfrey's text appears to foreground the same aspect of language: each idiolect pertains to a very specific geographical, cultural, or political territory. But, while the theme of linguistic perversion is counteracted in Langevin's novel through the highly territorial use of linguistic strategies, the English of the implied author in *The New Ancestors* is a non-territorial, homeless language. The fundamental territoriality of the language of *L'Elan d'Amérique* has been seen in its metaphoricity, its reliance on poetic and auditory strategies of text generation, and instances of linguistic licence (how does one translate 'Claire, comme la mer' into English, the language in which it is supposedly uttered?). The central symbolism inherent in the bilingual wordplay on *buck* and *élan* can be seen to perform a type of conjunction similar to the one operated by the symbolism of transubstantiation in Aquin's text, although less radical. Rather than being sylleptic, the word-play here is metaphoric: the different meanings of the words are actualized simultaneously, but instead of contributing to the undecidability of the text, they focus the reader's attention on the polysemy which carries the allegory and thus draw attention to the meaning-creating potential of language. *Beautiful Losers* is clearly founded on a similar belief in the generative power of language, although here it is the coincidence of signifiers that brings about the revelation. Cohen's text illustrates the distinction discussed by Benjamin and Derrida between vehicular translation as perversion, and the sacred transference of the signifier.

While both the rebus and the allegory depend on polysemy, the latter, as we have seen in *L'Elan d'Amérique*, unlike the former, at least strives towards transcendence. Saussure (and, of course, Derrida) may have done to our relationship to language what Copernicus (and Galileo) did to our relationship to the universe, and the writers and critics I have discussed here may be in a position similar to that of the sixteenth-century mannerists, who had to cope with the tension between the desire for geocentrism and the knowledge of its illusory nature. Are we caught in the trap between the desire for transcendence, for the transparent word, and the knowledge of its non-existence? Or has language simply replaced God as the 'transcendental signified' of our time, that beyond which we cannot go? That it precludes transcendence may paradoxically only align it more closely with the sacred: no one has shown more clearly than Cohen that meaning is *in* the word, not behind it.

The wordplay in *L'Elan d'Amérique* and the sacred signifier in *Beautiful Losers* function in much the same – anamorphic – way as the editorial commentary in *Trou de mémoire*, constituting a prism through which the meaning of the text can be perceived. They form nodal points in which the different 'levels' of the text – the political allegory and the psychological drama – converge, emphasizing the desire to preserve language's sacred powers of creation and meaning that Benjamin saw as typical of this kind of writing. This would corroborate Maureen Quilligan's claim that allegory can only be written in times when language has a sacred value, a view based on the acknowledgment of the importance of language and the generative power of the pun which always lies at the bottom of the allegorical narrative. Unlike Quilligan, however, I would argue that allegorical wordplay implies at least a striving towards transcendence, or rather, perhaps, that it acknowledges the sacred power *within* the word. Much of post-structural theory can, in fact, be characterized as allegorical, manifesting an ambivalent stance towards the sacredness of language.[1]

Walter Benjamin may have been right in claiming that 'Allegories are, in the realm of thoughts, what ruins are in the realm of things' (*The Origin of German Tragic Drama* 178), and a mannerist sense of decay and melancholy may be the mode of the allegorist, as of his/her analogue, the alchemist. Ruins are, as Craig Owens has indicated, the kind of traces that combine the site-specificity whose postmodern literary counterpart is the in-built referential obsolescence we have seen most clearly in *Beautiful Losers*, with the possibility to reconstruct an original. The resurrection of ruins – for which Cohen provides an appropriate metaphor in the reconstruction of the Akropolis – may be analogous to the restoration work implied in both the anamorphic and the alchemical enterprises we have witnessed in such novels as *Beautiful Losers* and *Trou de mémoire*.

My reading of *L'Elan d'Amérique* raised the question of the status of allegory as a postcolonial strategy. I classified the genre as essentially territorial insofar as it strives to transcend the divisions between sacred and profane, spiritual and material, personal and universal. It is irrefutable that the allegorical features that are clearly present in all of the novels participate in the collectivizing enterprise that Deleuze and Guattari define as specific to the minor literature, and hence as typical of marginality. The personal is directly plugged into the political in all of the novels I have read, most clearly in *L'Elan d'Amérique*, least obviously in *Gone Indian*. Yet the latter is without doubt more subversive in literary terms than the former. The anti-oedipal desiring machine is not necessarily politically effective; I would argue that the allegorical strategies of Langevin's text, with all their oedipal echoes, carry more political force than Cohen's pseudo-Deleuzean romance. And by the same token, the allegory is surely more *effective* as a political tool than the rebus of *Gone Indian*, notwithstanding the latter's obvious non-territoriality. All three strategies discussed here – allegory, anamorphosis, and rebus – are, in spite of the frequent critical insistence to the contrary, not simply effects of reading, and therefore to some extent a matter of choice, but intentional strategies with a didactic, even moral purpose. Of the three it is usually allegory that requires the least interpretative effort and which most clearly reveals the author's position; in my corpus *L'Elan d'Amérique* presents the least overwhelming challenge to the critic.

Although the author's 'signature' (as opposed to his position) is less obvious in *L'Elan d'Amérique* and *Beautiful Losers* than in *Trou de mémoire* and *Gone Indian*, it could perhaps be argued that in the former the text invades the author by way of the 'élan' encased in André *Lang*evin, a coincidence that may point to the generative power of the word in the text. In *The New Ancestors*, on the other hand, the affinity between the author and Michael Burdener can only be deduced from biographical information and Godfrey's own comments about his novel. In Aquin's and Kroetsch's novels, however, not only do the authors' names play a generating – rebus – role, but their specular identities – the Holy Ghost and the mad Adam – represent the two extremes of the dichotomy between naming/creation/ sacralization and unnaming/de-creation/desecration. The signature behind

Cohen's Zen riddle, while undoubtedly mirroring a serious quest for both self-knowledge and truth, also implies a wink to the reader, indicating the novel's balancing between high seriousness and dark comedy. It could be argued that the desperately looked-for 'tongue' is found only to be placed firmly in the author's cheek. What is indisputable is that the restoration of whatever 'perspectives curieuses' these three texts employ involves the resurrection of the author.

While all of the five novels I have read show evidence of both territorializing and deterritorializing tendencies, I would contend that my analyses indicate that in the Québécois texts the former are more crucial, while in the latter the reverse is true, with the possible exception of *Beautiful Losers* which, again, occupies an ambivalent middle position. Both *Trou de mémoire* and *L'Elan d'Amérique* are firmly anchored in an indigenous vernacular, referential, and sacred territory. The metaphoric dependency in Langevin's text stresses the conjunctive properties of the trope, tending towards identity rather than difference. The anamorphic technique of Aquin's text, with its potentially deterritorializing effect here serves to anchor the text in a profoundly religious territory whose mysterious conjunction of sacred and profane operates the same grounding as does Cohen's text but without leaving the vernacular. It is clear that ontological concerns in both precede the political, and that the cure for the alterity of the colonized is to be found in religious/aesthetic mystery.

The two extreme poles on my heuristic spectrum of territoriality are represented respectively by the conjunctive oxymoron – in *Trou de mémoire* and, to some extent, in *Beautiful Losers* and *L'Elan d'Amérique* – and the disjunctive syllepsis – in *Gone Indian*. The metamorphosis, which in Cohen's text operates the final conjunction and resurrection of the author, has the opposite outcome in *The New Ancestors*, where it becomes a clearly deterritorializing strategy. One of the most striking features shared by the Canadian texts is the preoccupation – whether foregrounded self-consciously or not – with the translation of the oral into print. This is not an unusual aspect of postmodernism; it is, as Linda Hutcheon has pointed out, an almost inevitable corollary to its self-consciousness, and as Derrida reminds us, it is always linked to the problematics of origin, authority, and presence. In *The New Ancestors* we saw, most clearly in the case of the proverbs, how the translation of the oral into the written deprives the word of its authenticity and perverts its truth. In *Gone Indian* it is Madham's transcription of Jeremy's spoken narrative that casts doubts on the authenticity of the story, and in the end allows him to appropriate it for his own purposes. In *Beautiful Losers* we again encounter a more ambivalent position, where the disjunction between oral and written is mystically redeemed through inscription – the pictorial rather than simply written – and the privileging of the receptive gaze. Typically, however, this can only be done by recourse to an extra-territorial language; the vernacular in itself is incapable of performing the sacred function.

The immediate objective of my study has been to suggest a practical methodology for analysing textual signs of alterity, hence my focus on close readings rather than general observations. My corpus has been limited and my approach clearly synchronic, concentrating on the formal treatment of one particular problem while paying little attention to historical develop-ments. Clearly a much more extensive investigation is needed before any significant conclusions can be drawn concerning the directions of the two literatures with regard to their position on a spectrum of territoriality. While I cannot do justice to the wide variety of fiction produced in both cultures during the decade following the publication of *Beautiful Losers*, a brief survey of texts that express a similar interest in the status of the culture from which they emanate may help throw some light on my findings.

Quebec

It is a commonplace to point to the preference in the literature of Quebec for myth and imagination as opposed to the realist bent of Canadian fiction. This distinction usually implies a view of a turn toward myth as a sign of the colonized's difficulty in representing reality and history, while realism is seen as a result of the writer's unproblematic relation to language and representation, a view I questioned in my own positioning of it nearer the non-territorial pole. While the novels I have discussed can hardly be said to participate in the presumed Canadian enthusiasm for 'realism,' it can be argued that the difficulty of reappropriating the 'stolen' history of Quebec – seen as a consequence of the cultural alienation of the colonized – does indeed often express itself through metaphor and allegory, which I have identified as tending towards territoriality. A difficulty in grappling with the past and a consequent turning away from 'realism' or historiography are not, per se, subversive or constitutive of a 'minor' literature; it is only the expression that difficulty takes that determines its territorial status. As I argued in chapter 1, the critical stance that claims allegory, for instance, to be inherently symptomatic of the minority situation puts the cart before the horse, when it concludes from this observation that the genre must be subversive. Although myth and allegory indeed seem to imply a collective gesture, connecting the personal with the social, that is not necessarily the

result of a revolutionary deterritorializing impulse. As we saw in *L'Elan
d'Amérique*, the linkage of the personal and the collective can also be a
territorial strategy which strengthens the bonds between the members of
the 'Gemeinschaft' in face of adversity; Langevin's use of stream-of-consciousness encourages the reader to identify with the protagonists.

In an extreme formulation, it could be claimed that the Québécois break
with the tradition of the 'roman de la terre' is a superficial phenomenon,
reflective of changes in literary convention rather than any real transformation of ideology, and the image of the colonized territory as abused woman
can be seen as yet another version of the traditional 'femme-pays.' The most
crucial difference between the new grounding in the territory and the old
may lie in the equation of 'pays' with language and the conscious revindication of the vernacular, whether *joual* or French, which can be said to
anchor the texts even more firmly in their cultural territory. It is perhaps
not surprising that the political literary challenge in Quebec largely began
in poetry (with poets like Gaston Miron, Paul Chamberland, and Michèle
Lalonde), and that the inevitably territorial 'roman-poème' – exemplified by
Langevin's novel – remained a major genre. The long silence of a poet like
Miron, for instance (as well as of Hubert Aquin in the early days of his
literary career), was no doubt a direct consequence of linguistic alienation.
During the period of renaissance I have investigated here, however, that
situation changed. Although Miron's *L'Homme rapaillé* (1970) speaks about
alterity perhaps more poignantly than any other contemporary work, the
poetic itinerary it describes is in itself a *mise en abyme* of the assumption
of the colonized identity, and the subsequent coming into majority of its
literature.

In fiction this journey is perhaps best illustrated in Jacques Godbout's
work, which, whatever its setting, is always concerned with the political
situation at home. From the early insularity of *L'Aquarium* (1962) to the
explicitly political *Les Têtes à Papineau* (1981), which is retroactively gaining
in prophetic force, the allegorical overtones are present. Even in the midst
of the bewilderment and homelessness of *Le Couteau sur la table* (1965),
with its generic affinity to the *nouveau roman*, the nostalgia for the 'pays'
is expressed in allegorical terms of the love of a woman; the narrator's
fascination with the cosmopolitan 'anglaise,' Patricia, gives way to his loyalty
towards Madeleine, the Québécoise (predictably killed by an American machine in the end). The assumption of a Franco-American identity begins
already in *Salut Galarneau!* (1967) where what in the earlier novel was
presented as the narrator's 'faute,' to be a French speaker in America, becomes an acknowledgment of the combination of *francité* and *américanité*

constituting the identity of 'le roi du hot dog.' The celebration of the vernacular continues in *D'Amour P.Q.* (1972) where *joual* is clearly linked to the territory – yet again represented by a woman – as the secretary, Mireille la Merveille, turns the tables on the highbrow author whose manuscript she is typing. The intertextual territory is inclusive, ranging from the Bible and *Paradise Lost* to comic strips and FLQ communiqués, but it is Mireille's vernacular that makes possible the sentimental 'révolution d'amour.' Godbout rejects the past as a burden and instead celebrates the new; the intellectual becomes a cartoon figure as pop art, in a conversion reminiscent of *Beautiful Losers*, becomes the new religion and Mireille the new saint. Disparate discourses and stories are mixed in typically postmodern fashion but they are in the end united under the sign of the vernacular; as the fictional author realizes: 'La libération du verbe ... passe par l'affirmation du français en Amérique. Il ne peut y avoir de littérature bilingue' (153).

Le Couteau sur la table is preceded by a year by Claude Jasmin's *Ethel et le terroriste*, which also draws the analogy between the separatist movement in Quebec and the black movement in the United States. Rather than furthering the revolutionary cause, however, Jasmin (like Godbout, in fact) cautions against the xenophobic aspect of Québécois nationalism – the 'appel de la race' variant we have encountered both in *Trou de mémoire* and the Parc Lafontaine incident in *Beautiful Losers* – by having his protagonist reject his Jewish girlfriend in favour of the cause. The implicit comparisons between the separatist movement and Nazism are obvious, and the hero's final decision to opt for love and Ethel rather than hate and the movement anticipates Godbout's 'révolution d'amour.' The sentimentality continues in *Pleure pas Germaine* (1965), where the image of the artist is presented in the portrait of a sculptress who never finishes her work; it is the creative process that counts, not the product, but this also means that politics are left behind. Jasmin's use of the vernacular as well as his characters here tend towards the stereotypical. The following two novels, *L'Outaragasipi* (1971) and *La Petite patrie* (1972), continue in the same vein; rejecting archival history, they are anchored in a personal and communal past, emphasizing genealogy and place as the primary facets of identity.

It may be argued that Godbout's (and Jasmin's) use of *joual* illustrates the disarming of an earlier potentially subversive gesture. When used by Jacques Renaud in *Le Cassé* (1964), as well as several of the writers linked to *Parti pris*, it had a defamiliarizing function and a rather shocking effect, reflecting the 'honte de soi' that Fanon and Sartre see as the first stage of the growth of the colonized's political consciousness. But the defiant vindication of the vernacular, when accepted as a literary technique, soon became a territorial strategy. It can also be argued that the use of *joual* becomes an elitist and colonizing strategy when it is appropriated by writers who do not speak it, writing for readers to whom, because of their class position, it is an alien or folkloric language.[2] The abandonment of its use by radical separatist writers coincided with its appropriation into the literary mainstream. The itinerary of *joual* thus demonstrates the speed with which a cultural establishment can defuse the subversive potential of a minor literature, and it may be illustrated in the works of Michel Tremblay, whose acclaimed *Les Belles-soeurs* brought the speech of the Montreal working class to the stage in 1968. While the use of *joual* on the stage was clearly designed as a political act, it also enhanced the social realism of his plays and by the time of the novel trilogy, beginning with *La Grosse femme d'à côté est enceinte* (1978), it has become a matter of serving the reality effect. Some of Tremblay's plays are set among marginals, at times on and around the Main. The saintly subculture of Cohen's 'desire apparatus' flourishes in *Sainte Carmen de la Main* (1976) and *Damnée Manon, sacrée Sandra* (1977), both of which operate the fusion of the profane and the sacred, as sexual perversion and religious ecstasy are shown as mirror versions of the same profound impulse, so that, as in Cohen's and Aquin's novels, the damned are also the sacred.

A telling instance of territorial reappropriation of a specific stolen history is found outside Quebec in Antonine Maillet's Acadian stories and plays. The metropolitan popularity of *Pélagie-la-charrette* (1979) – the first French-Canadian novel to win a Goncourt – is not due to its non-territoriality or political force but rather to its folkloric charm. Although Maillet's work abounds with pathos and compassion for the people of Acadia, the strategies she uses in *Pélagie* are clearly territorial: the recuperation of history is operated through a historical romance/epic, expressed in a fusion of myth, fact, and oral tradition, translated into an Acadian patois that is more notable for its poeticity and quaintness than its political force. In her earlier work, particularly the monologues that make up *La Sagouine* (1971), the political awareness of social injustice is less overshadowed by the territorial language which, because of the more contemporary setting, reflects the hybridization of the vernacular, even if its main function seems to be to forge a link with history instead of foregrounding the breach between past and present as did the early use of *joual*. The closest Acadian equivalent to *joual* might be the *chiac* spoken in the areas of greatest assimilation in New Brunswick (reminiscent of the hybridized French spoken in Godfrey's Mali), which has not, as far as I am aware, entered mainstream literature.

The language games played by Réjean Ducharme would, no doubt, offer another fertile field for an exploration along the lines suggested in my study.

The untranslatability of novels like *Le Nez qui voque* (1967) and *L'Océantume* (1968), for example, points to their rootedness in the language of writing, whose closeness to the vernacular is often evident in the play on an indigenous pronunciation and vocabulary. It is not surprising that Ducharme's fascinating novels have not gained a lot of popularity outside their linguistic territory.[3] The territorial nature of language is thematized already in his first published novel, *L'Avalée des avalés*, a contemporary of *Beautiful Losers* and equally shocking to the critical establishment. In it 'le bérénicien,' the private language based on the sense of fit between sound and sense (as in Bérénice's portmanteau name for her mother, 'Chamomor,' signifying 'Chat mort,' 'Chameau mort,' and 'Amour'), allows the heroine to express all her ambivalent feelings. Here, as in all of Ducharme's texts, language draws a magic circle around the initiates to the exclusion of others, particularly adults, in a territorializing movement that stands in opposition to an often encyclopedic intertextuality. While explicitly deconstructing conventional meaning, the play on signification here exploits the meaning-creating potential of language and works on both signifier and signified, as well as on the level of the sociolect. In coining words like 'patrillotisme' and 'matrimaniaque' (in *Le Nez qui voque*), for instance, Ducharme firmly grounds his text in the vernacular, poking fun at indigenous pronunciation, while at the same time satirizing the foibles of the Québécois society he describes.

Ducharme's own naming strategies are, like those of his protagonists, rather peculiar and highly improper, but they seem to corroborate rather than undermine or parody – as do most of Kroetsch's narratives, for instance – the mythological powers of the name. Many of his characters engage in name-games and frequently name themselves, thus assuming control over their fates, and the allegorical force of names like Mille Milles (*Le Nez qui voque*) or Constance Chlore (*L'Avalée des avalés*) is evident. The striving towards territoriality is also visible in Ducharme's obsession with the avoidance of oedipal splitting, expressed thematically in a way that brings to mind Poe's 'Annabel Lee': the ideal of a pre-sexual love in an enchanted territory, untouched by the realities of the adult world.

The frequency of child narrators in Québécois fiction (and film) is an interesting phenomenon in itself, and the fact that it is sometimes combined with a strong allegorical tendency, as in the texts of Marie-Claire Blais and Roch Carrier, would appear to corroborate its territorial character. The rejection of Québécois cultural stereotypes in Blais' *Une saison dans la vie d'Emmanuel* (1965) nevertheless relies heavily on an indigenous mythology and intertext, notably the by now familiar conjunction of sex and religion – seen also in Carrier's *La Guerre, Yes Sir!* (1968). The world of Blais' family is Rabelaisian and insular at the same time. The reference to the girls in the numerous family as 'les petites A' and 'les grandes A,' successors to Ducharme's 'trois A' in *Le Nez qui voque*, does not deny the force of naming but collectivizes and hence allegorizes it in a way similar to such affirmations of communion as Mille Milles' and Chateaugué's secret, communal alias, 'Tate.' It is perhaps symptomatic that one of the few named characters, and the only true individual in Blais' novel, Jean Le Maigre, does not survive. The universe seen through the eyes of baby Emmanuel is a timeless, cyclical one, where individuals are interchangeable types. Blais' ambivalent use of Québécois cultural stereotypes – taken to its extreme in her parodic *Un joualonais sa joualonie* (1973) – is similar to that of Carrier's trilogy whose itinerary resembles Godbout's novels, beginning in a rather harsh historic reality, combined with a dreamlike surrealism, in *La Guerre, Yes Sir!* (1968), retreating into a mythological and personal past in *Floralie, où es-tu?* (1969) and combining the two in a more immediate present in *Il est par là, le soleil* (1970). To both Blais and Carrier the family becomes the allegorical counterpart to society as a whole.

Perhaps the most ambitious effort at fusing the oral storytelling of a mythological, territorial culture with the requirements of the novel form is Gérard Bessette's *Les Anthropoïdes* (1977) in which the author tries to reconstruct a pre-literate universe (which could be that of the original 'A _____ s'). Bessette's attempt to recreate a truly oral universe rather than 'translating' it into modern terms (as does, for instance, William Golding in *The Inheritors*) produces a stylistic opacity that makes the text resistant to easy reading. The novel seems to aim at fusing the – recreated – vernacular with the sacredness inherent in that very unfamiliarity, thus creating an uncanny situation of communion between narrator and reader. The narrative is monologic insofar as even the metacommentary relating to storytelling etc. is carried out in the same mythical language. Bessette illustrates mythological naming by changing his characters' names according to their status in society, their distinguishing features, or the deeds they perform. The storyteller as precursor of the writer is a prominent figure charged with the collective memory of the tribe. The analogy between the 'paroleur' and the writer is made clear in the emphasis put on the teller's self-conscious anticipation of the reception of his stories, which parallels the writer's dependence on his critics. The story is told as a succession of initiations, and access to the 'parole' also gives access to women and power in an animate universe where the earth is clearly gendered feminine. Although Bessette's novel claims to be set in a purely imaginary territory and seems like a universally applicable fulfilment of the dream of a pre-oedipal society, the mention of the river 'Kebekouâ' on the last page does indeed seem to ground it retroactively in a specific geography.

The language games the author engages in to create the mythical/oral atmosphere are rooted in French and his return to myth is untainted by the irony that marks any such attempt made by his Canadian colleagues. Although there are lots of neologisms, or rather neo-archaisms, the wordplay is generated on the level of the signified, with an atmosphere of exoticism created by the use of compounds and spelling, particularly the use of the letter K instead of Q. Bessette's effort here is a good illustration of one of the most visible differences between the Canadian novels and their Québécois counterparts, insofar as his 'translation' of an oral culture into print presents relatively few problems. While the transposition is far from effortless, the French vernacular is sufficiently flexible to accommodate Guito's mythical 'parolade.'

Bessette's itinerary as a writer, although completely different in style from Godbout's, can be seen to follow a similar trend towards linguistic territorialization, and, like Langevin, he here leaves the realism of his earlier works in order to allegorize his cultural history and his own role as spokesman for a collectivity. By inventing a tribe and placing his narrative in a mythical version of his territory, thus enacting rather than analysing myth, Bessette avoids the colonizing gesture of which another chronicler of 'A ____ s' might be accused. From *Aaron* (1954) through the critical and commercial success of *Agaguk* (1958) to *Ashini* (1960) and the sequels to *Agaguk* (*Tayaout, fils d'Agaguk* [1969]; *Agoak, l'héritage d'Agaguk* [1975]), Yves Thériault's investigations of ethnic marginality imply a perspective that attempts to familiarize the unfamiliar through a quasi-anthropological inquiry from which, by necessity, the observer/author remains aloof. At least in Thériault's early novels, it is exoticism rather than marginality that interests the author.

The major status of Québécois literature and its language(s) allows a younger generation of writers – if not best, certainly most prolifically represented by Victor-Lévy Beaulieu – to indulge their fascination with American culture. Beaulieu's celebratory adoption of his colonial literary heritage from Victor Hugo to Herman Melville (and, less surprisingly, Jack Kerouac) is symptomatic of the victory over cultural alterity and the entrance into majority heralded by *Salut Galarneau!*. Beaulieu's vision of Québécois reality in his Beauchemin family saga, beginning with *Race de monde* in 1969, is a mixture of social realism and hallucinatory dream sequences, all couched in a clearly indigenous and spoken vernacular. Through frequent, territorial wordplay the French spoken in 'Morial Mort' expresses the assumption of a historically and geographically specific identity, and, as in the novels of Blais and Carrier, the family becomes metonymically related to the community as a whole. Beaulieu's choice of name for his tragicomically life-affirming protagonist, Abel Beauchemin, may be a challenge to Cartier's definition of Quebec as 'la terre de Caïn,' in the same vein as Aquin's rebuttal of 'je me souviens.'

Incorporating many diverse styles and frequently using pastiche and parody, *Race de monde* looks like a truly heteroglot text. The language is full of anglicisms and neologisms, but they are all finally territorialized in the vernacular, as is the parody which includes every possible indigenous stereotype, from the 'mère-poule' to the perverted priest. Much of Beaulieu's early work relies on puns and wordplay; in *Race de monde* the 'calembour' is referred to as 'une flèche' that will kill the father (56). While ostensibly subversive and antagonistic, the language of writing inscribes the very culture it claims to want to kill in an oedipal drama, which paradoxically perpetuates the gendered model we have seen so amply illustrated and which indeed seems to survive the explicit use of the colonization paradigm. In Beaulieu's version of the October crisis in *Un rêve québécois*, (1972) for example, the alterity experienced by the protagonist is only redeemed through the rape and murder of his wife, 'sa Jeanne d'Arc,' in a gruesome orgy of violence, anticipated in *Les Grands-pères* (1971). The freedom to move out of the territory seems to be gained at the expense of killing the 'femme-pays,' whose dismemberment is beginning not only to bear out Pierre X. Magnant's claim about the origin of literature but to emphasize its gender-specificity: the literature coming out of a society that perceives itself as colonized is built on the corpses of women.[4]

The inscription of the colonization paradigm in a pre-existing patriarchal ideology, which it seems often to exacerbate rather than question, no doubt goes some way towards explaining the reluctance of many women writers to adopt the literary politics of their male colleagues at the time. This does not mean, as used to be claimed, that their writing was apolitical; rather, as Patricia Smart has shown, feminist criticism is making visible the political in a literature that used quite different means and methods. Renowned authors like Anne Hébert, for instance, early on wrote against the 'roman de la terre' and questioned the ambivalent attitude towards women, perpetuated by the Church and the veneration of the mother, which so often led to revolt – and revulsion – continued in the works of Beaulieu, for instance.

Although Hébert's novels are less overtly political than most of the texts I have discussed, her attitude to her cultural territory may be symptomatic of someone who represents the 'double colonization' which makes the facile borrowing of metaphors of sexual violence so problematic. In her first long narrative, *Les Chambres de bois* (1958) Hébert seems to want to move away, both geographically and symbolically, from the narrow confines of Quebec to the metropolis. As the story moves from a childhood in rural Quebec to adulthood in Paris, however, the narrative (and, it may be argued, the writing itself) becomes more claustrophobic, before it opens up into a possibility of freedom. In *Kamouraska* (1970), perhaps her best-known work, Hébert moves into the heart of darkness of the feudal past of her home province, as well as of her family history, to illustrate the horrors of its repressed and insular life. In *Les Enfants du sabbat* (1975) the analogy between the profane and the sacred – religious devotion and blasphemy – is worked out thematically in a way reminiscent in intent, though not in style, of *Trou de mémoire*. Yet in spite of her rejection of a great deal of her cultural heritage, Hébert's attempts to move out of the familiar territory seem less successful, both narratively and aesthetically. It is significant that the only one of her novels entirely set in Paris, where she has lived most of her writing life, *Héloïse* (1980) – a bizarre story of vampirism set partly in the metro – is the least critically successful of her novels.

Hébert's return to Quebec in *Les Fous de Bassan*, which gained her a Prix Fémina in 1982, is interesting insofar as it more clearly than any of the earlier works fuses the historical and the mythical, while retaining many features of the 'roman-poème.' Again, the story is prompted by violence, the rape and murder of two young girls, but unlike in the novels written by the male writers – with the possible exception of RR's return in *Trou de mémoire* – the victim here begins to talk back from beyond the grave. The indirect cause of the crime is the wind from the sea, explicitly linked to women, passion, and madness, implicitly to sexual repression and religion, and both the victims and the murderer become *pharmakos* figures, acting out a collective sacrificial drama. The narrative gains in allegorical force through the narrations of the victims, both before and after the crime, which make reference to Genesis, yet again emphasizing the creative power of the corpse.

In territorial terms the novel resembles *L'Elan d'Amérique*; it is set among a linguistic and religious minority within Quebec. In spite of the narrative structure which divides the telling of the story among several narrators, the text is monologic, reflecting the presence of an authorial voice that supersedes the ostensible fragmentation. Exemplifying the language of passion and madness, it might be argued that the narrative voice is the wind itself – the (un)Holy Ghost? – which here, as in *L'Elan d'Amérique*, speaks French. With the exception of names, no concessions are made to the anglophone milieu, and the narrative exhibits the same anchoring in the language of writing as does Langevin's novel, highly dependent on metaphor and poetic principles of text generation. Like Langevin, Hébert prefers a metropolitan French, but her writing seems most 'at home' in Quebec. The debt owed to Faulkner, shared with Langevin and discernible in less tangible ways in earlier texts, here surfaces in the central intertextual presence of *The Sound and the Fury* (together with its source text, *Macbeth*). As in Faulkner, the 'tale told by an idiot' – Benjy's has a counterpart in Perceval's – may best represent life, but Hébert outdoes her predecessor in also letting the sound and fury be conveyed by a ghost, as she lets the victim talk back.

The often striking similarities between the literatures of Quebec and the American South are frequently seen in formal and thematic features which may well stem from their analogous histories: the myth of the glorious past, the trauma of the conquest, the presence of religion, agrarianism, and cultural isolation, etc. which in both lead to a similar fusion of the poetic with the grotesque. It is difficult to think of any regional literature within America that conveys a more distinct sense of community than that of the South, and it would be as difficult to argue for its status as minor or non-territorial as to claim the same for its Québécois counterpart.

After what seems like a fairly long period of intense territorialization on many fronts it is hardly surprising that, in 1979, Michel Morin and Claude Bertrand launched an appeal to the writers of Quebec to create a 'territoire imaginarie de la culture.' In what amounts to an individualistic reversal of Deleuze and Guattari's vision, they advocate a distantiation from the real territory and from what they see as the imprisonment in a narrow, basically introspective, and collective nationalism. It may be argued that a new generation of writers has moved in that direction, which in some cases entails a movement away from the political arena, which has been taken over by new 'marginals,' most visibly by women, as the postcolonial project has given place to the feminist enterprise of writers like Nicole Brossard, Louky Bersianik, and France Théoret. The struggle for an indigenous 'écriture féminine' is a project analogous to the earlier generation's quest for what might be called an 'écriture québécoise,' although fraught with quite different problems in a context where 'woman' has long been made to play a metaphoric role as victimized territory.[5] The radical experimentation in which many of these writers engage aims at deterritorializing language from its grounding in an external reference dominated by a patriarchal discourse, perpetuated in the colonization paradigm, and towards its subsequent regrounding in a physical reality and a real body (needless to say a body which shares few characteristics with that imaged in what at first glance might seem like an analogous endeavour in *Beautiful Losers*).

This brief survey seems to indicate that there exists in Quebec during the period I have been discussing a paradoxical relationship between a thematic postcolonial revindication of alterity and a simultaneous assertion of difference, a coexistence of a thematic cultural alienation with a linguistic 'at-homeness.' The Québécois identity searched for, no matter how marginal or transparent it is perceived to be, is anchored not so much in a historical and political context as in a mythical, referential, and vernacular territory. It may be argued that the recourse to myth and allegory in so many of the Québécois texts has, in a way, served to make the *literary* territory of Quebec more 'real' than perhaps it would have been if the historiographic endeavour had proven less problematic. While the two texts I analysed in depth, as well as many of the ones mentioned in passing, are undoubtedly political both in impulse and effect, the formal expressions taken by the postcolonial project here are primarily – though not exclusively – territorial, hence in the terms of Deleuze and Guattari symptomatic of a major literature.

It is difficult to think of a Québécois novel that shows signs of the same problems in translating the oral-vernacular into print that we encountered in all of the Canadian novels. My discussion has indicated that the discourse of colonization in Québécois literature is indeed contemporaneous with the vindication of the vernacular. It could be argued that in the situation of alienation that pertained in Quebec in the sixties, when the antagonist was identified with 'les anglais' – primarily referring to English Canada – rather than with a French-speaking metropolis, the existence of an indigenous vernacular absolved the writers from attempting the deterritorialization of the 'colonizer's' language which so many of their Canadian counterparts felt compelled to engage in.

Canada

In Canada the situation is somewhat different, and I will argue that, in the period concerned, several of the non-territorial features discussed in connection with *The New Ancestors* and *Gone Indian* dominate much of its fiction. The ambivalence towards language and its relationship to the – individual and cultural – territory is unwittingly expressed in an incident in Alden Nowlan's 'meta-mythologically' entitled novel, *Various Persons Named Kevin O'Brien* (1973) which may serve as a preface to my brief survey. On a visit to his childhood home the protagonist thinks: 'they would remember a boy named Kevin O'Brien. Common sense says I was that boy and nobody else. But, then, common sense is no more than what its name suggests: a consensus' (26–7). The arbitrariness of the name, which is such a source of anxiety for Kevin (or the various Kevins), is underscored as its link to the referent is shown to depend on convention. Yet at the same time the recourse to etymology in the very definition of that convention or consensus points to a desire to imbue language with the motivation and meaning it lacks, an allegorical desire that will remain unfulfilled except in Kevin's own fictionalized naming of his hometown in his memoir, Lockhartville.

The sense of entrapment in a 'foreign' language, a situation which would constitute a typical breeding ground for a minor literature, is perhaps most explicitly portrayed in Margaret Atwood's *Surfacing* (1972). The theme of alterity as exile is expressed by the narrator as she returns to her childhood home – an archetypal journey, it seems, in the quest for identity – in Northern Ontario: 'Now we're on my home ground, foreign territory' (11). The problematics of language are shown to lie at the bottom of the dilemma: 'If you look like them and think like them then you are them ... you speak their language, a language is everything that you do' (129). The question of identity is thus inextricably linked to the search for an idiom, a theme that also recurs frequently in Atwood's poetry. The heroine's quest takes her through a gradual metamorphosis, in which she rids herself of false representations but, having nothing with which to replace them, eventually loses all of the properties unique to her self, and the novel ends in silence and waiting. In Atwood's earlier novel, *The Edible Woman* (1969), the search is more specifically for a feminine voice, described in a way that brings to mind Deleuze's discussion of the dichotomy of speaking and eating in some cases of schizophrenia – speaking deterritorializes the organs of the body whose primary function is nourishment – so that eating or refusing to eat becomes a defence against the assault of language on the body, a phenomenon which may also be relevant to *Beautiful Losers* (*Logique du sens*). Atwood's metaphorical treatment of this theme, which converges with her literalization of metaphors of eating (of the type 'What's eating her?') and the play on the power of metaphor to turn people, especially women, into food, in both *The Edible Woman* and *Lady Oracle* (1976) anticipates the recent attention paid to eating disorders among women which are linked to problems of voice and self-representation.

It can be argued that *The Edible Woman* is prompted by the rebus principle; as Atwood translates Freudian clichés into culinary ones it is the *oedipal* woman who is symbolically sacrificed and eaten. The ritual beheading of the cake/woman near the end of the novel makes possible the restoration of a different order, in which metaphor is divested of its cannibalistic power and Marian is, at least potentially, metamorphosed into an anti-oedipal, non-edible woman, freed from the threat of being devoured.

It can be argued that Atwood's two first novels move towards the muteness Dennis Lee postulates as a necessary step in the colonized's need to clear a linguistic space ('Cadence, Country, Silence'). From this silence *Lady Oracle* emerges in a parodic assumption of extraterritoriality, where the metamorphic nature of identity is narrativized into 'a complex of possibilities' incorporating an intertextual collage of cosmopolitan canons and traditions. Atwood's nationalism is explicit in the early work, and in *Surfacing* 'American' becomes a metaphor for the figurative colonization/rape of nature expressed in imagery that brings to mind Langevin's – notably associated with hunting and guns. It is both ironic and symptomatic of the direction taken by the country's literature that Atwood is included, with no mention of her nationality, in the recent *Columbia Literary History of the United States* (1988).

The problem of language or voice is overtly thematized in a truly Canadian example of 'historiographic metafiction,' Rudy Wiebe's *The Temptations of Big Bear* (1973) which, in a way at times reminiscent of Godfrey's novel – though from a completely different ideological as well as formal angle – deals with a conflict between the mythological consciousness of the Indians and the legalistic mentality of British imperialism on which Canada is built, and which has led to the perpetuation of false representations of natives. While it attempts to recuperate a part of Canadian history from the point of view of the margin, the novel simultaneously undercuts its own enterprise by thematizing translation as perversion in a way similar to that described by Langevin. This has the effect of describing the language of the Indians (which is exclusively oral) as territorial while inevitably pointing to the unreliability of the author's own efforts at rendering it without bias. The novel shows English as a vehicular, abstract language pertaining to print, law, and bureaucracy while at the same time translating the Cree spoken by the natives into the writer's own English, an operation that requires a deterritorialization of the language of writing.

Like Cohen, Wiebe incorporates archival material to foreground the difference between his fictional recreation of events – and particularly of characters – and their representation by official history, thus showing them both to be equally uncertain. Wiebe's own enterprise is *mise en abyme* in the figure of the Métis translator who, occupying an uncomfortable middle ground, has to translate the legalistic language of the white men into the poetic discourse of the Indians and vice versa. The project points to the instability of the relationship between literal and figurative or, rather, that metaphor is in the eye of the beholder, as it were; Big Bear wonders why he has been accused of stealing the white grandmother's hat – he has committed crimes against the crown – in an almost Kafkaesque literalization of a dead metonymy. In the mythological consciousness, there exists no distinction between literal and figurative, just as there is no difference between words and things; the division between the literal – fact – and the figurative – fiction – is a white man's invention. This explains the Indians' inability to participate in the fundamentally semiotic process of lying, with its dependence on the detachability of words from things and signifiers from signifieds. Lying attests to the vehicularity of language, and it may be argued that the rebus, as *Gone Indian* illustrates, is a type of lie; it is that very detachability which makes it possible for language to become an alibi.

Many of Wiebe's other novels perform similar operations in revising or re-visioning history and recovering lost memories: of the Mennonites in *The Blue Mountains of China* (1970) and the Métis in *The Scorched-Wood People* (1977). The author self-consciously attempts to avoid repeating the appropriation perpetrated by earlier historiographers, an endeavour that requires formal experimentation; the inherent vehicularity of the English language precludes the immediacy demanded by an oral vernacular – English is no 'Hiro-Koue.' It is significant that Wiebe's interest in visionaries, while clearly linked to his religious beliefs, is expressed in an association between orality – often oratory – and vision, which again is reminiscent of the ideal of sainthood encountered in *Beautiful Losers* – a category to which figures like Big Bear and Riel belong (although it is questionable whether Wiebe would like to see them in the company of Cohen's saints).

Peter Such's *Riverrun* (1973) is another attempt at transposing a particularly obscure part of Indian history into modern novelistic form. Like Wiebe's novels, this one is based on historical documents and, in a way similar to both *Big Bear* and *The New Ancestors*, it juxtaposes two views of time, the cyclical and the linear, nature-time and history. The narrative is interspersed with a few phrases in the original Beothuk language, which are left untranslated, and hence – together with a proliferation of Indian names – serve the same 'sacred' function that we have seen in so many other cases. In his version of Beothuk consciousness Such uses generic features more reminiscent of the epic than the modern novel, and the text conveys the impression that it is the writer's English that has been translated into Beothuk – according to Hölderlin's and Benjamin's ideal model of sacred translation – rather than the other way around. The attempt to avoid appropriating or colonizing the language of the colonized is visibly turned against the language of the colonizer itself, and the result is a deterritorialization of the language of writing. It is not only the circularity that leads Such to modernism and Joyce (the allusion in the title is to *Finnegans Wake*) but also the attempt to turn English into (albeit only one) foreign language.

All of the strategies and concerns we have seen in the three Canadian novels I have analysed in depth are present in Robert Harlow's *Scann* (1972), the last of a trilogy beginning with *Royal Murdoch* (1962) and *A Gift of Echoes* (1965). An apparent chronicle of specific individuals and places, it blurs the boundaries between people, between people and places, and between history and fiction, as what begins as an attempt to map a specific geographical and historical territory becomes an exploration of the human mind and a quest for truth, the 'country that has no absolute borders' (128), for which Canada consequently becomes an apt metaphor. The main narrator, Amory (amorous and amorphous) Scann – split into the various roles he performs which never seem to coincide; he is editor Scann, writer Scann, critic Scann, even lover Scann – leaves his family from Easter Saturday to Easter Monday to hide in a hotel in the centre of his own town to write a chronicle about it. The limbo between death and resurrection becomes three days of 'Creation' in an allegorical Genesis, and Canada or the north becomes a metonymy for creation ex nihilo. Unlike the south (and we might add in light of the foregoing discussion, Quebec), which is engaged in 'ritualizing the metaphors that are left behind when an era and its seminal idea dies [*sic*]' (90), Canada never saw its birth as idea, and is forever caught in 'a moment of transition' (89), emblematized by the ungraspable moment between pitch and catch in an image resembling both Kroetsch's ski-jumper and Cohen's escaped ski. Although Scann's story does not make explicit use of the colonization paradigm, it talks about mapping and staking out territory – imaged as trapping – as a question of power relations and draws parallels between the treatment of Indians in Canada and slaves in the United States. As in Jeremy's and Mrs Beaver's dream, the colonized take revenge: nature through its own trickster figure, 'carcajou,' the wolverine, and the slaves by raping the daughters of the master. While this text thus genders the territory in the archetypal way it acknowledges that it can never be mapped and controlled.

As the many levels of narrative become conflated, the figures of history become 'real' while the people surrounding Scann in his daily life take on fictional qualities; identity breaks down in an imagery of dissemination very similar to the one found in *The New Ancestors*. No certainties are left, no beginnings and endings, and the manuscript of Scann's chronicle is burnt. As in Cohen's, Aquin's, and Kroetsch's novels, the idea of pure being or truth, which is always there as the goal of the quest, is represented by woman. In what seems like a transposition of Cohen's hourglass image into linguistic terms, truth/being/woman is here epitomized as the '-ing' of pure becoming, which, of course, cannot be documented.

As in Kroetsch's fictions, words often seem to precede and generate actions in this complex novel. Scann's figurative and literal scanning of the landscape never seems to penetrate surfaces, and it is again the signifier that engenders meaning. The beginning of the novel, for instance, concerns a visit to the dentist, which can be seen to spawn the frequent imagery of teeth, as well as the whole o(do)ntological quest of Scann's enterprise which has to do with molars-morals-mortals and that will eventually bring him to the 'saw-toothed edge of his world' (20).

The mapping of the Canadian territory that Scann sets out to perform, and that I have joined in my own way, has, of course, been carried out for as long as the country has existed, and, as in so much literature and theory preceded by the prefix post – from Borges to Baudrillard – the map, from being an emblem of colonization, has become a paradigmatic metaphor for the problematics of representation in general.[6] In the period I am discussing an implicit concern with the (im)possibility of mapping the Canadian territory is present even in the fictions of writers not often identified with either postmodernism or postcolonialism, except indirectly. Margaret Laurence's novels, for instance, are usually viewed as examples of the 'realism' so typical of Canada, and her Manawaka as a thinly disguised version of her hometown, Neepawa, metonymically representative of any small town, not unlike its Ontario counterparts in Alice Munro's stories, for instance. Yet the preoccupation with finding a way to express the experience of her protagonists is in many of Laurence's texts more central than the content of that experience. The search for a voice becomes particularly acute in *The Diviners* (1974), where Morag's writing is contingent on her quest for a past, a history, and a language that she can call her own. While Laurence does not do away with the traditional concept of character and does not engage in any radical formal experimentation, she thematizes the importance of language for identity through her insistence on the idiolect as perhaps the most crucial feature of characterization. Extraterritoriality is represented by Morag's Métis lover, Jules Tonnerre, 'with two languages lost, retaining only broken fragments of both French and Cree, and yet speaking English as though forever it must be a foreign tongue to him' (244). It is significant, of course, that it is the extraterritorial who represents the artist figure; like Jules and the diviner, Royland, Morag can only rely on her own powers, stake out her own territory from within the silence.

An interesting example of the intrusion of the sacred into the mimesis of everyday life is found in *A Jest of God* (1966), where Rachel Cameron to her shame and surprise breaks out in glossolalia in the tabernacle where she has accompanied her friend. As in the case of *Beautiful Losers* and *The New Ancestors*, the reproduction of the alien tongue (or tongues) emphasizes its mystery: 'Galamani halafka tabinota caragoya lal lal ufranti' (35). Rachel's attempts at dismissing the incident as a momentary fit of hysteria do not contradict but rather underscore its sacred power. It is clear that some kind of spirit has spoken through her body in a language of potential revelation, and her pentecostal speech stands in the same relation of opposition to her mother's 'magic word' of empty convention, 'please,' as Εὐχαιστω stands to 'thanks' in *Beautiful Losers*. The vernacular of Manawaka is a language of alibis; used to cover rather than discover and express feelings, it hides more than it reveals. In its conventionality it proves less territorial than its superficial insistence on community would suggest.

The search for a specific women's voice continues among writers who, like their counterparts in Quebec, go further in formal experimentation and for whom the colonization paradigm provides a more feasible analogy because of the slightly less violent misogyny of its adoption into the literature of their male peers. Often, however, the similarities between the explicit use of the paradigm by the male writers I have discussed, and its adoption into women's writing are largely superficial. Audrey Thomas' *Mrs. Blood* (1970) and *Blown Figures* (1974), for instance, are both set at least partly in Ghana and trace the almost schizophrenic breakdown of identity in a way reminiscent of Godfrey's (the reader familiar with *The New Ancestors* will be pleased to see several African expressions recur, although the familiarity with the earlier text will lessen their defamiliarizing effect). Both of Thomas' novels depict writing as a *pharmakon*; causing pain by bringing into consciousness painful memories, it also serves as cure. As in *Beautiful Losers* the protagonist is weighed down by memory, expressed in bodily symptoms specific to the female experience and symbolized by blood: notably childbirth and miscarriage. While Thomas' texts are visibly postmodern in their incorporation of a number of discourses, both literary and paraliterary, they are difficult to characterize as either particularly Canadian or postcolonial. It is significant that what in Cohen's and Aquin's novels, for instance, would be metaphoric, is here primarily literal: the emphasis is on the physical experience. Even Cohen's narrator's shit is more metaphorical than Isobel's blood in *Blown Figures*, for instance; the drama of identity is played out in and on the body, as Thomas speaks back at Freud by de-allegorizing his notion of female sexuality as 'the dark continent.'

Thomas' use of different discourses and languages is a radical attempt at uprooting language, resulting in a deterritorialization where it is difficult to discern a specific vernacular, and where the boundaries between the different registers of language become confused in complete heteroglossia.

The recourse to a foreign language at a sacred moment that we have already seen in Cohen, Godfrey, and Laurence, also occurs in Kroetsch's *The Studhorse Man* (1970) where a mysterious origin is heralded with a spoken, untranslated Cree phrase: 'Kis-see-wus-kut-tã-o' (69) as Poseidon, the studhorse, is 'born' from the water of Wildfire lake in a baptism of fire and water. The rebus principle is at work in this novel, whose picaresque journey is a parodic actualization (similar in impulse if not in form to Aquin's rebuttal of 'je me souviens') of the Canadian motto, 'a mari usque ad mare,' which is 'translated' – through a transference of the signifier – into a fabulous journey from mare to mare which remains unconsummated. Like Scann's quest, that of the studhorse man, Hazard Lepage, goes in circles, ending where it began, having engendered not a new breed of horses but a proliferation of signifiers uprooted, like their counterparts in *Gone Indian*, from their signifieds. As Poseidon's quest for a mare proceeds, Hazard follows – *par hasard*, as it were – from Marie to Martha, also without issue. The attempt at arriving at an end and establishing an origin, a new dynasty of horses, is thwarted by the incessant movement of desire from object to object, actualized narratively in the sliding of the signifier from signified to signified. It is in the nature of desire that its consummation kills it. This process is literalized when Poseidon's striving to sire becomes a de-siring, in what must be the funniest and most paradoxical in Kroetsch's considerable inventory of comical images: Poesy's role is to keep a stableful of mares constantly pregnant in the service of preventing pregnancy: PMU – pregnant mare's urine – is a crucial ingredient in birth control pills. This image becomes paradigmatic of the eternal gestation of the Canadian quest which never seems to be carried to term; the desired identity never sees its birth. The jest God plays on Rachel in Laurence's novel may be a variant of this; her supposed pregnancy turns out to be a benign tumour. Kroetsch's career as a novelist is almost emblematic of the Canadian search for identity, and it is perhaps not surprising that he is also one of the foremost critics of the country's literature. The beginning and (provisional) end of the quest is encapsulated in his titles, with their insistence on extraterritoriality: from *But We Are Exiles* (1965) to *Alibi* (1983).

While the preoccupation with the problem of recuperating history and the past prevails in the works of writers as different in temperament as Timothy Findley and Jack Hodgins, for instance, a shift in focus and direction can be discerned after 1975. The search for analogues to the situation in Canada, which earlier so often led to Africa, continues but in more exclusively literary or textual terms, without undergoing the same metaphorization into politics. It may be argued that since the mid-sixties Canada has become more postmodern and cosmopolitan than postcolonial: the metropolitan part of the collective psyche has won out over the colonial. The thematic failure of the quest for the Canadian identity and the consequent assumption of extraterritoriality by the generation of writers I have discussed may have freed the next one to travel abroad; like so many other things free trade entered literature before it entered politics. The major influence on writers like Hodgins, as well as on Kroetsch in *What the Crow Said* (1978), is no doubt Garcia Marquez. Although magic realism (exemplified not only by Marquez but also Salman Rushdie) is sometimes seen as typical of postcolonialism, I do not think the fascination of Canadian writers with works like *A Hundred Years of Solitude* can be attributed solely to a shared concern with postcolonialism.

The influence of the magic realists goes much further than the postcolonial 'margin,' and Canadian interest in them is more than just political. Hodgins' *The Invention of the World* (1977) may seem like a Canadian version of Marquez' story, but its indebtedness to Flann O'Brien's earlier works may be even greater. In this fantastic novel the concern with the relationship between history and myth finally leads to a conflation of all possible types of discourse; myth, legend, history are all shown as inventions existing because of the creative – inventive – powers of the author who, in a typically postmodern manner, thus becomes the arbiter of 'truth.' Timothy Findley's *Famous Last Words* (1981) shows a similar disregard for generic boundaries, but rather than celebrating the liberation from history and the consequent discovery that 'whatsoever is truth,' Findley sounds a note of caution that may indeed be relevant to our discussion; literary innovation is not necessarily inimical to political conservatism, or even fascism, and some 'truths' are more pernicious than others.

Canada as a whole has often represented a 'territoire imaginaire' for outsiders; it has served as a kind of Cathay to European writers and readers, a mythical territory whose name one would be surprised to encounter on a real map. In Michel Tournier's words: 'Le Canada reste toujours, pour moi, cet au-delà qui frappe de nullité les dérisoires misères qui m'emprisonnent' (*Le Roi des aulnes*). This was very much my own feeling, nourished on Ernest Thompson Seton and Lucy Maud Montgomery, before setting out on my own journey to the country, which turned into a wild-goose chase, as I found myself, rather like Jeremy Sadness, in what seemed like a centreless labyrinth. It was an unsettling discovery to find that, much less romantically, Canada seemed as elusive to its inhabitants as to imaginary travellers like myself.

It is impossible to do justice to the literary production of Canada in the decade following the publication of *Beautiful Losers*, with which I began my inquiry, and my corpus has yet again been admittedly eclectic. Each methodology invents its own object, every canon is a creation of a certain way of seeing; the critic creates her own anamorphosis and writes her own allegory. If any conclusion can be drawn from this selective survey of the two literatures, it would seem to be quite simple: the possession of a language unique in the North American context facilitated the Québécois naming of a specific cultural territory and the affirmation of an identity distinct from the Canadian and American ones. The entrapment in the English shared with the major presence on the continent at the same time drove Canadian writers to subvert and metamorphose their language and to 'unname' a world, in order to, eventually and tentatively, (re-)name their own. The commonality of the paradigm of colonization shared between the two cultures has led to thematic similarities which have sometimes been attributed to a 'common national mystique' (Sutherland 26), but the different expressions this shared concern has taken indicate, I believe, that the postcolonial endeavour is both more relevant and more visible in the Québécois texts, with their emphasis on the 'recuperative work' on the level of language, which is inevitably reflected in territorial strategies, while the homelessness of their Canadian counterparts is mirrored in the non-territorial strategies that attest to the diffuseness of its contestatory position. It might be argued that the literature of Quebec during the crucial period in question identified with the colonial part of the dual identity of the metropolitan colony, while the literature of Canada leaned towards an – unwitting – identification with the metropolitan part of the national psyche. This conclusion does not, however, lay to rest the question of the respective identification and valorization of the two movements in critical discourse, a thorny problem I can no longer avoid addressing.

Reading in the Margin

The theories that inform the methodology I have proposed here are based on two more or less explicit presuppositions: literary subversion is analogous to ideological defiance, and postcolonialism and postmodernism are both aesthetics of marginality. It would be reassuring to be able to state unequivocally at the end of the investigation that the, undoubtedly politically motivated, postcolonial project is indeed also aesthetically revolutionary, and that the postmodern stance is truly marginal. A different picture has emerged, however, and we may be left with more questions than answers. The political force of all of the novels I have studied, perhaps the Québécois ones in particular, puts into question the analogy between literary and political radicalism. It could, in fact, be argued that my corpus has shown the two as opposed and that a novel like *L'Elan d'Amérique* carries greater political force than *Gone Indian*, for instance, in spite of the latter's more radical subversion of literary convention. By the same token, a close reading shows the seemingly both thematically and aesthetically revolutionary *Trou de mémoire* to be fundamentally religious and, it may even be argued, politically reactionary. The correlation in Deleuze and Guattari's theories between 'minor literatures' and ideological subversion results, I would argue, from an a priori valorization of a certain aesthetics and its subsequent translation/perversion into the realm of politics, a kind of category mistake or wishful thinking which, it seems, every generation insists on repeating; a comparison with the literary radicals of modernism provides a sobering reminder.

How, then, can we distinguish between the two projects? Although the paradigm of colonization occurs in some form in all of the novels I have read, postcolonial concerns are most explicit in *Trou de mémoire*, *The New Ancestors*, and *L'Elan d'Amérique*. All of these use allegorical features in a way that gives credence both to the genre's claim to a privileged position within postcolonial counter-discourse and to its collective force. Yet the rhetorical and linguistic strategies used vary greatly. While both Québécois texts privilege territorial strategies and rely on the language of writing to carry meaning, there is no doubt that Aquin's novel is a great deal more formally 'revolutionary' than Langevin's which falls somewhere between a modernist and a postmodernist aesthetic. *The New Ancestors*, on the other hand, demonstrates mostly non-territorial features which are carried even further in *Gone Indian*, the least overtly political of all the texts I have read. It could be argued that literary experimentation may detract from the 'message' which must be perceived in order for the text to be politically effective. In the case of *Trou de mémoire*, for instance, the revolutionary thematics are more immediately visible than the religious impulse I have detected behind it.

With its clear participation in both postcolonialism and postmodernism Aquin's novel may indeed provide the best object for the litmus test this study seems to need. The overt – thematic – concern with colonialism and its expression in territorial strategies, which ground the discussion in a specific reference and participate in the recuperation and assumption of alterity, point to its position within the first. Dependent on its contestatory position vis-à-vis a centre defined in political/referential terms, it carries on a struggle from a cultural/linguistic margin which it vindicates and valorizes. I suggested in chapter 1 that the ambivalence of postmodernism, in particular with regard to its political stance, may result from the nebulous character of its antagonistic 'centre,' which is, I would argue, primarily an aesthetic construct. The subversion of 'realist representation,' demonstrated in the uprooting of language from its referential dependency, shows its affinity with post-structuralist theory and its equally apparent difference from the recuperation and territorialization characteristic of the postcolonial enterprise. Yet at the same time, the decentring of the subject that is at the 'centre' of most contemporary theoretical scepticism is, in the texts of writers like Cohen, Aquin, and Kroetsch, counteracted by the reinscription of authorial control. All of these texts are alibis; through the manipulative strategies of the anamorphosis and the rebus they testify to language's ability to be elsewhere, which is not anywhere at all but a specific place determined by the author. Rather than illustrating the deconstructive potential of language, these writers challenge the view of the subject as constituted in and through language by, more or less overtly, wresting control away from it.

L'Elan d'Amérique, on the other hand, affirms the post-structuralist view of language as that which speaks us; the writer may be self-conscious about his craft but accepts without question his place within a linguistic territory. I suggested in my introduction that the final answer to the question of the relationship between the two movements – postcolonialism and postmodernism – may lie in the author's position in the text which is symptomatic of his or her position within the language of writing. In order to manipulate language one has to perceive it as alien, to be as far removed from the mythological position 'en deça' as possible. The controlling author who sits in the middle of the textual labyrinth and directs the reader's way through it is, by definition, to some degree an extraterritorial, someone who is capable of using language as an instrument or a tool. This would be the condition of the postmodernist. As my readings have shown, this does not mean that this stance is more inherently subversive than postcolonialism, but rather that the contestation works on different aspects of the texts.

I am not the only critic to identify the vindication of the writing subject as one of the distinguishing features of postmodernist fiction; it is implicit in its literary self-consciousness. But its particular expression in the controlling strategies we have seen in my chosen corpus follows, I would argue, from a contestation not of a political situation, or even of a literary canon, so much as of a critical establishment that, for the last several decades, has relegated the author to the margin. The manipulative strategies of those texts most easily labelled postmodern attest to the writer's desire for mastery in an age where he – again, I use the pronoun advisedly – has been reduced to an effect, rather than a cause, of reading. It is no longer the great figures in the literary canon that must be figuratively killed – pace Harold Bloom – but the appropriators, myself and my colleagues. Although critics are becoming increasingly willing to acknowledge the manipulative nature of many postmodern texts, its cause and effect have not been sufficiently explored, possibly because of the critical taboo against 'the intentional fallacy.' The prevailing focus on openness and the reluctance to deal with the politics of manipulation are both, I would argue, paradoxically facilitated by the appropriation (from margin to centre) – as opposed to the original intent – of much post-structuralist theory into a critical establishment which makes it conform to its own desires. Although no self-respecting critic would any longer lay claim to objectivity, it is often easier to domesticate ideologically troublesome texts than to profess one's love for, or fascination with, books that an increasingly puritanical – in the sense of politically prescriptive – critical establishment has marked for its figurative burnings.

At any given time a certain number of allegories and metaphors are accepted into mainstream criticism as explanatory paradigms while others are censored. Like the literary texts themselves, the critical treatment of them, including my own, validates Kafka's despair over our dependency on metaphor; it is as necessary and as impossible as translation and as potentially corrupting. The territoriality of metaphor means, as I have shown, the grounding of expression in reference, but a split one (with all the violent connotations of the word), a simultaneous naming and gesture towards unnaming, a kind of maiming similar to that so often perpetrated against the representatives of territory in my corpus. If 'language is a violence we do to things,' as Nietzsche claims, then metaphor, like translation, is a specific type of violence for which, within his own patriarchal discourse (notwithstanding Derrida's deconstruction of the great man into woman) rape might be an appropriate 'meta-metaphor.'

The reliance on metaphor, which neither my methodology nor any of the sampled texts have succeeded in shaking off (although, I would argue, the only writer in my main corpus not bothered by this is Langevin) reflects the impasse of marginal writing as well as of its criticism: there are no paradigms outside the centre, and extraterritoriality is, strictly speaking, an impossibility. The subversion of language cannot take place outside its territory, because the outside does not exist; resistance can only move towards the linguistic margin, pushing the difference inherent in metaphor as far as possible toward its disjunctive pole and yet stopping short of the complete loss of reference which would undermine political effectiveness. Language, as we know it, could not exist without naming and metaphor, but, as Robert Kroetsch has shown in his texts, the 'originary supplement' with its oxymoronic and territorial indication of sacred potential can be metamorphosed into a sylleptic gesture of deterritorialization. Or, to paraphrase my academic precursor, the good professor Madham, if bullshit can be turned into truth, the reverse is equally possible (although what this means for my own discussion, I shudder to think). To flee the realm of metaphor is as impossible as to leave the magic circle of language, and the metropolitan colonial writer and critic who cannot step out of that of the 'colonizer' can only strive to make the circle as centreless as possible.

My own discussion is, by necessity, no more immune to the corruptive potential of its metaphoric underpinnings than any other. The textual corpus has proved to be littered with corpses and rape victims, whose pain has been reduced to territorial symbolism, illustrating time and again the bias inherent in the sexual tropology that almost invariably accompanies the adoption of the colonization paradigm into a discourse still dominated by a 'centrist,' patriarchal ideology. The fact that I have myself adopted the territory metaphor makes me particularly vulnerable to accusations of collusion, and the question I raised in the introduction about its usefulness for the analysis of other types of marginality – particularly one based on gender – presents itself ever more urgently. Some critics argue that the situation in settler colonies, such as Canada and Quebec, provides a good model for feminism, insofar as the linguistic situation in which a sense of place has to be constructed from within a language inherently alien to the territory is similar to the situation of women's writing (cf. Ashcroft). The descriptions provided in essays by Gaston Miron, Hubert Aquin, Dennis Lee, and Robert Kroetsch, as well as the novels of Margaret Atwood, for instance, of the silence at the heart of the Québécois and Canadian experience are indeed reminiscent of many women's accounts of their attempts to carve out a linguistic space within a 'foreign' territory.

To some, Canada has come to be equated with the 'ex-centricity' typical of postmodernism which, in turn, is emblematized in the female voice (Hutcheon *The Canadian Postmodern*; Irvine *Sub/version*). In other words, Canada itself – more so than Quebec – has become a metaphor for marginality. In spite of the number of prominent female authors in the country, however, the great majority of those writers clearly identifiable as either postmodern or postcolonial are – as my corpus has illustrated – (white) men. A survey of books on postmodernist fiction shows this to be equally true outside Canada. This paradox again demonstrates the entrapment of much of this debate in metaphor; how can women, natives and ethnic writers preserve the reality, and the difference, of their experience if their specific marginalities are constantly metaphorized? The critical insistence on turning postmodernism into a marginal phenomenon leads to metaphor which, at the extreme, denies the reality of that very marginality. The postmodern writer names himself; a margin/alias, his marginality becomes an aesthetic choice rather than a political reality. In my own opinion (and here I join Linda Hutcheon) a writer like Robert Kroetsch is much more representative of postmodernism than both his contemporary female colleagues and the many minority writers that have come into prominence more recently. As my corpus has demonstrated, Canadian and Québécois postmodernism is best represented by an ethnic and sexual mainstream for which marginality is more figurative than real. It could be argued, of course, that this may be another chicken-and-egg question (and I might well be the chicken). Discussions about definitions are always to some extent circular; my conclusions may stem from a desire to identify postmodernism's distinction from postcolonialism so as to vouchsafe the political integrity of the latter (and of myself?).

If postmodernism can be seen as a metaphorization of postcolonialism, or as a translation of the centre/margin dialectic from a political into an aesthetic register, neither of the two, at least in my case-study, has left the parameters of a fundamentally centrist, patriarchal ideology. The most troubling aspect – at least to me, as a female reader – of the use of the colonial paradigm in the novels I have read is the metaphorization of territorial aggression as rape, whose inherent misogyny is so succinctly illustrated in the critical reaction to Langevin's text (as opposed to his own fairly sympathetic treatment of it) as well as in Cohen's and Aquin's allegorical exploitation of their female protagonists. This is symptomatic of its translation into a pre-existing master narrative of sexual relationships, where the submissive position is marked feminine. Even where the rape metaphor allows for the victims' revenge, as in *Gone Indian* (and *Scann*), it is still inscribed in the same paradigm. It could be argued that the Manichean allegory with its clear dualities – positive and negative, good and evil, same and other – continues to structure much of the textual and critical discourse of marginality but that in the metropolitan colony its racist foundation has been replaced by a sexist one, where the centre is marked masculine, the margin feminine.

As I found myself constantly 'marginalized' and manipulated by these texts, positioned in a place shown me by what Mary Anne Caws calls 'the finger in the text' with little freedom of movement, it became increasingly clear that a writing in the margin – whether postcolonial or postmodern – demands a reading in the margin, if not always actualized as literally as in *Trou de mémoire*. Allegory, alibi, alias, as well as apocryphy and the aleatory power of signifiers, are all related to alienation and alterity, indicating the potential of language to manipulate, to be elsewhere, and to place both speaker and listener, author and reader, in the position of the Other. The critical interest in alterity is accompanied by a focus on the possibility of reading 'otherwise,' that is to read from the position of the Other. It may be argued that postcolonial and postmodernist texts force us to do so. In *L'Elan d'Amérique* the reader is asked to see as the Other sees by experiencing the alterity of the protagonists through the identification demanded by the stream-of-consciousness narration. In *Gone Indian*, she is again invited to see as the Other sees, but this time by repeating the movements of the author rather than the protagonist. While the two impulses are distinct and demand a different investment, both position the reader in a similar way.

The manipulative strategies of the brand of postmodernism exemplified by Aquin's anamorphosis and Kroetsch's rebus have an important self-reflexive function in pointing to the potential for manipulation that always inheres in the relation between author and reader, and an argument can be made for the postmodernist's only making explicit what is always already the case. To stop here, however, is to skirt a potentially uncomfortable issue. The negative connotations surrounding the terms I have used to describe the type of postmodernism encountered here – manipulation, constraint, mannerism – result from the a priori critical valorization of openness and freedom (and the consequent marginalization, or redefinition, of techniques and genres that refuse to conform to these criteria), on which is seen to depend the 'jouissance' we are led to expect from postmodern texts. Rather than attempt to redefine them I prefer to see these strategies as symptomatic of a certain postmodern erotics of reading, and I would argue that manipulation is not incompatible with pleasure.

My claim that criticism may well reveal more about the critic's desire than about its presumed object now forces me to face the question why I enjoy these texts. What has my own choice of metaphors – as well as my choice of corpus – revealed about my own desire? Am I by nature inclined to let myself be manipulated or am I, through my own inevitable gendering, already indoctrinated 'willingly' to assume the marginal position, thus enacting the double fate reserved for me since time immemorial and perpetuated in the texts I have just read, as the ultimate beautiful loser – the postmodern version of madonna and whore – saint and rape victim? Like most critics, I do not take pleasure in readings that present no challenge, and some of the texts I have tackled here have indeed proved hard nuts to crack (does my metaphor here, for instance, reveal a desire for revenge? If so, for what?).

In fact, my desire to engage with a text is often inversely proportionate to its resistance – a peculiar fact that places me in a position gendered masculine in relation to the text in an age-old myth of seduction which suddenly seems to contradict the argument I have built up. How can I be positioned as both submissive and aggressive vis-à-vis the text? It could be answered that, like Aquin's perfect crime, the perfectly executed mannerist novel would be a contradiction in terms; only when the manipulation involved is revealed is the author's mastery ascertained. The detective/reader's decoding must second-guess the criminal/author's encoding, an enterprise which, if met with success, at the same time confirms the mastery of the former; the two fulfil each other's desire both to master and to submit. The author's assumption of control and defiance of the critic are prompted by a desire to touch and be touched; it is not coincidental that writers like Aquin and Kroetsch are openly concerned – in the case of the former almost to the point of obsession – with the reception of their work. To be manipulated also means to be handled and touched or seduced. Aquin describes his relationship to the reader as 'une "danse de séduction"' or an embrace that turns into rape (quoted by Hutcheon *Narcissistic Narrative* 159 n7). The easy confusion of the two – at least from the object's point of view – fundamentally different phenomena is symptomatic of the patriarchal translation/perversion of erotics into pornography.

According to Benjamin, 'It is indeed characteristic of the sadist that he humiliates his object and then – or thereby – satisfies it. And that is what the allegorist does' (*The Origin of German Tragic Drama* 184–5). In spite of my warnings in chapter 1 against turning allegory into a reading practice, my own project has shown that this is indeed the fate of criticism. Whichever version of Manicheanism we choose, we inevitably perpetuate the cruelty to which these texts subject us, and this may be the lesson they teach (yes, there is – almost – as much didacticism in their endeavour as in my own). As long as the centre/margin dialectic is inscribed in a dominant discourse which sees any power relationship as based on a primordial, 'natural,' sexual hierarchy which entails the subjection of one – always the same – partner, sado-masochism may indeed provide the appropriate allegory. The saintly masochism which is the desired position for the reader in this postmodern dance may demand an act of willing submission to the author, but this is at the same time a mutual recognition, a confirmation of the subjecthood of both. As the reader submits to the mastery of the author, the latter submits to the cruelty of the critic. Only when the sparring game between the two has been liberated from the ideological strait-jacket which inscribes the submission to mastery in an allegory where (because of its gendering?) it is always negatively valorized will it be possible for the reader to admit to wanting to 'be had,' to take her – or his – place in the margin, and to exclaim, as I have often wanted to in my encounters with these texts: 'Touchée!'

Notes

CHAPTER ONE: Mapping the Territory

1 Derrida's translator's (Joseph F. Graham) choice – 'transferability' – though probably the closest equivalent, causes problems, considering Derrida's view of the sacred text as 'intransférable.'
2 To claim, as does Roland Barthes, for instance, that myth is a secondary modeling system and the vehicle for ideology does not change the fact that the individual who adheres to it is always, in Lévi-Strauss' term, 'en deça.'
3 Paul de Man, quoted by Patricia Parker in 'The Metaphorical Plot,' in *Metaphor: Problems and Perspectives*, ed. David S. Miall
4 See 'The Uncanny,' in *The Standard Edition of the Complete Psychological Works of Sigmund Freud*, vol. 17.
5 Lacan has also recounted an intriguing case of early metonymy-formation by a young child (see *Séminaire 3*: 260–1).
6 See 'L'Instance de la lettre dans l'inconscient, ou la raison depuis Freud,' in *Ecrits*, and 'Métaphore et métonymie,' in *Séminaire 3*.
7 See also Girard, 'Differentiation and Undifferentiation in Lévi-Strauss and Current Critical Theory.'
8 See Freud, *Totem and Taboo* 181–9, 199, and *Moses and Monotheism* 135, 207.
9 The use of entropy as a literary topos is particularly insistent in early American postmodernism, the most notorious examples being Thomas Pynchon's short story 'Entropy' and his classic *The Crying of Lot 49*. For a discussion of the thermodynamic concept of entropy in postmodern literature, see Kuehl, *Alternate Worlds* chap. 10.
10 It is true that metamorphoses in fairy-tales are not usually accompanied by an uncanny effect. As opposed to the case of the fantastic, where the reader is left in a state of uncertainty, the tale restores a reassuring order.

11 Jean-Charles Falardeau, quoted by Robert Major in 'Le Joual comme langue littéraire'

12 See the article on 'Anamorphosis' in Abraham Rees, *The Cyclopedia or Universal Dictionary of Arts, Sciences and Literature*, vol. 2 (London: Straham 1819).

13 It is significant that several of Salvador Dali's surreal paintings use anamorphic techniques; in one instance he copies the same anamorphosis that is used on the cover of *Trou de mémoire*.

14 Lacan's example of anamorphic art is the younger Hans Holbein's *The Ambassadors*, which plays a central role in *Trou de mémoire*. Panofsky suggests that the painter 'signs' his work in the anamorphic figure of a hollow bone ('Hol-bein') which constitutes the centre of the painting and points out that the sixteenth century was as fond of puns as of anamorphoses (14 n1). Holbein's signature is also an example of the rebus principle which I will discuss at length in chapter 6; the visual pun harks back to the hieroglyphic 'cartouche,' the transformation of the name into a picture puzzle. The suggested isomorphism of punning and anamorphosis will prove pertinent to my analysis of Aquin's novel. (It is, incidentally, not by accident that I use the pronoun 'he' in the discussion of anamorphosis; this manipulative brand of postmodern fiction seems to be a particularly male phenomenon.)

CHAPTER TWO: *Beautiful Losers*

1 I adopt the term *mise en abyme* rather loosely from Lucien Dällenbach to indicate any textual strategy that performs an interior duplication of narrative patterns.

2 Stephen Scobie points to the analogy between the submission of the victim in the sado-masochistic relationship and the submission to the will of God which constitutes sainthood in a provocative article juxtaposing Cohen's novel with the pornographic *Story of O*. The analogy will prove equally applicable to Aquin, whom Patricia Merivale has characterized as a 'highbrow pornographer.'

3 Stephen Scobie has pointed out the parallels between 'I's' initiation, the legend of Oscotarach and the myth of Osiris, Isis' husband, in yet another link with Isis, significantly operated through a play on Greek words (Gnarowski 107).

4 As a model for aleatory yet meaningful transformations, the *I Ching* is a kind of archetype for the postmodern text (see e.g. Gregory Ulmer, 'The Object of Post-Criticism,' in Foster, ed. *The Anti-Aesthetic*).

5 It may be more than a coincidence that Heracleitus' example of how a single

substance can be perceived differently depending on the perceiver's position is sea-water – harmful to humans, it is beneficial to fish.

6 Stephen Scobie has pointed to the eucharistic allusion here. His claim that it is the English word that is transformed into the sacred Greek is, however, to my mind, a result of reading the wrong way (*Leonard Cohen* 120).

7 Rosmarin Heidenreich points to a Faustian allusion in this episode which links F. with Mephistopheles, thus emphasizing his demonic role (Heidenreich 88). Like F., the D.V. is both God and the *devil*.

8 Various translations have been suggested by Douglas Barbour, based on R.E. Witt's *Isis in the Graeco-Roman World* (Gnarowski 142). The one quoted here is preferred also by Desmond Pacey (Gnarowski 88) and Dennis Lee (*Savage Fields* 70). The quotation seems, in fact, to contain a grammatical error (the adjectives are in the neuter form rather than the feminine). This may be explained by a comparison with Plutarch's version of the inscription, which, although attributed to both Athena and Isis, does not include a name but simply says: 'I am all that has been, and is, and shall be, and my robe no mortal has yet uncovered.' (The translation is from the Loeb edition of Plutarch.) I am grateful to Dr Drew Griffith for his assistance with the intricacies of the Greek in the text, although I assume responsibility for any misuses to which I may have put it.

9 The relationship between F. and 'I' anticipates that between the narrator, Madham, and his 'tool' Jeremy in *Gone Indian* and is typical of much postmodern fiction. Robert Kroetsch's latest novel, *Alibi*, plays more explicitly with the idea of agency as the execution of somebody's will; other famous examples are found, for instance, in John Fowles' *The Magus* and Thomas Pynchon's *The Crying of Lot 49*.

10 F.M. Macri points to this pun in '*Beautiful Losers* and the Canadian Experience' 93.

11 To McHale, postmodernism is distinguished by its preoccupation with ontological questions (*Postmodernist Fiction*).

CHAPTER THREE: *Trou de mémoire*

1 The editor's footnoted insistence on the race of the monkeys and his long-winded refutation of Magnant's claim that they belong to the species rhesus serve to foreground that word. The rhesus monkey is frequently used in experimental medicine, but it is also the only mammal, besides humans, to possess the crucial Rh factor which can result in sanguinary incompatibility and prevent procreation. Hence perhaps the description of the murder, preceded by intercourse, as a 'court-circuit sanguin' (85).

2 The novel, first published in 1938, has been translated as *Laughter in the Dark*.

3 Aquin here points inadvertently to allegory as the foundation of literature; only as corpse can the character enter what Benjamin significantly calls 'the homeland of allegory' (*The Origin of German Tragic Drama* 217), because only when deprived of its individual biography can it be made an emblem.

4 Marilyn Randall has pointed out that the perfect crime is paradoxical insofar as it requires the criminal's confession in order to be perceived. In that sense it is analogous to plagiarism, of which Aquin seems to be guilty; it only succeeds to the extent that it is unsuccessful (*Le Contexte littéraire* 211). In other words, plagiarism, like crime, does not exist until it is discovered; hence perfection is by definition incompatible with either crime.

5 For a closer analysis of this, see my article, 'Hubert Aquin et le mystère de l'anamorphose.'

6 See C.G. Jung, *Psychology and Alchemy*, on transubstantiation 308–13; on the stone/Christ parallel 345–431.

7 C.G. Jung, *Mysterium Coniunctionis*, which contains the Latin original of the *Aurora Consurgens* with a German translation

8 Quoted by Georges Bataille in *La Littérature et le mal* 191

9 Fanon has commented on the near absence of suicides in colonized societies, as opposed to the frequency of murder and violence toward others (in *Les Damnés de la terre*).

10 Aquin has written two essays on Papineau. In 'L'Art de la défaite,' written before *Trou de mémoire*, he seems to share Magnant's contempt, but in 'La Mort de l'écrivain maudit,' written in 1969, he defines Papineau as the blasphemous revolutionary of his time. Both essays are found in *Blocs erratiques*.

11 See Mason Wade, *The French Canadians 1760–1967* 1: 43.

12 The frequent references to the baroque in the text have led most critics to identify Aquin's anamorphic techniques with that period. As indicated above, however, anamorphosis, unlike metamorphosis, pertains particularly to mannerism. A particularly useful discussion on the relationship between anamorphosis and mannerism is offered by M-Pierrette Malcuzynski in her doctoral dissertation and her article 'Anamorphose, perception carnavalisante et modalités polyphoniques dans *Trou de mémoire*' in *Voix et images* 33 (1986).

13 Anthony Wall has pointed out that RR's final 'truth' is itself false, since, in fact, some of the works she claims are apocryphal are not, and that her commentary includes as many inaccuracies as does the rest of the text. This does not, however, annul the *mise en abyme* function of her annotation.

14 Under Bakunin's confession is a note handwritten by Nicolas I: 'Je consens à ce qu'il revoie son père et sa soeur en Présence de G. Nabokow' (283).

15 Rosmarin Heidenreich has pointed out several similarities between the two novels.

16 Mullahy may also bear a relation to an Irish 'Papineau,' R.J. Mulcahy, who, after leading the Fine Gael and representing the Sinn Fein in the House of Commons, ended up fighting the IRA as commander of the 'Free State Army.' Heidenreich has suggested that Pierre *Xavier* Magnant and *Charles* Mullahy allude to Charles Xavier, the Zemblan alter ego of John Shade in Nabokov's *Pale Fire* (Heidenreich 117).

17 Lucie Brind'Amour suggests that an inverted R resembles the Russian sign for 'I' (565 n4). 'Ruskin' is similar to the Russian word for 'Russian,' and the double-agent aspect is twice foregrounded in RR's name. (Visualized 'in Russian,' where R is rendered by what looks like a P, Magnant's own name translates the permanent revolution into the automobile code: his initials would read 'revolutions per minute.') The name also harks back to the Botkin-Kinbote connection from *Pale Fire*.

18 Although St Joan was never referred to by this epithet, she was commonly called 'la pucelle,' for instance by Voltaire in *La Pucelle* and by Shakespeare in *Henry VI*.

19 The biography of Ghezzo shows him to be another ambiguous Papineau figure; he collaborated with the slave traders in Dahomey.

20 This possibility was first suggested by Lucie Brind'Amour (567 n37) and has been confirmed by Marilyn Randall who points to existing correspondence between the two writers (*Le Contexte littéraire* 153).

CHAPTER FOUR: *The New Ancestors*

1 Page references are given both to the 1970 New Press edition and the 1972 paperback edition of *The New Ancestors*.

2 See also 'Differentiation and Undifferentiation.'

3 On 1 August 1962 Kwame Nkrumah was the target of an assassination attempt at Kulungugu, which eventually led to the dismissal of Chief Justice Korsah, who presided over the trial and acquitted three CPP members of plotting against the life of the president.

4 For a dissenting view see A.C. Morrell.

5 I am indebted to Egya Sangmuah for this translation.

6 In Armah's *The Beautyful Ones Are Not Yet Born*, 'the last shall be the first' enters the narrator's mind as he encounters a 'shitman' who could have been Samuels' stepfather (Armah 121). Armah's novel in many ways complements Godfrey's; it takes up where *The New Ancestors* ends, depicting the time

leading to the coup that ousted Nkrumah, and its aftermath. There are many subtle parallels between the two novels.

7 Godfrey has referred to Silone's novel as one of many parodied in *The New Ancestors* (Gibson 174).

8 Godfrey also claims to parody Robbe-Grillet's novel (Caroline Bayard and Nick Power 93).

CHAPTER FIVE: *L'Elan d'Amérique*

1 See e.g. Gérard Bessette, Denis Saint-Jacques, Gabrielle Pascal, Richard G. Hodgson, and David J. Bond.

2 For a thorough analysis of the form of the novel, see André Brochu.

3 It is disturbing that most critics have, almost completely, overlooked the significance of the rape scene, and that those who have commented frequently subscribe to the myth of rape as self-imposed. Thus, Gérard Bessette brushes aside the brutality of the incident by laconically stating: 'Mlle Smith s'est fait déflorer ... A la suite de quoi notre héroïne – suivant les traces de sa mère – semble avoir forniqué avec assiduité' (14). André Gaulin, in 'La Vision du monde d'André Langevin,' calls Claire a 'nymphomane', without in any way defining the term, who, after the rape pursues 'sa vocation de femme violée et de putain' (166). His turn of phrase, besides revealing the stereotypical equation of prostitution and rape, imparts an active assumption on Claire's part of the role of prostitute. The choice of the word 'vocation' resonates with another clichéd equation of saint and whore. Claire, of course, is neither. In fact, the same critics who accuse her of actively assuming her role at the same time agree that she has no identity at all. Gaulin does stress the metaphoric value of the rape and insists that all characters are raped, including Antoine who, in what must be the most astounding metaphorization of rape, is 'violé par le refus de sa femme' (in 'Le Romancier et l'essayiste d'un peuple orphelin'). He goes even further when he claims that Claire has mortally abused David, thus turning her into a 'rapist' guilty of a much worse crime than that of her male counterparts. Denis Saint-Jacques is not quite so harsh but talks about Claire's encounter with 'un Allan dont malgré l'agression elle se délivre aisément' (267). This line of reasoning is doubly ironic coming from critics who often accuse Langevin of misogyny.

The only female critic who has written at length on *L'Elan d'Amérique* is Gabrielle Pascal, who calls Claire 'le personnage féminin le plus autonome de Langevin' (70). She also brushes over the rape, however, and attributes Claire's lack of identity to the absence of the father.

4 André Brochu's careful reconstruction of the chronology of the diegesis

shows that it is possible, although unlikely, that Peabody is Claire's father (234).

5 The legend tells of a pact made between the devil and the lumberjacks in camp far away from home, by which they can fly in the devil's canoe to see their sweethearts for the night on condition that they avoid church spires and refrain from mentioning God's name. Honoré Beaugrand's account of the legend, together with some others, including 'Le Loup garou,' has been published in *La Chasse-galerie* (Montréal: Fides 1979). Beaugrand's version was first published in *La Patrie* in 1891.

6 This intertext has been pointed out by Brochu (239).

7 Giraudoux's play contains a crucial incident involving the death of a bullfinch belonging to the fiancée of Ondine's beloved Hans. Bertha, who is Ondine's opposite and rival, claims that the bird, which she was holding, died because Hans squeezed her hand too hard, while Ondine maintains that 'Le poing de la plus faible femme devient une coque de marbre pour protéger un oiseau' (Giraudoux 114). This incident recalls Claire's killing her canary and her submissive acceptance of guilt.

8 See e.g. Bessette, Hodgson and Harger-Grinling, and Brochu.

CHAPTER SIX: *Gone Indian*

1 This function of the epigraph has been suggested by Russell M. Brown in 'Crossing Borders' 160.

2 Kroetsch does refer to novels as labyrinths (Neuman and Wilson 78). And when Jeremy arrives in Edmonton, he is greeted by 'the Shadbolt painting of a labyrinthine airport ... a labyrinth' (11). His arrival in Canada and at the carnival is his entry into the labyrinth of the novel.

3 The similarity between the anamorphic techniques used by Aquin, for instance, and the rebus strategies used in this text is inadvertently revealed in the *Encyclopedia Britannica*'s definition of the phenomenon: 'Rebuses may convey direct meanings ... or they may deliberately conceal meanings, to inform only the initiated or to puzzle and amuse.'

4 The image of passing through the looking-glass is, according to Gilles Deleuze, appropriate for a text that seeks to do away with vertical relationships of reference and meaning: 'Passer de l'autre côté du miroir, c'est passer du rapport de désignation au rapport d'expression ... C'est arriver dans une région où le langage n'a plus de rapport avec des désignés, mais seulement avec des exprimés, c'est-à-dire avec le sens' (*Logique du sens* 38). In other words, the world on the other side of the mirror is a rebus.

5 This metaphor brings to mind Nietzsche's efforts to literalize Christian sym-

bolism, such as the 'flock' or the 'herd.' Thus spake Zarathustra: 'Except we turn back and become as cows, we shall not enter the kingdom of heaven. For we ought to learn one thing from them: chewing the cud. And verily, what would it profit a man if he gained the whole world and did not learn this one thing: chewing the cud!' Quoted by Paul Cantor, 'Friedrich Nietzsche: The Use and Abuse of Metaphor' in Miall 71-88 (83)

6 The equation between shitting yourself and inventing yourself returns more explicitly in *What the Crow Said*, where Liebhaber finally invents himself into his own story by performing the rather unpleasant, if natural, act in a moment of terror. In so doing, he liberates himself from the tyranny of the printing press.

7 The possibility that Madham is Sunderman's new identity has been presented by Arnold E. Davidson in his short but incisive essay 'Will the Real R. Mark Madham Please Stand Up: A Note on Robert Kroetsch's *Gone Indian.*'

8 Madham's name is particularly appropriate for his position in the novel in the light of Gilles Deleuze's definition of the esoteric word, of which the *mot valise* is a variant: 'Le mot ésoterique en général renvoie à la fois à la case vide et à l'occupant sans place' (*Logique du sens* 62).

9 The importance of rising and falling is foregrounded also in Jeremy's misquoting the title of Gibbon's famous work as '*The Rise and the Fall*' (55).

10 The disagreement concerning the definition of syllepsis and zeugma can be traced to differences between the French and the Anglo-Saxon traditions. Derrida's examples of syllepsis (such as Mallarmé's 'hymen' and Plato's 'pharmakon') correspond to Dumarsais' rather vague definition: 'une figure par laquelle le même mot, dans la même phrase, est pris tout-à-la fois dans le sens propre et dans un sens figuré, qui se rapporte ou à la métonymie, ou à la synecdoque, ou à la métaphore' (Dumarsais-Fontanier *Les Tropes* 2 [Genève: Slatkine Reprints 1967]: 174). The examples presented by Dumarsais, however, comprise primarily sentences where the two are either actualized syntagmatically ('Rome n'est plus dans Rome, elle est toute où je suis'), or where the metaphoric intent is evident ('Du coup qui vous attend je mourrai plus que vous'). This type of syllepsis is, unlike the Derridean pun, dependent on the syntagmatic context and carries no greater weight of undecidability than any other trope.

To Puttenham, the syllepsis is more specific than the zeugma, which comprises any kind of yoking of two words or phrases by means of one word. A syllepsis is specifically the yoking of expressions that are of different 'natures' (*The Arte of English Poesie* ed. Gladys Doidge Willcock and Alice Walker [Cambridge University Press 1936] 165). Although his examples are also quite different from those of the *Princeton Encyclopedia*, his definition is akin to the one I am adopting here.

CHAPTER SEVEN: Retracing the Map

1 See e.g. Gregory Ulmer's discussion of Derrida ('The Object of Post-Criticism,' in Foster, ed. *The Anti-Aesthetic*) and Joel Fineman's of psychoanalysis.

2 For an interesting discussion of the politics of the use of *joual* in literature, see Kwaterko.

3 *L'Avalée des avalés*, perhaps the most translatable of Ducharme's books, has, in fact, been translated into Swedish, with interesting but bizarre results. Needless to say the translation, though faithful and competent, was neither a commercial nor a critical success.

4 For a more extensive discussion of alterity being turned into violence against women in the literature of Quebec, see Patricia Smart, *Ecrire dans la maison du père* (chap. 6). Smart also points to the implicit link between literature and the pornography paradigm that I will return to in my conclusion.

5 An analogy drawn between the two paradigms by Madeleine Gagnon (inadvertently?) reveals a patriarchal bias by juxtaposing Freud's question 'Que veut la femme?' with the colonizer's question: 'What does Quebec want?' (quoted in Randall, 'L'Ecriture féministe: Une poétique du plagiat?' 265). The parallel is thus placed within a discourse which, faced with a mysterious (and exasperating) Other, aims at representing her rather than allowing her to represent herself.

6 See e.g. Huggan 'Decolonizing the Map.' On the Canadian obsession with mapping, see E.D. Blodgett.

Works Cited

Aquin, Hubert. *Blocs erratiques*, ed. René Lapierre. Collection Prose entière. Montréal: Quinze 1977
– *Trou de mémoire*. Montréal: Le Cercle du livre de France 1968
Armah, Ayi Kwei. *The Beautyful Ones Are Not Yet Born*. Boston: Houghton Mifflin 1968
Ashcroft, Bill, Gareth Griffiths, and Helen Tiffin. *The Empire Writes Back: Theory and Practice in Post-Colonial Literatures*. London-New York: Routledge, 1989
Ashcroft, W.D. 'Intersecting Marginalities: Post-Colonialism and Feminism.' *Kunapipi* 11:2 (1989): 23–33
Atwood, Margaret. *Surfacing*. 1972; Don Mills: PaperJacks 1973
Autret, Jean. *L'Influence de Ruskin sur la vie, les idées et l'oeuvre de Marcel Proust*. Genève: Droz 1955
Bakhtin, Mikhail. *Rabelais and His World*, trans. Helene Iswolsky. Cambridge, Mass.: MIT 1968
Bakounine, Michel. *Confession*, trans. Paulette Brupbacher. Paris: Rieder 1932
Baltrusaitis, Jurgis. *Anamorphoses ou magie artificielle des effets merveilleux*. 1955; Paris: Olivier Perrin 1969
Barthes, Roland. *S/Z*. Collection Points. Paris: Seuil 1970
Bataille, Georges. *La Littérature et le mal*. Paris: Gallimard 1957
Bayard, Caroline, and Nick Power. 'Interview with Dave Godfrey.' *Open Letter* 3rd series. 3 (1975): 81–91
Beaulieu, Victor-Lévy. *Race de Monde*. Montréal: Editions du jour 1969
Benjamin, Walter. *Illuminations*, trans. Harry Zohn. New York: Schocken 1969
– *The Origin of German Tragic Drama*, trans. John Osborne. London: NLB 1977
Benstock, Shari. 'At the Margins of Discourse: Footnotes in the Fictional Text.' *PMLA* 98 (1983): 204–55

Bessette, Gérard. 'L'Elan d'Amérique dans l'oeuvre d'André Langevin.' Livres et auteurs québécois (1972): 12–33

Bhêly-Quénum, Olympe. Un piège sans fin. Paris: Stock 1960

Blodgett, E.D. Configuration: Essays in the Canadian Literatures. Downsview: ECW 1982

Bond, David J. The Temptation of Despair: A Study of the Quebec Novelist André Langevin. Fredericton: York 1982

Booth, Wayne. 'Metaphor as Rhetoric: The Problem of Evaluation.' In On Metaphor, ed. Sheldon Sacks. Chicago: University of Chicago Press 1979

Brind'Amour, Lucie. 'Sur Trou de mémoire: le révolutionnaire pris au piège.' Voix et images 5 (1978): 557–67

Brochu, André. L'Evasion tragique: essai sur les romans d'André Langevin. Cahiers du Québec: Collection Littérature. Montréal: Hurtubise HMH 1985

Brown, Russell M. 'Crossing Borders.' Essays on Canadian Writing 22 (1981): 154–68

– 'Freedom to Depart.' Review of Gone Indian by Robert Kroetsch. Canadian Literature 61 (1974): 103–04

– 'An Interview with Robert Kroetsch.' University of Windsor Review 7.2 (1972): 1–18

Cameron, Donald A. Conversations with Canadian Novelists. Toronto: Macmillan 1973

Cassirer, Ernst. Language and Myth, trans. Susanne K. Langer. New York: Harper & Brothers 1946

– Mythical Thought, trans. Ralph Manheim. Vol. 2 of The Philosophy of Symbolic Forms (3 vols). 1955; New Haven: Yale University Press 1966

Caws, Mary Ann. The Eye in the Text: Essays on Perception, Mannerist to Modern. Princeton: Princeton University Press 1981

Cellier, Léon. 'D'une rhétorique profonde: Baudelaire et l'oxymoron.' Cahiers internationaux de symbolisme 8 (1965): 3–14

Cohen, Leonard. Beautiful Losers. New York: Bantam Books 1966

Dällenbach, Lucien. Le Récit spéculaire: Essai sur la mise en abyme. Paris: Seuil 1977

Davidson, Arnold E. 'Will the Real R. Mark Madham Please Stand Up: A Note on Robert Kroetsch's Gone Indian.' Studies in Canadian Literature 6 (1981): 135–9

Debrunner, Hans W. Witchcraft in Ghana. 1959; London: Brown, Knight & Truscott, 1961

Deleuze, Gilles. Logique du sens. Paris: Minuit 1969

Deleuze, Gilles, and Félix Guattari. Capitalisme et schizophrénie: L'Anti-Oedipe. Collection Critique. Paris: Minuit 1972

- *Kafka: pour une littérature mineure*. Paris: Minuit 1975
De Quincey, Thomas. 'On the Knocking at the Gate in *Macbeth*.' *The Collected Writings of Thomas De Quincey*, ed. David Masson. 14 vols. 10: 389–94. London: Black 1897
- 'On Murder Considered as One of the Fine Arts.' In *The Collected Writings*. 13: 9–124
Derrida, Jacques. *De la grammatologie*. Paris: Minuit 1967
- 'La Pharmacie de Platon.' In *La Dissémination*, 69–196. Paris: Seuil 1972
- 'Des Tours de Babel.' In *Difference in Translation*, ed. Joseph F. Graham 209–48. Ithaca: Cornell University Press 1985
Downey, Deane E.D. 'The Canadian Identity & African Nationalism.' *Canadian Literature* 75 (1977): 15–26
During, Simon. 'Postmodernism or Postcolonialism?' *Landfall 155* 39:3 (1985): 366–80
Eliade, Mircea. *Rites and Symbols of Initiation: The Mysteries of Birth and Rebirth* (1958), trans. Willard R. Trask. New York: Harper & Row 1965
Falardeau, Jean-Charles. *Notre société et son roman*. Montréal: HMH 1967
Fineman, Joel. 'The Structure of Allegorical Desire.' In *Allegory and Representation*, ed. Stephen J. Greenblatt 26–60. Baltimore and London: Johns Hopkins University Press 1981
Fishman, Joshua. *Language and Nationalism*. Rowley: Newbury House 1972
Fletcher, Angus. *Allegory: The Theory of a Symbolic Mode*. Ithaca: Cornell University Press 1964
Foster, Hal, ed. *The Anti-Aesthetic: Essays on Postmodern Culture*. Port Townsend, Washington: Bay Press 1983
Freud, Sigmund. 'Beyond the Pleasure Principle' (1920). *The Standard Edition of the Complete Psychological Works of Sigmund Freud*, trans. and ed. James Strachey. 24 vols. 18: 1–64. London: Hogarth and the Institute of Psycho-Analysis 1955
- *Moses and Monotheism* (1932), trans. Katherine Jones. The International Psycho-analytical Library, no. 33. London: Hogarth 1951
- *Totem and Taboo* (1946), trans. A.A. Brill. New York: Random House, Vintage Books 1961
- 'The Uncanny' (1919). In *The Standard Edition* 17: 217–56
Frye, Northrop. *The Great Code: The Bible and Literature*. New York: Harcourt, Brace, Jovanovich 1982
Gardiner, Alan. *The Theory of Proper Names*. London: Oxford University Press 1954
Gaulin, André. 'Le Romancier et l'essayiste d'un peuple orphelin.' *Québec français* 22 (1976): 24–8

– 'La Vision du monde d'André Langevin.' *Etudes littéraires* 6 (1973): 153–67

Gibson, Graeme. *Eleven Canadian Novelists*. Toronto: Anansi 1973

Girard, René. 'Differentiation and Undifferentiation in Lévi-Strauss and Current Critical Theory.' In *Directions for Criticism: Structuralism and Its Alternatives*, ed. Murray Krieger and L.S. Dembo, 111–36. Madison: University of Wisconsin Press 1977

– *La Violence et le sacré*. Paris: Bernard Grasset 1972

Giraudoux, Jean. *Ondine*. Paris: Bernard Grasset 1939

Gnarowski, Michael, ed. *Leonard Cohen: The Artist and His Critics*. Toronto: McGraw-Hill Ryerson 1976

Gobard, Henri. *L'Aliénation linguistique: analyse tétraglossique*. Paris: Flammarion 1976

Godbout, Jacques. *D'Amour, P.Q.* Paris: Seuil 1972

Godfrey, Dave. *The New Ancestors*. Toronto: New Press 1970 and 1972

Hallyn, Fernand. 'Holbein: la mort en abyme.' *Romanica Gandensia* 17 (1980): 165–81

Hancock, Geoff. 'An Interview with Robert Kroetsch.' *Canadian Fiction Magazine* 24/25 (1977): 33–52

Harlow, Robert. *Scann*. 1972; Toronto: NCL 1977

Hartman, Geoffrey H. 'Psychoanalysis: The French Connection.' In *Psychoanalysis and the Question of the Text*, ed. G.H. Hartman, 86–113. Baltimore: Johns Hopkins University Press 1978

Heidenreich, Rosmarin. *The Postwar Novel in Canada: Narrative Patterns and Reader Response*. Waterloo: Wilfrid Laurier University Press 1989

Hodgson, Richard G. 'Time and Space in André Langevin's *L'Elan d'Amérique*.' *Canadian Literature* 88 (1981): 31–8

– With Virginia Harger-Grinling. '*L'Elan d'Amérique* by André Langevin: Silence Articulate.' *Comparison* 12 (1981): 3–14

Huggan, Graham. 'Decolonizing the Map: Post-Colonialism, Post-Structuralism and the Cartographic Connection.' *Ariel: A Review of International English Literature* 20:4 (October 1989): 115–31

Hutcheon, Linda. *The Canadian Postmodern: A Study of Contemporary English-Canadian Fiction*. Toronto: Oxford University Press 1988

– '"Circling the Downspout of Empire": Post-Colonialism and Postmodernism.' *Ariel* 20:4 (October 1989): 149–75

– *Narcissistic Narrative: The Metafictional Paradox*. Waterloo: Wilfrid Laurier University Press 1984

– *A Poetics of Postmodernism: History, Theory, Fiction*. New York and London: Routledge 1988

– *The Politics of Postmodernism*. New York and London: Routledge 1989

Irvine, Lorna. *Sub/version: Canadian Fictions by Women*. Toronto: ECW 1986

Jahn, Jahnheintz. *Muntu: An Outline of Neo-African Culture*. 1958; London: Faber and Faber 1961

Jakobson, Roman. 'On Linguistic Aspects of Translation.' In *On Translation*, ed. Reuben A. Brower, 232–9. New York: Oxford University Press 1966

– 'Shifters, Verbal Categories, and the Russian Verb.' *Selected Writings*. 2 vols. 2: 130–47. The Hague: Mouton 1971

– 'Two Aspects of Language and Two Types of Aphasic Disturbances.' In *Fundamentals of Language*, by Jakobson and Morris Halle, 55–82. The Hague: Mouton 1956

Jameson, Fredric. 'Third-World Literature in the Era of Multinational Capitalism.' *Social Text* 15 (1986): 65–88

JanMohamed, Abdul R. 'The Economy of Manichean Allegory: The Function of Racial Difference in Colonialist Literature.' *Critical Inquiry* 12.1 (1985): 59–87

Jung, C.G. *Mysterium Coniunctionis: Untersuchung über die Trennung und Zusammensetzung der seelischen Gegensätze in der Alchemie*. Band 12 der *Psychologischen Abhandlungen*. 3 vols. Dritter Teil ('Aurora Consurgens'), edited by M.-L. von Franz. Zürich und Stuttgart: Rascher 1957

– *Psychology and Alchemy*, trans. R.F.C. Hull. Vol. 12 of *The Collected Works of C.G. Jung*, edited by Herbert Read et al. Bollingen series 20. Princeton NJ: Princeton University Press 1968

Kafka, Franz. *Diaries of Franz Kafka*, ed. Max Brod. New York: Schocken Books 1949

Kermode, Frank. *The Sense of an Ending: Studies in the Theory of Fiction*. 1966; New York: Oxford University Press 1968

Kripke, Saul. *Naming and Necessity*. 1972; Cambridge, Mass.: Harvard University Press 1980

Kroetsch, Robert. *Gone Indian*. Toronto: New Press 1973

– *The Studhorse Man*. 1970; Markham: PaperJacks 1977

– 'Unhiding the Hidden: Recent Canadian Fiction.' *Journal of Canadian Fiction* 3.3 (1974): 43–5

– With James Bacque and Pierre Gravel. *Creation*. Toronto: New Press 1970

Kuehl, John. *Alternate Worlds: A Study of Postmodern Antirealist American Fiction*. New York and London: New York University Press 1989

Kwaterko, Jozef. *Le Roman québécois de 1960 à 1975: idéologie et représentation littéraire*. Montréal: Le Préambule 1989

Labov, William. *Language in the Inner City*. Philadelphia: University of Pennsylvania Press 1972

Lacan, Jacques. *The Four Fundamental Concepts of Psychoanalysis*, trans. Alan Sheridan. New York: W.W. Norton 1978

- 'L'Instance de la lettre dans l'inconscient ou la raison depuis Freud.' *Ecrits*, 493–528. Paris: Seuil 1966
- *Le Séminaire de Jacques Lacan* (Book 3), ed. Jacques-Alain Miller. Paris: Seuil 1981
Laguerre, Michel S. *Voodoo Heritage*. Beverly Hills: Sage 1980
Langevin, André. *L'Elan d'Amérique*. Montréal: Le Cercle du livre de France 1972
Laurence, Margaret. *The Diviners*. 1974; Toronto, New York, London: Bantam 1975
- *A Jest of God*. 1966; Toronto: NCL 1974
Lecker, Robert. 'Relocating *The New Ancestors*.' *Studies in Canadian Literature* 2 (1977): 82–92
Lee, Dennis. 'Cadence, Country, Silence: Writing in Colonial Space.' *Boundary 2* 3:1 (1974): 151–68
- *Savage Fields: An Essay in Literature and Cosmology*. Toronto: Anansi 1977
Leney, Jane E. '"In the Fifth City," an Integral Chapter of *The New Ancestors*.' *Canadian Literature* 96 (1983): 72–80
Lévi-Strauss, Claude. *La Pensée sauvage*. Paris: Plon 1962
Lodge, David. *The Modes of Modern Writing: Metaphor, Metonymy, and the Typology of Modern Literature*. London: Edward Arnold 1977
Lotman, Yuri, and Boris Uspenskij. 'Myth – Name – Culture.' In *Soviet Semiotics*, ed. Daniel P. Lucid 233–52. Baltimore: Johns Hopkins University Press 1977
- 'On the Semiotic Mechanism of Culture.' *New Literary History* 9 (1978): 211–31
Maccabée-Iqbal, Françoise. *Hubert Aquin, romancier*. Québec: Les Presses de l'Université Laval 1978
McHale, Brian. *Postmodernist Fiction*. New York and London: Methuen 1987
Macri, F.M. '*Beautiful Losers* and the Canadian Experience.' *Journal of Canadian Fiction* 8 (1973): 88–96
Major, Robert. 'Le Joual comme langue littéraire.' *Canadian Literature* 75 (1977): 41–51
Malcuzynski, M-Pierrette. 'Anamorphose, perception carnavalisante et modalités polyphoniques dans *Trou de mémoire*.' *Voix et images* 33 (1986): 475–94
- 'La Fiction néobaroque aux Amériques, 1960–1970. Littérature carnavalisée et aliénation narrative chez Hubert Aquin, Guillermo Cabrera Infante et Thomas Pynchon.' Diss. McGill University 1981
Margeson, Robert. 'A Preliminary Interpretation of *The New Ancestors*.' *Journal of Canadian Fiction* 4.1 (1975): 96–109
Memmi, Albert. *Portrait du colonisé*. Montréal: Etincelle 1972
Merivale, Patricia. 'Hubert Aquin and Highbrow Pornography: The Aesthetics of

Perversion.' *Essays in Canadian Writing* 26 (1983): 1–12

Miall, David S., ed. *Metaphor: Problems and Perspectives*. Sussex: Harvester 1982

Miner, Horace. *The Primitive City of Timbuctoo*. Princeton: Princeton University Press 1953

Monkman, Leslie. '*Beautiful Losers*: Mohawk Myth and Jesuit Legend.' *Journal of Canadian Fiction* 3.3 (1974): 57–9

Morin, Michel, and Claude Bertrand. *Le Territoire imaginaire de la culture*. Collection Brèches. Lasalle: Hurtubise HMH 1979

Morrell, A.C. 'The I and the Eye in the Desert: The Political and Philosophical Key to Dave Godfrey's *The New Ancestors*.' *Studies in Canadian Literature* 12.2 (1987): 264–72

Murray, Timothy C. 'A Marvelous Guide to Anamorphosis: Cendrillon ou la petite pantoufle de verre.' *Modern Language Notes* 91 (1976): 1276–95

Neuman, Shirley, and Robert Wilson. *Labyrinths of Voice: Conversations with Robert Kroetsch*. Edmonton: NeWest 1982

New, William. *Articulating West: Essays on Purpose and Form in Modern Canadian Literature*. Toronto: New Press 1972

– 'Canadian Literature and Commonwealth Responses.' *Canadian Literature* 66 (1975): 14–30

Nouveau roman: hier, aujourd'hui. 2 vols. Colloque de Cerisy 1971 (Collection 10/18). Paris: Union générale des éditions 1972

Nowlan, Alden. *Various Persons Named Kevin O'Brien: A Fictional Memoir*. Toronto: Clarke, Irwin 1973

Ogden, C.K. *Bentham's Theory of Fiction*. London: Kegan Paul, Trench, Trubner 1932

O'Hagan, Howard. *Tay John*. NCL 105. 1960; Toronto: McClelland and Stewart 1974

Panofsky, Erwin, ed. *Galileo as a Critic of the Arts*. The Hague: Martinus Nijhoff 1954

Parker, Patricia. 'The (Self-)Identity of the Literary Text: Property, Propriety, Proper Place, and Proper Name in *Wuthering Heights*.' In *Identity of the Literary Text*, ed. Mario Valdés and Owen Miller, 92–116. Toronto: University of Toronto Press 1985

Pascal, Gabrielle. *La Quête de l'identité chez André Langevin*. Montréal: Aquila 1976

Pynchon, Thomas. *The Crying of Lot 49*. 1967; New York: Bantam 1972

– *V.* 1961; Philadelphia and New York: Lippincott 1963

Quilligan, Maureen. *The Language of Allegory: Defining the Genre*. Ithaca: Cornell University Press 1979

Randall, Marilyn. *Le Contexte littéraire: lecture pragmatique de Hubert Aquin et de*

Réjean Ducharme. Collection L'Univers des discours. Longueuil: Le Préambule 1990
- 'L'Ecriture féministe: une poétique du plagiat?' *Queen's Quarterly* 96:2 (Summer 1989): 263–78
Redmond, Donald. *Sherlock Holmes, a Study in Sources*. Kingston and Montreal: McGill-Queen's University Press 1982
Ricoeur, Paul. *La Métaphore vive*. Paris: Seuil, 1975.
Sacks, Sheldon, ed. *On Metaphor*. Chicago: University of Chicago Press 1979
Saint-Jacques, Denis. '*L'Elan d'Amérique*.' *Etudes littéraires* 6 (1973): 257–68
Scobie, Stephen. *Leonard Cohen*. Vancouver: Douglas & McIntyre 1978
- 'Magic, Not Magicians: "Beautiful Losers" and "Story of O".' *Canadian Literature* 45 (1970): 56–60
Sebeok, Thomas. 'Naming in Animals with Reference to Playing: A Hypothesis.' *Recherches sémiotiques/Semiotic Inquiry* 1 (1981): 121–35
Sephiha, Vidal. 'Introduction à l'étude de l'intensif.' *Langages* 18 (1970): 104–20
Slemon, Stephen. 'Modernism's Last Post.' *Ariel* 20: 4 (October 1989): 3–17
- 'Monuments of Empire: Allegory/Counter-Discourse/Post-Colonial Writing.' *Kunapipi* 9.3 (1987): 1–15
- 'Post-Colonial Allegory and the Transformation of History.' *Journal of Commonwealth Literature* 23:1 (1988): 157–68
Smart, Patricia. *Ecrire dans la maison du père: l'émergence du féminin dans la tradition littéraire du Québec*. Montréal: Editions Québec/Amérique 1988. Translated by Patricia Smart, under the title *Writing in the Father's House: The Emergence of the Feminine in the Quebec Literary Tradition*. Toronto: University of Toronto Press 1991
- *Hubert Aquin, agent double*. Montréal: Les Presses de l'Université de Montréal 1973
Söderlind, Sylvia. 'Hubert Aquin et le mystère de l'anamorphose.' *Voix et images* 9.3 (1984): 103–11
Steiner, George. *After Babel: Aspects of Language and Translation*. 1975; London: Oxford University Press 1977
- *Extraterritorial: Papers on Literature and the Language Revolution*. 1968; New York: Atheneum 1971
Sterne, Laurence. *The Life and Opinions of Tristram Shandy, Gentleman* (1760), ed. Ian Campbell Ross. Oxford: Clarendon 1983
Sutherland, Ronald. *Second Image: Comparative Studies in Quebec/Canadian Literature*. Toronto: New Press 1971
Thomas, Louis-Vincent, and René Luneau. *Les Religions d'Afrique noire: textes et traditions sacrés*. Paris: Fayard/Denoël 1969
Thomas, Peter. *Robert Kroetsch*. Vancouver: Douglas & McIntyre 1980

Thompson, Stith. *The Folktale*. New York: Dryden 1951

Todorov, Tzvetan. *Introduction à la littérature fantastique*. Collection Points. Paris: Seuil 1970

Wade, Mason. *The French Canadians 1760–1967*. 2 vols. Toronto: Macmillan 1968

Wall, Anthony. 'Prisonnier dans ce trou, ce *Trou de mémoire*.' *Voix et images* 41:2 (hiver 1989): 301–20

Watt, Ian. *The Rise of the Novel: Studies in Defoe, Richardson and Fielding*. 1957; London: Chatto & Windus 1963

Index

Hölderlin, Johann Christian Friedrich, 12, 222
Holmes, Sherlock, 86, 87, 97, 101, 175
Holy Ghost, 91, 142, 202–3, 207. *See also* Pentecost
Hutcheon, Linda: ex-centricity, 233; 'narcissistic narrative,' 21, 236; postmodernism, 5, 39, 41, 208
Huyssen, Andreas, 58

I Ching, 54, 174, 180, 238n4
identity: apocryphal or false, 92, 155, 178, 181, 196; dissolution or loss of, 51, 53, 140–1, 168, 179, 205, 225; and genealogy, 115; and metamorphosis, 28–32; and myth, 28; and naming, 21–2, 204; quest for, 4, 6, 200, 220; specular, 103, 120, 178–80, 185, 192, 207; and story-telling, 182. *See also* difference; initiation
imperialism, 39, 46, 116, 131, 138–9, 221
Indian: allegorical role of, 143–6, 152, 164, 165; becoming, 178, 184, 188, 193, 196; colonizing of, 49, 54; history of, 22; language, 221–2. *See also* mythologies
initiation: and death, 118–19; and identity, 48, 49, 121; and naming, 21; in *The New Ancestors*, 117–20; and sacrifice, 56, 117, 153. *See also* rape
inscription, 65–7, 132, 209
intensity: and expression, 52, 59, 105; and metamorphosis, 33–4; and natural narrative, 34; and poetry, 167; and repetition, 134

intention, intentionality, 6, 37, 38, 200, 207, 231
intertexts: in *Beautiful Losers*, 43–9; in *L'Elan d'Amérique* 156–62; in *Gone Indian*, 173, 185–7, 196; in *The New Ancestors*, 113, 128, 130, 136–41; in *Trou de mémoire*, 96–100
intertextuality, 9, 16, 213
irony: and inversion, 172; and myth, 18, 204; in postcolonialism, 18; in postmodernism, 6, 17–18, 31; and naming, 204
Isis, 47, 55, 59, 60, 63, 66, 202–3

Jakobson, Roman, 24–5, 34
Jameson, Fredric, 37, 39
JanMohamed, Abdul, 36
Jasmin, Claude, 211
Jerome, St, 12
Joan, St, 101, 102, 241n18
Joseph Andrews, 20
joual, 10, 33, 93, 166, 210–12
Joyce, James, 29, 103; *Finnegans Wake*, 35, 101, 104, 223
Jung, Carl Gustav, 88

Kafka, Franz, 15, 32–4, 198, 222, 232
kairos, 17, 139, 155, 176
Kermode, Frank, 16–18, 175
Kripke, Saul, 19
Kroetsch, Robert: *Alibi*, 143, 195, 196, 199, 226, 239n9; *But We Are Exiles*, 183, 226; *Gone Indian*, 170–99, and passim; 'The Sad Phoenician,' 117–18; *The Studhorse Man*, 143, 172, 196, 226; *What the Crow Said*, 183, 203, 227, 244n6; *The Words of My Roaring*, 143, 181

Labov, William, 33

Lacan, Jacques: anamorphosis, 35, 38, 238n14; corps morcelé, 31; metaphor, 24, 27; metonymy, 27, 194–5, 237n5; mirror stage, 21, 79; primacy of signifier, 29; sliding signified, 50
Lalonde, Michèle,165, 210
Langevin, André: *L'Elan d'Amérique*, 143–69, and passim; *Poussière sur la ville*, 143
Laurence, Margaret, 224–6
Lecker, Robert, 139
Lee, Dennis, 15, 221, 233
legends. *See* mythologies
Leney, Jane E., 128
Lévi-Strauss, Claude, 17, 237n2
literalization, 32–3, 220, 222, 226; in *Beautiful Losers*, 44, 46–8, 60, 61, 69, 90; in *Gone Indian*, 198; of marginal writing, 60; in *The New Ancestors*, 117; in *Trou de mémoire*, 83
Lodge, David, 27–8
Lotman, Yuri, and Boris Uspenskij, 13–14, 16, 18, 25, 127
Lowry, Malcolm, 140

macaronic writing, 35
Maccabée-Iqbal, Françoise, 100, 105
McHale, Brian, 69
'machine désirante,' 45. *See also* desiring machine
magic, 13, 26, 89, 137, 162; in *Beautiful Losers* 51–2, 59, 67; in *Gone Indian*, 180
Maignan, Père, 88, 100
Maillet, Antonine, 212
Manicheanism. *See* allegory
mannerism, 87, 206, 235, 240n11
Margeson, Robert, 123, 131–2

margin: and centre, 6, 37, 39, 117, 230, 233–4, 236; critical shift to, 3; literal writing in, 60, 104; reading in, 234–5; without centre, 183
margin/alias, 3, 233
marginality: aesthetics of, 229; canonization of, 29; and colonization, 3–4, 8; and metaphorization, 3, 233; and postmodernism, 229–30, 233; and subversion, 4; and territoriality, 39. *See also* alterity; otherness
marginalization, 114, 122.
marginal literature, 15, 29, 40, 232. *See also* minor literature
Marquez. *See* Garcia
Marxism, 90, 96, 113, 130
master narrative, 3, 5, 36, 234
Memmi, Albert, 71, 91, 92, 118
memory: collective, 9, 13, 214; and history, 62; loss of, 46, 66, 71, 92, 107, 108, 117, 155; and pharmakon, 66; repression and return of, 94, 125, 153. *See also* kairos; Proust
metafiction, 35; historiographic, 221
metamorphosis: 28–33, 34–5; in *Beautiful Losers*, 54–8; in *Gone Indian*, 177–85, 193–4; in *The New Ancestors*, 78, 112–29, 133, 141; reading and writing, 88. *See also* carnival; translation; transubstantiation
metaphor, 23–8; in allegory, 37; in *Beautiful Losers*, 50, 52; and criticism, 231–2; in *L'Elan d'Amérique*, 145–52; Kafka on, 32; subversion of, 197; and violence, 232
metonymy, 24–8; and laterality, 198; and multiplicity, 195–6; and syllepsis, 198. *See also* Lacan
minor literature, 15, 29, 37, 207, 209, 212, 220

THEORY/CULTURE SERIES